IF YOUR LETTER MESSAGE DEALS WITH	LOOK AT MODEL(S)
For Free Catalog	8-1
For Free Products	8-3
About Housing	11-3
For Information from a Commercial Credit Applicant	21-2
For Information from References	21-3
For Information on Services	8-15
About New Product	8-5, 8-7
About Prices/Discounts	8-9
About Residence/Vacation Property	11-5
About Training Materials	8-13
Congratulations	
To Boss	32-7
To Customers	19-11
To Employees	32-1 to 32-4, 32-6, 33-1
To New Members	32-5
On Opening a New Store	19-15
Confirmation	
Of Appointment	13-3
Of Oral Instructions	13-1
Of Prices and Discounts	13-2
Of Travel Arrangements	13-4
Employee Relations	
Discharging and Demoting Due to Economic Conditions	29-8, 29-9
Memorandum to Managers	24-2, 24-5
Offering Congratulations	32-1 to 32-7
Offering Good Wishes	33-2
Offering Sympathy	33-3, 34-1, 34-2
Receiving Request from Employee to Attend a Convention	24-3
Terminating Employee	36-3
Warning Employee	36-2
Formal Invitations	
Accepting a Formal Invitation	39-3
To Attend an Annual Banquet	39-2
Expressing Regrets to a Formal Invitation	39-5
To Honor a New President	39-1
Ghost-Writing for the Executive	
Disavowing a "True" Rumor	30-6
Follow-Up Letter to a Company Executive	30-5

IF YOUR LETTER MESSAGE DEALS WITH	LOOK AT MODEL(S)
Handling a Request	30-2
"Holding" Letter About a Purchasing Decision	30-4
Referring Problems to Others	30-3
Using Discretion	30-1
Giving Thanks	
To Customer for Courtesies to Sales Representative	19-3
To Customer for Payment and Order	19-8
To Customer for Receiving a Sales Representative	19-16
To Customer for Referral	19-7
To a Friend	19-14
For Hospitality	41-2
To a Long-Time Customer	19-17
For Past Support	19-9
For a Personal Favor	41-1
To a Reader for Favorable Comments	31-6
To a Reference	38-2
Informal Invitations	
Accepting an Informal Invitation	40-2
Expressing Regrets to an Informal Invitation	40-3
Informal Invitation to Dinner	40-1
Invitations	
Declining Invitation	26-5
To Keynote Speaker	26-7
To Open House	16-1
To Panel Participant— Modest Fee Offered	26-4
To Professional Speaker	26-1
Response to Invitation	26-2
To "Second Choice" Panelist	26-6
To Use Credit	19-19
Job Resumes	
Change of Career	37-2
High-Level Position	37-3
Little Related Experience	37-4
Middle Management Position	37-1
Memorandums as Reports	
About Centralization of Department	25-4
On Customer Correspondence	25-2
On Heavy Turnover in Regional Office	25-1

THE McGRAW-HILL HANDBOOK OF BUSINESS LETTERS

ROY W. POE

THIRD EDITION

McGraw-Hill, Inc.

New York   San Francisco   Washington, D.C.   Auckland   Bogotá
Caracas   Lisbon   London   Madrid   Mexico City   Milan
Montreal   New Delhi   San Juan   Singapore
Sydney   Tokyo   Toronto

ss Cataloging-in-Publication Data

Hill handbook of business letters / Roy W. Poe.—3rd
ed.
        p.   cm.
      Includes index.
      ISBN 0-07-050425-3 (HC) :   —ISBN 0-07-050451-2 (PB)
      1. Commercial correspondence—Handbooks, manuals, etc. I. Title.
II. Title: Handbook of business letters.
HF5726.P55 1994
808'.066651—dc20   93-24986
                                                              CIP

   2 3 4 5 6 7 8 9 0   DOC/DOC   9 9 8 7 6 5

ISBN 0-07-050425-3 (HC)
ISBN 0-07-050451-2 (PB)

   3 4 5 6 7 8 9 0   DOC/DOC   9 9 8 7 6 5

*The sponsoring editor for this book was Betsy Brown, the editing supervisor was
Fred Dahl, the designer was Inkwell Publishing Services, and the production
supervisor was Suzanne Babeuf. It was set in Palatino by Inkwell Publishing
Services.*

Printed and bound by R.R. Donnelley & Sons Company.

This book is printed on recycled, acid-free paper containing a
minimum of 50% recycled de-inked fiber.

Contents

About This Handbook / xv

A Gallery of Letters / xvii

Part 1   THE LETTER WRITER'S CRAFT / 1

   Section 1   What a Good Business Letter Is—and Is Not / 2

   Section 2   Consider Goodwill in Your Communications / 7

   Section 3   Don't Waste Words / 12

   Section 4   Keep the Language Lively and Simple / 21

   Section 5   Personalize Your Letters / 28

   Section 6   Emphasize the Positive / 36

   Section 7   Use the Correct Letter Form / 44

Part 2   REQUEST LETTERS AND RESPONSES TO REQUEST LETTERS / 53

   Section 8   Asking for Information About Materials, Prices, and Discounts / 54

   8-1   Asking for a Free Catalog / 55
   8-2   Responding to a Request for a Free Catalog / 56
   8-3   Requesting Free Products / 57
   8-4   Responding to a Request for Free Products / 58
   8-5   Asking About a New Product / 59
   8-6   Responding to a Request for Information About a New Product / 60
   8-7   Asking About a Product and the Name of a Dealer / 60
   8-8   Supplying Information About a Product and the Name of a Dealer / 61
   8-9   Asking About Prices and Discounts / 62
   8-10   Responding to an Inquiry About Prices and Discounts / 63

8-11   Requesting Advice and Product Inspection / **64**
8-12   Responding to a Request for Advice and Product Inspection / **65**
8-13   Asking About Training Materials / **66**
8-14   Supplying Information About Training Materials / **67**
8-15   Asking for Detailed Information on a Service / **68**
8-16   Supplying Detailed Information on a Service / **69**

Section 9   Requests to Reproduce Printed Materials / **70**

9-1   Requesting Magazine Reprints or Permission to Reproduce / **71**
9-2   Responding to a Request for Reprints or Permission to Reproduce / **72**
9-3   Requesting Free Reproduction Privileges of a Book Illustration / **73**
9-4   Responding to a Request for Free Reproduction Privileges / **74**
9-5   Requesting Reproduction Privileges for Commercial Use / **75**
9-6   Responding to a Request for Reproduction Privileges for Commercial Use / **76**
9-7   Requesting Permission to Reproduce Noncopyrighted Materials / **77**
9-8   Responding to a Request for Permission to Reproduce Noncopyrighted Materials / **78**
9-9   Requesting a Copy of a Speech for Distribution / **79**
9-10 Responding to a Request for a Copy of a Speech for Distribution / **79**

Section 10   Letters Asking for an Appointment / **80**

10-1   Asking to Visit Showrooms / **81**
10-2   Responding to a Request to Visit Showrooms / **82**
10-3   Asking for an Appointment to See a Computer Operation / **83**
10-4   Responding to a Request for an Appointment to See a Computer Operation / **84**

Section 11   Other "Asking" Letters / **85**

11-1   Asking About Conference Accommodations / **86**
11-2   Supplying Information About Conference Accommodations / **87**
11-3   Asking About Housing / **88**
11-4   Responding to a Letter About Housing / **89**
11-5   Asking About Residence and Vacation Property / **89**
11-6   Responding to an Inquiry About Residence and Vacation Property / **90**

Part 3   TRANSMITTAL, CONFIRMATION, AND "ANNOUNCING" LETTERS / **91**

Section 12   Transmittal Letters / **92**

12-1   Transmitting Payment on Account / **93**
12-2   Transmitting Final Payment on Account / **93**

12-3   Transmitting Payment—Discrepancy Explained / **94**
12-4   Transmitting a Contract / **95**
12-5   Transmitting a Program Draft for Approval / **96**
12-6   Transmitting Materials Separately / **97**

Section 13   Confirmation Letters / **98**

13-1   Confirming Oral Instructions / **99**
13-2   Confirming Prices and Discounts / **100**
13-3   Confirming an Appointment / **101**
13-4   Confirming Travel Arrangements / **102**

Section 14   "Announcing" Letters / **103**

14-1   Announcing a New Product / **104**
14-2   Announcing an Acquisition / **105**
14-3   Announcing an Anniversary / **106**

Part 4   SALES COMMUNICATIONS / **107**

Section 15   Writing Sales Letters / **108**

15-1   Selling a Product / **110**
15-2   Selling an Educational Course / **111**
15-3   Selling a Book / **112**
15-4   Selling Conference Accommodations / **113**
15-5   Selling a "Retirement Concept" of Living / **114**

Section 16   Writing Sales Promotion Communications / **115**

16-1   Invitation to an Open House / **116**
16-2   Formalized Invitation to a Special Exhibit / **117**
16-3   Follow-Up to an Exhibit Visitor / **118**
16-4   Announcing New Products and Services / **119**
16-5   Announcing a New Location / **120**
16-6   Welcoming a Newcomer to the Community / **121**

Part 5   LETTERS FROM CUSTOMERS TO SUPPLIERS / **123**

Section 17   General Letters from Customers to Suppliers / **124**

17-1   Placing a Cash Order / **125**
17-2   Placing a COD Order / **126**
17-3   Placing a Credit Card Order / **127**
17-4   Praising a Supplier's Sales Representative / **128**
17-5   Thanking a Supplier for Service and Support / **129**

Section 18   Problem Letters from Customers to Suppliers / **130**

18-1   Receipt of a Low-Quality Office Product / **131**
18-2   Response to Letter About Receipt of a Low-Quality Office Product / **132**
18-3   Error in an Invoice / **133**
18-4   Response Regarding Error in an Invoice / **133**
18-5   Complaint About a Supplier's Sales Representative / **134**
18-6   Response to Complaint About a Supplier's Sales Representative / **135**
18-7   Poor Service on a Special Order / **136**
18-8   Response to a Letter Regarding Poor Service on a Special Order / **137**
18-9   Poor Performance on a Service Contract / **138**
18-10   Responding to a Letter About Poor Performance on a Service Contract / **139**
18-11   Receipt of an Unacceptable Substitute / **140**
18-12   Response to Letter About an Unacceptable Substitute / **141**
18-13   Customer Receives a "Pay-or-Else" Letter in Error / **142**
18-14   Response to a Complaint About "Pay-or-Else" Letter / **143**
18-15   Irate Customer Accuses Supplier of Sloppy Record Keeping / **144**
18-16   Response to Customer About Sloppy Record Keeping / **145**
18-17   Response by an Irate Customer Who Discovers an Error / **145**
18-18   Complaint About Loss of Conference Materials / **146**
18-19   Response to Complaint About Loss of Conference Materials / **147**
18-20   Customer Not Given an Expected Discount / **148**
18-21   Response to a Customer Who Is Not Given an Expected Discount / **149**

Part 6   LETTERS FROM SUPPLIERS TO CUSTOMERS / **151**

Section 19   General Letters from Suppliers to Customers / **153**

19-1   Introducing a New Sales Representative / **154**
19-2   Follow-Up of a Sales Representative's Call / **155**
19-3   Thanking a Customer for Courtesies to a Sales Representative / **156**
19-4   Acknowledging a First Order / **157**
19-5   Follow-Up After Services Have Been Rendered / **158**
19-6   Follow-Up on a Previous Order / **159**
19-7   Thanking a Customer for a Referral / **160**
19-8   Thanking a Customer for Payment and for an Order / **161**
19-9   Expressing Appreciation for Past Support / **162**
19-10   Acknowledging a Large Order / **163**
19-11   Congratulating a Customer on a Professional Achievement / **164**
19-12   Writing to a Customer Who Has Stopped Buying / **165**
19-13   Winning Back an Inactive Customer / **166**
19-14   Thank-You Letter for Sending a Friend / **167**
19-15   Congratulations on Opening a New Store / **168**
19-16   Thanking a Customer for Receiving a Sales Representative / **169**

19-17 Thanking a Person Who Has Been a Satisfied Customer for
       20 Years / **170**
19-18 Letter to a Customer About the Illness of a Sales Representative / **171**
19-19 Inviting a Cash Customer to Use Credit / **172**

Section 20 Problem Letters from Suppliers to Customers / **173**

20-1   Delayed Shipment / **174**
20-2   Unexpectedly Out of Stock / **175**
20-3   Mistake in Filling an Order / **176**
20-4   Wrong Size Shipped Twice / **177**
20-5   Error in an Invoice / **178**
20-6   Wrong Merchandise Sent—Customer Primarily to Blame / **179**
20-7   Customer Takes an Unearned Discount / **180**
20-8   Unauthorized Return of Merchandise / **181**
20-9   Damaged Stock Returned for Credit / **182**
20-10 Unauthorized Use of Service Personnel / **183**
20-11 Damaged Shipment—Carrier Perhaps to Blame / **184**
20-12 Damaged Shipment—Customer Definitely to Blame / **185**
20-13 Suggesting a Substitute / **186**
20-14 Returning an Unsigned Check for Signature / **187**
20-15 Response to an Irate Customer About Sloppy Record Keeping / **188**
20-16 Bending Company Policy to Say "Yes" to a Customer / **189**
20-17 Saying "No" to a Customer / **190**

Part 7 CREDIT AND COLLECTION LETTERS / **191**

Section 21 Credit Letters / **192**

21-1   Requesting Commercial Credit / **194**
21-2   Requesting Information from a Commercial Credit Applicant / **195**
21-3   Requesting Information from References Supplied / **196**
21-4   Accepting an Applicant for Commercial Credit / **197**
21-5   Turning Down an Applicant for Commercial Credit / **198**
21-6   Another Letter Denying Credit / **199**
21-7   Accepting an Applicant for Consumer Credit / **200**
21-8   Turning Down an Applicant for Consumer Credit / **201**

Section 22 Collection Letters / **202**

22-1   First Reminder After Monthly Statement / **203**
22-2   Second Reminder / **204**
22-3   Third Reminder / **204**
22-4   Fourth Reminder—Telephone Call / **205**

22-5 Fifth Reminder—Telegram / **205**

22-6 Sixth Reminder—Personal Letter / **206**

22-7 Seventh Reminder—The Final Letter / **206**

Part 8 INTEROFFICE LETTERS (MEMORANDUMS) / **207**

Section 23 "Announcing" Memorandums / **208**

23-1 Announcing a Meeting / **209**

23-2 Announcing a Moratorium on Staff Additions / **210**

23-3 Announcing a New Library / **211**

23-4 Announcing Final Plans for New Warehousing / **213**

23-5 Announcing a New High-Level Position / **214**

23-6 Announcing the Promotion of an Executive / **215**

Section 24 Procedural Memorandums / **216**

24-1 Writing a Confirmation Memorandum / **217**

24-2 Reviewing the Importance of Merit Ratings / **218**

24-3 Employee Request to Attend a Convention / **219**

24-4 Requesting Permission to Establish a New Position / **220**

24-5 The Company President Writes About a "Grabbag" of Valuable Leftovers / **221**

Section 25 Memorandums as Reports / **222**

25-1 Reporting on Heavy Turnover in a Regional Office / **223**

25-2 Report on Customer Correspondence / **224**

25-3 Suggestions for Improving the Company House Organ / **226**

25-4 Report About Centralization of a Department / **228**

Part 9 LETTERS CONCERNING GUEST SPEAKERS / **231**

Section 26 Inviting Guest Speakers / **232**

26-1 Inviting a Professional Speaker / **233**

26-2 Professional Speaker's Response to an Invitation / **234**

26-3 Responding to the Letter from a Professional Speaker / **235**

26-4 Inviting a Panel Participant—Modest Fee Offered / **236**

26-5 Panel Participant's Negative Response to an Invitation / **237**

26-6 Inviting a "Second-Choice" Panelist / **238**

26-7 Inviting a Keynote Speaker—No Funds Available / **239**

Section 27   Thanking Guest Speakers / **240**

27-1   Thanking an Outstanding Professional Speaker / **241**
27-2   Thanking a Successful Keynote Speaker / **242**
27-3   Thanking a Successful Speaker and Requesting Copies / **243**
27-4   Thanking an After-Dinner Speaker / **244**
27-5   Thanking an Ineffective Luncheon Speaker / **245**
27-6   Thanking a Disappointing Substitute Speaker / **246**

Part 10   PUBLIC RELATIONS AND PERSONNEL LETTERS / **247**

Section 28   General Public Relations Letters / **248**

28-1   Handling a Special Request / **249**
28-2   Refusing a Request to Buy Advertising / **250**
28-3   Acknowledging a Request for a Donation / **251**
28-4   Turning Down a Request for a Donation / **252**
28-5   Responding to a Friendly Critic / **253**
28-6   Responding to an Outraged Critic / **254**
28-7   Turning Down a Request for Confidential Information / **255**
28-8   Apologizing for Inconveniences / **256**

Section 29   Personal Letters / **257**

29-1   Responding to a Qualified Applicant—No Position Available / **258**
29-2   Responding to an Unqualified Applicant—Position Available / **259**
29-3   Writing to an Applicant Who Failed to Qualify / **260**
29-4   Responding to a Partially Qualified Applicant / **261**
29-5   Requesting Information About a Job Applicant / **262**
29-6   Offering an Executive Position to a Qualified Person / **263**
29-7   Announcing an Important Appointment—News Release / **265**
29-8   Writing a Valuable Worker Being Discharged Because of Unfavorable Economic Conditions / **266**
29-9   Demotion of a Field Sales Manager Because of Economic Conditions / **267**

Part 11   WRITING RESPONSIBILITIES OF EXECUTIVE ASSISTANTS / **269**

Section 30   When-the-Executive-Is-Away Letters / **270**

30-1   Using Discretion in Writing for the Executive / **271**
30-2   Handling a Request to Participate in a Convention Program / **272**
30-3   Referring Problems to Others / **273**
30-4   "Holding" Letter About a Purchasing Decision / **274**

30-5   Follow-Up Letter to a Company Executive / **275**
30-6   Disavowing a "True" Rumor / **276**

Section 31   Writing for the Executive's Signature / **277**

31-1   Accepting a Speaking Invitation / **278**
31-2   Saying "No" to a Request for Support / **279**
31-3   Writing a Major Stockholder / **280**
31-4   Suggesting an Alternate Speaker / **281**
31-5   Responding to a Letter of Praise About a Speech / **282**
31-6   Thanking a Reader for Favorable Comments / **283**

Part 12   EMPLOYEE RELATIONS LETTERS / **285**

Section 32   Letters of Congratulation and Appreciation / **286**

32-1   Congratulating an Employee on a Job Well Done / **287**
32-2   Congratulating an Employee on a New Management Concept / **288**
32-3   Congratulating an Employee for an Outstanding Report / **289**
32-4   Congratulating an Employee on an Anniversary / **290**
32-5   Congratulating a New Member of the Twenty-Five-Year Club / **291**
32-6   Congratulating an Employee for Community Recognition / **292**
32-7   Writing a Letter of Congratulation to the Boss / **293**
32-8   Responding to Congratulations on a Promotion / **294**

Section 33   Letters on Retirement / **295**

33-1   Congratulating an Employee on Retirement—a Happy Occasion / **296**
33-2   Extending Good Wishes to a Reluctant Retiree / **297**
33-3   Writing an Employee Retiring for Health Reasons / **298**

Section 34   Letters of Sympathy / **299**

34-1   Death of an Immediate Supervisor and Close Friend / **300**
34-2   Sympathy on the Event of a Serious Illness / **301**
34-3   Serious Injury of a Close Friend and Employee and Her Family / **302**

Section 35   Letters of Recommendation / **303**

35-1   Unqualified Recommendation of a Former Employee / **304**
35-2   Qualified Recommendation of a Former Employee / **305**

Section 36   Unfavorable Reference Letters and Warnings to Employees / **306**

36-1   Responding to a Request for Information About an Unsatisfactory Former Employee / **308**

36-2   Warning Letter to an Employee / **309**

36-3   Terminating an Employee by Letter / **310**

Part 13   JOB-GETTING LETTERS AND OTHER EMPLOYMENT COMMUNICATIONS / **311**

Section 37   Job-Getting Communications / **312**

37-1   Job Résumé—Middle-Management Position / **318**

37-2   Job Résumé—Change of Career / **320**

37-3   Job Résumé—High-Level Position / **322**

37-4   Job Résumé—Little Related Job Experience / **324**

37-5   Application Letter for Middle-Management Position / **327**

37-6   Application Letter for Change of Career / **328**

37-7   Application Letter for High-Level Position / **329**

37-8   Application Letter for a Position Requiring Different Backgound / **330**

Section 38   Other Employment Communications / **331**

38-1   Requesting Permission to Use a Person as a Reference / **332**

38-2   Thanking a Reference / **333**

38-3   Follow-Up for Reason of Elapsed Time / **334**

38-4   Follow-Up to Present Additional Information / **334**

38-5   Accepting a Job Offer / **335**

38-6   Rejecting a Job Offer—Better Opportunity / **337**

38-7   Rejecting a Job Offer—No Interest in the Position / **338**

38-8   Letter of Resignation—Dislike for Travel / **339**

38-9   Letter of Resignation—No Opportunity for Growth / **340**

38-10 Letter of Resignation—Bypassed for Promotion / **341**

38-11 Letter of Resignation—Better Job Offer / **342**

38-12 Letter of Resignation—Personal Conflict / **343**

Part 14   SOCIAL CORRESPONDENCE / **345**

Section 39   Formal Invitations and Responses / **346**

39-1   Formal Invitation to Honor a New President / **347**

39-2   Formal Invitation to an Annual Banquet / **348**

39-3 Accepting a Formal Invitation / **349**
39-4 Accepting a Formal Invitation with a Qualification / **350**
39-5 Expressing Regrets to a Formal Invitation / **351**

Section 40 Informal Invitations and Responses / **352**

40-1 Informal Invitation to Dinner / **353**
40-2 Accepting an Informal Invitation / **354**
40-3 Expressing Regrets to an Informal Invitation / **355**

Section 41 "Bread-and-Butter" Letters / **356**

41-1 Expressing Thanks for a Personal Favor / **357**
41-2 Expressing Thanks for Generous Hospitality / **358**

Index / **359**

About This Handbook

Nearly everyone with writing responsibilities occasionally faces a problem of composing "just the right letter" in a situation that he or she has not met before. This statement can be verified by librarians, bookstore proprietors, communications specialists, and others who frequently receive requests for a certain model that will guide the writer in framing the appropriate letter.

Interestingly, some of the writers who face what-to-say dilemmas are experienced communicators. Others are novices whose exposure to even everyday writing situations is very limited. To some, then, this handbook will probably serve as an occasional reference; to others, it will become a much-used source of new ideas.

When *The McGraw-Hill Handbook of Business Letters* was first published in 1983, it was met with enthusiastic approval by thousands of people in business offices, libraries, bookstores, and the general public. Shortly after publication, this handbook was honored as the main monthly selection of the Fortune Book Club and was later translated into Japanese and Chinese. Given encouragement by this satisfying record, we undertook a second and now an enlarged, updated third edition.

In this latest edition, we hasten to say that three of the features that make this handbook a unique reference remain intact:

1. A wide variety of letter-writing situations are covered—from asking for special favors to saying no with the least possible offense, to terminating an employee by mail.

2. The situation that precedes each model tells the reader why the letter was written and what the writer hoped to achieve in composing it.

3. The number and title of each communication make it easy to locate the precise model that you're looking for.

A Final Word

Although this is primarily a reference book, we strongly encourage you to give careful attention at the outset to the general discussions—all of Part 1 and the kick-off material for each of the remaining parts and sections. It is here that the basic principles of good letter writing are emphasized. These principles will provide you with a solid foundation for communicating effectively and help you create your own letters with greater confidence and independence.

Roy W. Poe

A Gallery of Letters

SHOW-VOELKER CORPORATION
972 Caswell Avenue
Berkeley, California 94707

July 30, 19XX

Ms. Pamela R. Madison
320 NW 7th Street
Anderson, Indiana 07713

Dear Ms. Madison:

The film you asked for, "Filing and Finding," is certainly available, and I'll be happy to send you six copies immediately.

However, you might like to know that we have just released a new 16-mm color film, "Modern Records Management." The new film covers the traditional methods of "paper" filing--alphabetic, subject, numeric, and geographic--along with the procedures and equipment accompanying these methods. But it also presents the many new aspects of records management that have emerged in recent years--in short, "electronic record keeping." As you know, records management has undergone a dramatic revolution, triggered, of course, by the advance in computer technology and the advent of film (microfilm, etc.). I think you and your students will find "Modern Records Management" exciting and highly informative. A booklet describing these materials is enclosed.

May I send you this new film instead of "Filing and Finding"? I expect a sample copy to be available within the next ten days, and I will reserve it for you if you wish (use the enclosed postcard). There is no charge, of course, but we do ask that you return it within a week--the demand for the film is very great.

Thank you for writing.

Cordially yours,

M. M. Hightower
Sales Representative

Enclosures

A Sales Letter

TENNIS INTERNATIONAL
435 South Ironwood Drive
South Bend, Indiana 46675

May 1, 19XX

Dear Friend:

Ivan Lendl ... Boris Becker ... Steffi Graf ... Jim Courier ... Jimmy Connors ... Stefan Edburg ... Pete Sampras ... John McEnroe ... Monica Seles ... Michael Chang ... Andre Agassi ... John Newcomb ... Jack Kramer ... Martina Navratilova

Pardon me for name-dropping, but I have exciting news about these and other all-time tennis greats that I want to share with *Tennis International* readers. You know, of course, that each of these players blazed the pro circuit in one era or another, leaving an indelible imprint on tennis history. But did you know that they were also prolific commentators on the subject?

Tennis International has arranged to issue in book form the major writings of 20 of the greatest names in tennis. The first is *Ivan Lendl on Tennis*, followed by similar books by those named above, plus many of today's headliners whose names are instantly recognized by every tennis enthusiast.

I think you'll find every volume in this series immensely exciting. Each will be profusely illustrated by America's leading tennis artist, Eklund Nillsen, and will be handsomely bound in a rich-looking leatherlike cover. The price of each book will be only $18.95, including postage.

Use the enclosed card to order your copy of *Ivan Lendl on Tennis*. I'll accept your personal check now, or I can bill you later. As each volume is released, I'll send you advance notice. I don't think you'll want to miss a single one!

SPECIAL BONUS! If your order reaches me before May 15, I'll include--absolutely free--a beautifully illustrated 24-page booklet, *Back to Fundamentals*. It could make a big difference in your game.

Sincerely,

William Martin
Marketing Manager

Enclosure

A Sales Promotion Letter

Stacey's
1670 Broad Street
Newark, New Jersey 07102

June 29, 19XX

Mrs. Virginia Cranshaw
28 Blanford Place
Verona, New Jersey 07044

You've earned	
50 cents	Dear Mrs. Cranshaw:

50 cents
$ 1.00   Is it worth 50 cents a line to you to read this
           letter?

$ 1.50   We'll gladly pay you that amount--but only if you
$ 2.00   read the entire letter.

$ 2.50   Now, we reason it this way: You really are a valued
$ 3.00   customer, although lately you haven't been in even
$ 3.50   to say "Howdy." We would like you to come back to
$ 4.00   Stacey's; we would like to see you often; we would
$ 4.50   like to reopen your account. We think that it is
$ 5.00   better for us to have a long-time customer like you
$ 5.50   on our books than a customer we don't even know. And
$ 6.00   since it would cost us at least $11 to open a new
$ 6.50   account, we would rather pass the amount on to you.

$ 7.00   So, we say, "Here's an $11 check on the house. Come
$ 7.50   in and select anything you want to up to $50 or more,
$ 8.00   from our extensive stock of nationally advertised
$ 8.50   apparel for the entire family. Or select a household
$ 9.00   article--toaster, iron, lamp, or chair--you've been
$ 9.50   thinking about. Or, do your gift shopping early for
$10.00   such items as watches, silver bowls, or stereo records.

$10.50   The enclosed "check" is your down payment.

$11.00   Why not come in tomorrow?

                    Cordially yours,

                    Phyllis Moore
Enclosure   Customer Relations

Explaining a Price Increase

EUREKA AUTOMOTIVE PARTS
2003 East Pershing Street
Springfield, Missouri 68503

February 28, 19XX

Mr. G. Henry Richert
Rick's Auto Parts
1610 Center Street
Joplin, Missouri 64801

Dear Rick:

I've had several letters from good customers like you about our recent price increases on auto parts, and I'll tell you what I told the others.

I assure you, Rick, that we do not raise prices indiscriminately. But when we have to, we have to. Have you bought new suits or shoes lately, or a new automobile, or shopped at your local supermarket? If you have, you are as shocked as I am with the "outrageous" prices. But why pick on clothing manufacturers or automobile manufacturers or food suppliers? Everybody's doing it. I can remember just a few years back when a person could buy a nice house for $40,000. That same house today could cost over $100,000!

Our prices on automotive parts are just a reflection of what is happening to everything you and I buy. I remember when a fellow could get a change of oil and a new filter for a little over $8. Today we'd pay about $32 for the same purchase.

Enough. I really think that, if you compare our prices with those of other automotive supply houses, you will find that we are right in line with our competitors--perhaps even lower for the same quality. Granted, some supply houses can beat our prices because the quality of parts is much lower. But you must consider quality in everything you buy.

Thank you for writing me, Rick. I hope I haven't sounded uncaring. Certainly I do care, but I can't do anything about it except to give you a fair price.

Very cordially yours,

Donald Halston
Business Manager

Enclosure

Follow-Up to an Invitation to Speak

Consolidated Paper Corporation
463 Vista Boulevard NE
Albuquerque, New Mexico 87066

February 23, 19XX

Mr. Byron Hefley, President
Hefley Consultants, Inc.
10950 East Bella Vista
Scottsdale, Arizona 85259

Dear Mr. Hefley:

Everyone is delighted that you can be with us in Albuquerque on March 23. Thank you for accepting our invitation.

Enclosed is a rough draft of the program. You will see that the luncheon at which you are to speak begins at 12:15, and your talk should get under way about 1:30 p.m. I will introduce you. (Would you please send me a brief biographical sketch that I may refer to?)

I know that our workshop participants will be very much interested in your varied experience in the business arena. I'm sure you have some amusing stories to tell, and a bit of humor will be perfectly in order. I hope you'll devote some time, however, to giving us your view of the role of the executive assistant and how she or he can prepare for further advancement into management.

As I mentioned earlier, our meeting will be at the Rio Ranchero. If you plan to fly, let me know the airline and flight number, and I'll meet you at the airport. Or if you plan to drive, I'm certain you know how to get to the Rio Ranchero. You'll find our meeting room posted on the "Today's Events" board in the lobby.

In the meantime, please let me know if there is anything I can do to help you. We want to make your visit with us thoroughly enjoyable.

Sincerely yours,

Cynthia Murphy
Program Coordinator

Enclosure

Praising a Supplier for Services

THE RANIER HARDWARE COMPANY
1305 London Road • Duluth • Minnesota • 55811

October 15, 19XX

Mr. George Honeycutt
214 Steward Avenue
Kalamazoo, Minnesota 48912

Dear George:

Generally, it's the customer who gets all the attention.

When we held our Golden Jubilee Anniversary last month, we had a wonderful celebration. One of the things we thought of first was to write a couple of hundred of our retail customers to thank them for their loyal support over the years. Without them, we said, we couldn't possibly have become what we are; in fact, we wouldn't even be around to celebrate those 50 years. Of course, we meant it; you know the importance of loyal friends as well as we do.

But later we got to thinking: What about those poeple who kept us supplied with quality hardware products that dealers wanted to buy and did buy time and time again? Don't they deserve some credit, too? We've been buying hammers, saws, blades, wrenches, and a couple of dozen other Mikkelson-brand products from you for how long--35 years? And you've always given us genuine quality at a fair price, plus outstanding service. What more can a wholesaler ask from a manufacturer? Sure, we've had our minor squabbles from time to time, and your attitude was that the customer is always right (in our case, he often wasn't). Whatever the problems were--I forget--they haven't detracted one bit from our high opinion of your company, your products, and your people.

So, on at least one occasion, I want to direct my full attention not to our important customers, but to our important suppliers. Mikkelson stands very high on our list of those to whom we owe a great big thank you. Thank you!

Sincerely,

James R. Fernandez
Purchasing Manager

P.S.: When a small crisis arises between us--and it will--you won't hold over my head the nice things I've said, will you?

Letter of Recommendation

BRUNSWICK LIGHTING CORPORATION
1250 Avenue of the Americas
New York, New York 10020

August 10, 19XX

Mrs. Wynema Noblett
160 North Avenue
New Rochelle, New York 10901

Dear Mrs. Noblett:

I'm delighted to speak on behalf of Eileen Davis for the position of administrative assistant in your company.

Eileen has been my personal secretary for three years, and I have never had a better one. She was actually my administrative assistant in every sense of the term--we just don't have this job title at Brunswick Lighting Corporation. At any rate, Eileen was my "right arm" during the time she was here. She was excellent in her telephone communications, outstanding in dictation and transcription, and an excellent writer (she wrote many of the letters, memorandums, and reports that I signed).

I'm sorry that she resigned this position here, but I understand the reason was the long commute from her home in Westport--not only the distance but also the cost. What distressed her the most was the early rising hour and the late getting-home hour.

In closing, let me say this about Eileen Davis: If she were available to me, I would rehire her in a minute.

Sincerely yours,

Jennifer Webb
Controller

THE _____
McGRAW-HILL
HANDBOOK OF
BUSINESS
LETTERS

Part 1

THE LETTER WRITER'S CRAFT

Over the years, a lot of fuss has been made over the high cost of business letters. And with justification. When you think about such elements as stationery and postage, the writer's time, and overhead expenses, the cost of a single letter can boggle the mind (perhaps $15 each!).

We are frank to admit that letter-writing costs are much too high in many companies. A few people write letters that are longer than they need to be.

But let's be realistic. The dollars *spent* to put a letter in the mail can be inconsequential when compared to the dollars *lost* by writing a bad letter (or no letter at all). A terse, quickly tossed-off message to a highly valued customer may delight the cost accountant with its economy, but could result in a dimunition or total loss of that customer's business. Thus it could be an incredibly expensive "inexpensive" letter.

Letters are not merely mediums of communication. They are effective substitutes for face-to-face visits, making and keeping friends, attracting and holding customers, and building a favorable image for your company.

In this part, we offer several suggestions on how you can make your letters do all these things, with emphasis on triggering greater profits by writing effective messages.

Section 1

What a Good Business Letter Is—and Is Not

A letter may be thought of as a substitute for a personal visit. Just about everybody finds it impossible to meet and talk with every person with whom he or she wants to communicate—whether friends or relatives in a distant town, fellow employees just three floors or one building away, or customers, clients, and suppliers scattered everywhere. And the telephone is not always a satisfactory means of communicating. This fact alone makes the letter a powerful medium of communication in all walks of life.

But even if we could handle all our business and social communications on a face-to-face basis, we would still need to prepare written communications. One reason is that we often need a permanent record of what was said, to whom, by whom, and on what date. Equally, if not more, important is that written communications often do a far better job than the spoken word.

There are many other reasons for being able to write effective business letters. In the first place, your value to your organization will be greatly enhanced, which often means faster progress up the promotion ladder. (Competent writers are not as plentiful as you might imagine, and someone who shows a special talent for writing stands out like a beacon.)

Second, those who can compose effective business letters make new friends and keep old ones for the organization, thereby increasing sales and profits, which all businesses need for survival.

Third, a good writer can save a great deal of time and effort for an organization. A great deal of money is wasted each year by people who write windy and garbled messages that befuddle and exhaust their readers.

Finally, your rating as an employee—which hinges greatly on your skill in working harmoniously with the people around you—shoots up dramatically when you master the art of writing sensible, tactful, and finely honed communications.

If you have ever taken a course in business letter writing, chances are that you learned that a good letter is just right in length, personal, tactful, courteous, clear, conversational, and interesting. You were probably told that every letter you write is a sales letter; that is, you're always selling something—a product, a company image, an idea, or yourself. And you were cautioned to handle responses to all communications promptly, meaning within a day or two.

It's hard to quarrel with these rules because most of them make good sense for most letters. But watch that phrase, *for most letters*.

It's easy to make lists of rules for doing things—anybody can do it. Rules for writing good letters are no exception. Many large companies publish manuals for letter writers that are essentially style books. Although they may contain a few examples of good letters, the rules and examples supplied don't always work. The reason is that they are usually established to fit ideal conditions, and, as we know, conditions are rarely ideal. If you're answering an inquiry from a potential customer who is genuinely interested in your company's products, you can simply turn to your list of rules, and you're off and running. Your letter is friendly, tactful, personal, courteous, sales-structured, and the rest. But what if you're a credit manager and you have to write a sixth letter to a customer who appears to have no intention of paying the $2500 that is now six months past due? What happens to your warmth, friendliness, tact, courtesy, and the rest of "the rules"? Here you can close your style book. Nothing is going to work: You've used up all the "good" rules in the first five letters. Now you're going to have to write an "or-else" letter that will sound about as friendly as a wounded grizzly.

What Is a Good Letter?

Maybe you think we've started off this discussion negatively, talking about the unpleasant side of letter writing. Certainly we don't want to give the impression that letter writers are Simon Legrees at heart. But we're just as anxious that you don't get the impression that good letters are always tidings of great joy. Many excellent letters are neither brief, friendly, interesting, salesy, nor even courteous. You know that, in your own daily dealings with people, there are sometimes strong differences of opinion, that some individuals are cranky and unreasonable, that tempers flare when silly mistakes generate agonizing crises. On the other hand, most employees are intelligent enough to know that it's a lot more fun to work in a place where harmony and good cheer prevail, that surliness and bickering affect not only attitudes but productivity as well. So thank goodness most workers bring their "company manners" (learned at home) to the workplace.

If utopia is not likely to be found in any organization where there are pressures for performance, profits, or productivity, why should it be expected to exist *between* organizations? So, when it comes to business letters, writers should display their best "company" behavior, striving very hard to keep friends, generate goodwill, and enhance sales opportunities.

What *is* a good business letter? *A good business letter is one that obtains the results the writer hoped for.* To make the definition work, we have to assume that the writer wants what is best for (1) the organization she or he works for and (2) the individual to whom the letter is addressed.

Reader-Writer Relationships

The definition of a good business letter sounds simple and workable. But don't be misled; a good letter can be very difficult to write. One reason is that people are so different.

Not only people, but circumstances, can affect the reaction you receive. Let's say you write a beautifully apologetic letter to Customer A, explaining why for the fourth time in two months the wrong merchandise was shipped. The response you receive is something like this: *That's understandable; we make our share of mistakes, too. Think nothing of it.*

"Wow," you think, "that was *some* letter I wrote." And justifiably so. The reaction you got was exactly what you'd hoped for.

But Customer B gets the same elegant explanation for four similar boners, and the response you get from her is: *I'm fed up. No matter what you say, I can't ignore the shabby way you've handled my four orders. I've lost a lot of business because of you, and I want nothing more to do with you.*

How is it possible to win and lose with the same letter? The two recipients and/or circumstances may be entirely different. Customer A may have had plenty of stock in the warehouse and was not inconvenienced much by getting the wrong merchandise. Or he may be a long-time satisfied customer, with several personal friends in the company. Or he may owe you a favor for some special service in the past. Or perhaps he's just a person who doesn't rile easily.

On the other hand, Customer B may own a small business with a limited inventory, and any delay in getting the right merchandise could be disastrous. Or she may be a new customer who has placed only four orders with your company, all of which were fouled up. Or she may simply have a short fuse, not uncommon among harried small business owners.

So writing a letter is a very personal process. Communications are written by and to people, and the content of a particular message depends on how the writers feel about their subject, how well they know their reader, and what attitudes and policies are set by the organization they represent.

Suppose, out of an audience of 50 people, a dozen who heard the speaker at a large convention decide to write her about her talk. Although all 12 letters may have some common characteristics—complimentary, tactful, friendly, and so on—no two will be exactly alike. They will vary in approach, length, and emphasis. Although each letter will be different, all may be "good" letters, depending on what each writer wants her or his message to convey.

Following is a letter you may have written, assuming you are not personally acquainted with the speaker.

Dear Mrs. Garvin:

I thoroughly enjoyed your talk at the ASTD convention in Sacramento, and was especially interested in the new series of sales motivation films your company is soon to release.

Would you please send me complete details? If I could borrow one of the films temporarily, I will see that it is returned within a week.

Thank you!

Cordially yours,

That's a good letter. No wasted words but specific and friendly. But suppose the speaker you heard in Sacramento turned out to be an old college friend whom you haven't seen for four or five years. You had no chance to talk with her, but you want more information on the films she spoke about.

Dear Carla:

It was great seeing you at the ASTD convention in Sacramento—what a pleasant surprise! I thought your talk was super, and the rest of the audience was obviously equally impressed.

As training director here at Halliburton's, I'm always searching for new things. We're not happy with our sales training materials, and I'm intrigued by your series of motivational films.

Would you send me complete details? What are the chances of my borrowing one of the films for viewing by several people here? I promise to take good care of it and get it back within a week.

I'm sorry we didn't have a chance to visit in Sacramento, but you were mobbed as soon as the meeting broke up, and I had to dash for a plane. If you ever get to Cincinnati or I to Monterey, we've got a lot of catching up to do! Did you know that Agnes Richards is the managing director of the Singapore Hilton?

Cheers!

Although there are very few hard and fast rules for good letter writing, most people will respond favorably to your letters if you observe the following guidelines when possible:

---

1. *Consider goodwill in your business communications.*
2. *Don't waste words.*
3. *Keep the language lively and simple.*
4. *Personalize your letters.*
5. *Emphasize the positive.*
6. *Use correct letter form.*

We will cover each of these guidelines in Secs. 2 through 7.

Section 2

Consider Goodwill in Your Communications

Goodwill is a *friendly feeling*, or a feeling of confidence, that makes a customer buy from one firm rather than another. Although many people think of goodwill as an intangible thing, it is looked upon as an asset in computing the worth of a business. So it is a very valuable "intangible." Goodwill is greatly enhanced by a firm's reputation for:

- Turning out products or services that will appeal to customers.
- Selling at fair prices.
- Dealing fairly with employees, customers, and suppliers.
- Giving prompt attention to the needs of people.
- Supporting local community activities.
- Donating money or services to worthy causes.
- Being honest and aboveboard with everyone.

Of course, the opposite is also true. A company's goodwill is negative if it has a reputation for shoddy products, unfair prices, and a lofty attitude toward people. Owners and executives know that a poor public image will eventually be translated into poor sales and low profits. Understandably, then, more and more companies spend a lot of money in an effort to establish and maintain good "people relations," another name for goodwill. Without friends and supporters—without goodwill—the typical business will eventually perish.

Perhaps you enjoy shopping in a favorite store. Probably you prefer this store because it gives excellent, friendly service. Or it may be more conveniently located than other stores, or the prices appeal to you, or the people who wait on you are cheerful and courteous. The owners want you to think of them when you need merchandise or services.

Building goodwill—and holding it—are important requirements of the business letter. Many of the people you write never enter your place of business, never see you, never talk to you. Their impressions of your business and their attitude toward it are formed entirely through the letters they receive. A business letter, therefore, is not only a representative; it is also an ambassador.

Typical goodwill letters are those that say "thank you," "we appreciate," "we congratulate," and "we're sorry" (about an error), and so on. Whether or not you believe such letters are worthwhile, the fact remains that many world-famous companies use them to continue building their enterprises. If you were to investigate the progress of a company committed to a better letters program for building goodwill, you will almost certainly find it a step ahead of its competitors.

Although we can easily understand what goodwill means, it is sometimes difficult for many firms to achieve it. However, executives agree that letters certainly can contribute to a firm's goodwill, sometimes referred to as "favorable public relations." Good letters make a positive contribution; poorly written letters make a negative contribution. Letters that build goodwill are friendly, helpful, courteous, and tactful. And letter writers must be especially sensitive to people's needs and feelings if they are to be effective and build goodwill.

The Audiences for Goodwill Letters

There are four different audiences for goodwill letters: employees, customers, the public, and suppliers.

Employees

When management speaks and/or writes a letter complimenting an employee for outstanding achievement, it helps to build good employee relations. In turn, happy employees do their best in dealing with customers and the general public.

Following is a letter written to an employee by her supervisor. (Remember, a written message is often much more effective than a spoken one.)

Dear Jan:

I was so impressed with your presentation to the Long-Range Planning Committee that I couldn't resist telling you so in writing.

It was obvious to me that you hit it off admirably with your audience. And this statement is seconded by the number of listeners taking notes during your talk.

Congratulations!

Sincerely,

Customers

Good relations with customers can be highly profitable. These are the people who keep the company in business, and nothing is too good for them. The following letter was written by the president celebrating the fiftieth anniversary of the company.

Dear Bill:

As we approach our fiftieth anniversary, we are selfishly congratulating ourselves on this great achievement. However, it occurred to me that it would be a grievous error if we failed to give credit to those loyal customers who helped us to succeed—indeed, to flourish in the carpeting business. Oh, we had a few lean years at the beginning, but thanks to people like you, we pulled out of them and landed on solid footing.

All of us here at Bobbins Carpeting International thank you sincerely for standing by us so loyally. Could we have succeeded so well without people like you? No way!

Cordially yours,

Dear Mr. Stein:

I want to thank you again for choosing the Biltmore as your headquarters during the three days of the NOMA convention. It's people like you who make the hotel business rewarding and satisfying.

Of course, I happen to know that you didn't choose the Biltmore just because it was the headquarters of the NOMA convention. You have made it a habit of choosing us whenever you are in Hartford, and, of course, we are delighted to have you any time you visit our fair city.

You may be confident, Mr. Stein, that we shall leave no stone unturned to provide you with the most comfortable rooms, delightful cuisine, and personal attention that you have a right to demand.

I hope you arrived home safely in Bakersfield and found things to your liking at Marvello Products Corporation.

Sincerely yours,

The Public   Aside from customers and employees, it is also profitable to have successful public relations within the local community.

Dear Dr. Orsini:

I was in the audience when you spoke to the Commonwealth Club last evening, and I want you to know how much I enjoyed your talk.

I agree with you when you say that it's time we have a full-time salaried manager in the drive to construct and maintain a Senior Citizens Recreation Center in Shelbyville. Did you know that Linda Lopez has resigned as director of the Educational Adult Committee? From what I hear and observe, I think she has done an outstanding job there. And if you sell your idea to the City Council, Linda might be a good choice for the job of heading this drive and, upon its completion, managing it.

I close to remark that I admire your participation in the civic affairs of Shelbyville. You are needed!

Very sincerely yours,

Suppliers   Dear Mrs. Owens:

I have just finished writing a thank-you letter to our loyal customers on the event of our fiftieth anniversary. Suddenly it occurred to me to get a letter out immediately to our major suppliers without whose support we probably wouldn't have survived.

Over the years, I can recall many situations in which your company helped us out in filling a large rush order from an important customer. Without your help, heaven knows how many orders we would have lost! This reminds me of the statement we often make to customers: Without you we would not be in business. I now take the opportunity to say it better to our marvelous suppliers: Never in our business history has so much been owed to so few.

Thank you!

Cordially yours,

A Business House Promotes Goodwill

Following is a letter from a mail order men's furnishing house in which goodwill is mentioned.

L U X O R
A Proud Tradition for Over 82 Years

Dear Mr. Fisher:

Throughout the U.S.A. more than 17 million people rely on Luxor for quality, value, and service ... and they've made us the largest direct mail fashion houses in the world!

We recognize that our greatest asset is the continued goodwill of our customers. To this end, we are constantly searching for the finest quality merchandise at the lowest direct-to-you prices. Of the many thousands of items we consider each year, only those which meet our rigid standards of excellence are offered to our customers. We wouldn't dare do less, because each item is offered with a free trial *before* you decide to keep or return it.

For your convenience, we've developed the Luxor Easy Payment Plan. With it you can spread out the payments for your Luxor purchases and stay within your budget. That's one more way you can fight inflation when you shop Luxor.

We look forward with pleasure to serving you once again. You may be sure your order will be handled carefully and promptly. That's how we've maintained our reputation for more than 82 years.

Incidentally, our retail store here in Brandywine is open all year 'round. We'd be delighted to have you stop in and say "Hello," whenever you're visiting our area.

Cordially yours,

Section 3

Don't Waste Words

The writer who takes 100 words to say what might have been said just as well in 40 is a nuisance, a time waster. It is estimated that about one-third of the words in the typical business letter are wasted words.

Don't get the idea, though, that you should write in a telegraphic style. Sometimes you may want to include words that aren't really necessary, but that do add warmth and friendliness, resulting in a full-page letter. That's fine. The wasted words we refer to are those that clutter your message without adding anything to it—indeed, that detract from your letter.

Clutter Words and Phrases

If you want to be an effective letter writer, start now to edit your writing to eliminate nonsense words and phrases, repetition, and redundancies. For example:

Original (Unedited)   With reference to your request for an extension on your note under date of March 20, we have considered the matter carefully and are pleased to tell you that we will be willing to allow you an additional 90 days to make payment on your note.

Original (Edited)   ~~With reference to your request for an extension on your note under date of March 20, we have considered the matter carefully and~~ are pleased to ~~tell you that we will be willing to~~ allow you an additional 90 days to ~~make~~ ~~payment on~~ your note dated March 20 We

The edited version now reads as follows:

We are pleased to allow you an additional 90 days to pay your note dated March 20.

Note that the original paragraph contains 46 words, the revision 17. As you can see, there was no sacrifice in clarity by eliminating the clutter words and phrases; indeed, the message has been strengthened by this surgery.

Other examples follow.

Original (56 Words)

With reference to your recent request for 20 reprints of "How Good Are Sales Aptitude Tests?" in the May issue of *Modern Marketing Management*, these copies are enclosed for your convenience.

With appreciation for your kind remarks about this article and trusting you will find it very useful in your recruitment seminar in October, I remain,

Yours very truly,

Edited (31 Words)

Here are your 20 reprints of "How Good Are Sales Aptitude Tests?" I'm pleased you like the article and hope it will be exactly what you need for your recruitment seminar.

Sincerely yours,

Original (115 Words)

In looking at your current catalog, I notice that the emergency couch on page 50 (No. 273-1960) is shown in the illustration in the color of blue. However, in the description provided under the illustration, the colors listed as being available are black, ivory, green, and red. Does this mean that the color of the couch in the illustration is not available at this time?

If I could obtain the blue vinyl, which would match our decor, I would place an order in the near future for four at the price of $118.50 each. But I do not wish to order any of the other colors that you list in your description in the catalog.

Very cordially yours,

Edited (39 Words)

Is the emergency couch on page 50 of your catalog available in the blue vinyl illustrated? The colors listed as available do not include blue.

If the blue vinyl couch is available, I will place an order for four.

Very cordially yours,

Compare the following:

Unedited	Edited
Your check in the amount of $360	Your check for $360
Keep in mind the fact that	Remember that
Engaged in making a salary study	Making a salary study
Held a meeting to discuss	Met to discuss

Unedited	Edited
During the course of our research, we learned that	Our research revealed that
Until such time as you are in a position to	When you are able to
At this point in time	At this time
An extremely important element in building employee morale is the matter of recognition.	Recognition is extremely important in building employee morale.
In the event that	If
A large segment of the employees are of the opinion that	Many employees believe that
The size of the report is 112 pages in length.	The report contains 112 pages.
I hope you will be able to put in a brief appearance.	I hope you can drop in for a few minutes.
It is the recommendation of the operations committee that	The operations committee rcommends that
The treasurer made the announcement that	The treasurer announced that
There was only one objection to your proposal, and that was the matter of timing.	The only objection to your proposal was timing.
The manufacturing costs were quite a bit lower than any of us thought they would be.	The manufacturing costs were much lower than expected.
I hope that you will be in a position to make a decision within a short time.	I hope you can decide soon.
The difficulty with the present stock control system is that it cannot be depended on.	The present stock control system is not dependable.
Upon completion, please mail the application in the envelope that is being enclosed.	Please mail the completed application in the envelope enclosed.
These tractors are being sold at a price of $2995.	These tractors are priced at $2995.

Repetition

A common fault of some letter writers is repeating themselves. Following are examples:

Repetitive

1. Most industrial relations specialists recommend that *employees participate* in job evaluation, although many employers think that *employee participation* is not desirable.

2. *Although it is our policy to accept returned merchandise* that is in good condition, *returned merchandise* that is not salable cannot be *accepted*.

3. When we print your *form letters,* your customers will not recognize them as *form letters*. The *letters* will appear to be individually type-written.

4. It is *possible,* of course, that the damage occurred because of faulty packing. An even greater *possibility* is that the *shipper* was careless in storing the merchandise for safe *shipment*. In any event, we'll do everything *possible* to *ship* a replacement this week.

Edited

1. Most industrial relations specialists recommend that employees participate in job evaluation, although many employers do not share this point of view.

2. We accept only merchandise that can be resold.

3. When we print your form letters, your customers will think they are individually typewritten.

4. It is possible, of course, that the damage was the result of faulty packing. More likely, however, the carton was stored improperly by the shipper. In any event, we'll try to send a replacement this week.

Another form of repetition—redundancy—is illustrated in the following:

Redundant

Meets Thursday mornings at 10:00 o'clock a.m.

First and foremost

Prompt and speedy

Assemble together

Edited

Meets Thursday mornings at ten (*or* 10:00)

First *or* foremost

Prompt *or* speedy

Assemble

Redundant	Edited
Consensus of opinion	Consensus
Baffling and puzzling	Baffling *or* puzzling
Invisible to the eye	Invisible
The only other alternative	The only alternative
Repeat again	Repeat
The new procedure will begin to be initiated	The new procedure will begin (*or* take effect)
Contractual agreement	Contract *or* agreement
Fiscal financial year	Fiscal year
Agree and concur	Agree *or* concur
Free gratis	Free *or* gratis
Massively large	Massive *or* large
True facts	Facts
Vitally essential	Vital *or* essential
And etc.	Etc.
Endorse on the back	Endorse
Revert back	Revert

We said earlier, don't waste words. Compare the following.

Wordy	Better
At an early date	Soon (or give date)
At that time	Then
Due to the fact that	Because, since
In the event that	In case, if
Up to this writing	Until now
And etc.	Etc.
Both alike	Alike
Complete monoply	Monopoly
Cooperate together	Cooperate
Customary practice	Practice
Depreciate in value	Depreciate
During the course of	During
Endorse on the back	Endorse

Wordy	Better
Final completion	Completion
Lose out	Lose
May perhaps	May
New beginner	Beginner
Past experience	Experience
Over with	Over
Rarely ever	Rarely
Refer back	Refer
At all times	Always
In the near future	Soon (or give date)
Inasmuch as	Since

Brevity versus Common Sense

Because of our no-nos, you may by now have the idea that brevity is a cardinal virtue in business letters. Not so! Brevity can be a curse if you leave something out of your letters or wind up with a message that has no life.

Suppose you are writing to thank a speaker for an address before the Centerville Optimists Club Monday evening. If you want to be brief, you might write a letter like this:

Dear Mr. Weber:

This is to thank you for addressing the Centerville Optimists Club Monday evening. Your talk was well received, and I am grateful that you could be with us. The honorarium I promised is enclosed.

Very truly yours,

Not a bad letter—in fact, pretty good. But the writer is almost telegraphic in expressing appreciation to the speaker. Now let's look at another.

Dear Mr. Weber:

The members and guests of the Centerville Optimists Club to whom you spoke Monday evening are still talking about your superb presentation Monday evening. All those with whom I talked reported that they learned much from your talk, "Centerville in the 1990s."

Thank you, Mr. Weber, for sharing your insights into Centerville's future. How exciting! You certainly opened our eyes, and I speak for all the members of the Centerville Optimists Club when I say, "Well done!"

Sincerely,

P.S. The modest honorarium I promised is enclosed.

Sentence Length

The length and structure of your sentences are important factors in making your letters easy and interesting to read. Probably no other single writing fault hinders readability as much as the long, rambling sentence. For example:

Because of our limited warehousing facilities, we are studying the possibility of contracting with public warehouses and handling facilities, charging their customers only for the space occupied and the length of time it is used.

With only slight adjustments, the message above can be simplified:

Because of our limited warehousing facilities, we are studying the possibility of using public warehouses. Several in this area offer storage and handling facilities. Most charge only for the space occupied and the length of time it is used.

Paragraph Length

Be wary of "fat" paragraphs that give the reader no visual breather. Solid blocks of type are hurdles for the reader, and the writer should look for ways to break them up. Note the following example:

Many dictators simplify their planning by sorting incoming correspondence according to some particular method—for example, by subject matter. All letters that pertain to one topic are dictated before the dictator moves on to another topic. These writers say that separating the correspondence by subject matter improves their concentration and enables them to achieve the proper mood for each particular type of letter. Other successful dictators prefer to sort their correspondence according to difficulty. Some take the easy ones first; others, the tougher ones. There seems to be no hard-and-fast rule about this. And a third method of sorting mail to be attended to is according to urgency—the most pressing items first, regardless of subject matter or level of difficulty, and executives who are frequently interrupted in their dictation maintain that this type of sorting is a must.

Difficult reading? Yes. The paragraph is too long and needs to be broken down. Notice the following.

Most dictators simplify their planning by sorting correspondence according to three yardsticks—subject matter, difficulty, and urgency.

Subject Matter

Here all letters that pertain to one topic are dictated before the dictator moves on to another topic. Those who use this plan say it improves their concentration and enables them to achieve the proper mood for each type of letter.

Difficulty

Other successful dictators prefer to sort their correspondence according to difficulty. Some take the easy ones first; others, the tougher ones.

Urgency

A third method of sorting mail to be attended to is according to urgency—the most pressing items first, regardless of subject matter or level of difficulty. Executives who are frequently interrupted in their dictation maintain that this type of sorting is a must.

In very routine situations, the length of your letters is a matter of personal preference. Suppose, for example, you saw an advertisement in a financial magazine for readers to write the senior vice president for a copy of the company's latest annual report. Here is the letter you might write:

Dear Mr. Weber:

Please send me your latest annual report.

Sincerely yours,

Mr. Weber, or perhaps a subordinate who takes care of such matters, will know what you want and, assuming you write on your company's letterhead, where to send it.

Another person might write quite a different letter:

Dear Mr. Weber:

Please send me the latest annual report of Bardex, Inc., referred to in your ad in the June issue of *Financial Monthly*.

I have been following with great interest the growth of Bardex in recent years and am eager to learn more about its increasing involvement in energy conservation.

Sincerely yours,

Is the second letter better? Not necessarily. It is likely to elicit the same response as the first one in this instance because the chances are good that neither Weber nor anyone else with whom you will ever do business again will see the letter. So the choice boils down to what *you* think you ought to say.

Section 4

Keep the Language Lively and Simple

Some letter writers have the notion that big words are a sign of literacy. No matter how many communication experts warn against bigwordism, government people, college professors, sociologists, educators, business executives, and others merrily continue to communicate in an unknown tongue. It seems to be a game in which the winners are those who can speak and write the foggiest prose.

We do not discount the importance of a rich vocabulary. For many a useful "big word," there is no satisfactory substitute. As long as you use the word correctly and are certain that your readers or listeners are not baffled by it, go right ahead. The occasional polysyllable can add spice to your writing.

But in most of your letters, put away your lexicon (a fancy word for dictionary) and choose the word that you know is familiar to most people. Nearly everybody responds more warmly to the word *home* than to *abode* or *domicile*. Practically nobody in a crowded theater will rush to the exit if someone yells, "Conflagration!" But watch them make tracks when they hear the word, "Fire!" Recall the often told tale about P. T. Barnum, who had a hard time getting crowds to leave his sideshows once they paid to get in. To make room for other customers waiting in line, he posted the sign, "This way to the egress." Thinking this was another gigantic attraction, lingering visitors made their way to the sign—only to find themselves outside the tent. *Egress*, of course, is a fancy word for *exit*.

When you're writing a letter, express yourself pretty much as you would if you were facing your reader. Would you say to your boss: "My analytical evaluation of the incentive plan that has been instituted revealed myriad discrepancies and inconsistencies, with the inevitable result that serious inequities prevail among personnel"?

Of course, you wouldn't! Here is probably what you would say: "I've studied our present incentive plan carefully, and I think some changes are in order. What bothers me most about it is that the plan is very fair to some, but not at all fair to others."

Stuffy, overblown language has become so common that a name has been coined for it: *federalese*. This is because many federal government writers have a special fondness for abstruse expressions (*abstruse* is federalese for *hard to understand*).

Even when you know that the person you are writing to is highly literate, it's still a good idea to choose the simple word over the showy one—not because the reader won't understand you, but because conversational writing is livelier and more interesting. Following is a short list that illustrates what we mean.

Somewhat Showy	*Conversational*
Cogitate upon	Think about
Be cognizant of	Know that
Comprehend	See, understand
Comprised	Made up of
Conjecture	Think, believe
Consummate	Wind up, agree to
Corroborate	Confirm, make sure
Deliberate upon	Think about
Disbursements	Payments
Increment	Increase, raise
Maximal	Fullest
Initial	First
Nominal	Small, little
Obviate	Make unnecessary
Origination	Beginning
Proclivity	Leaning, tendency
Predicated	Based
Ratify	Approve, confirm
Rationale	Basis, reason
Remunerate	Pay
Scrutinize	Read, examine, inspect, look at
Transpire	Happen, take place
Ultimate	Final

Now let's look at examples of federalese writing:

Federalese	Natural Style
1. The contract enclosed herewith requires your signature before it can be executed and should be directed to the undersigned.	1. Please sign the contract enclosed and return it to me.
2. Due to a low inventory situation, we are reluctantly compelled to transmit a partial shipment of 5 Crescent motors in lieu of the 12 that were requested. We anticipate shipment of the remainder subsequent.	2. I'm sending 5 Crescent motors today. The remaining 7 will go out to you just as soon as we get a new shipment—probably next week.
3. The expeditious manner in which you executed our high-priority order for maple seedlings is hereby gratefully acknowledged.	3. The maple seedlings arrived this morning, and I can't thank you enough for this fast service.
4. Commensurate with standard practice in the industry, as a wholesale enterprise our organization must decline direct distribution to consumers. Undoubtedly you can satisfy your requirements at a local retail establishment in the Atlanta area.	4. As wholesalers, we sell only to retail stores and other distributors. However, you can buy Oneida appliances in several Atlanta stores. Most are listed in the *Yellow Pages*.
5. Your recalcitrance in expediting payment of your obligations obviates consideration of further extension of credit privileges, and we foresee no viable alternative than cancellation of aforesaid privileges.	5. I'm sorry, Mr. Baxter, that we are not able to offer you additional credit. I'm sure you know the reason: You still owe us money that we haven't been able to collect.

Coining New Words

An executive who wanted employees to give priority in their planning to cost control issued the directive that "the matter must be prioritized." People understood what *prioritized* meant, although they had never seen the word before. They had simply become accustomed to strange terms that people think up to "save time."

Ize words, as in *prioritize*, are favorites for federalese writers. Did you ever see the word *definitize*? Someone thought it up as a substitute for make definite. And more and more we see such terms as *legitimize, politicize, factionalize, strategize, accessorize, finalize, maximize, circularize,* and so on. Of course, there are many *ize* words that are perfectly acceptable—*standardize, visualize, jeopardize, economize, pressurize,* for example. But let a good dictionary guide you when you are tempted to tack on *ize* indiscriminately. (Or, should we say, when you are tempted to *oversyllabize*?)

There's also a growing tendency to tack on *wise* whenever possible: *policywise, procedurewise, weightwise, personnelwise,* and the classic *sizewise* (!). Wise endings make ugly words; people probably use them simply to prove that they are not strangers to the "in" jargon of officialdom.

Here are a few examples of "wise-itis" and their plain-talk equivalents:

"Wise-itis"

1. *Newscaster:* "Weatherwise, it looks like a damp, humid weekend."

2. This appears to be the right thing to do profitwise.

3. Costwise, it is inadvisable for sales representatives to concentrate on sparsely populated areas.

4. Distancewise, it's a toss-up between Colfax and Denton as a new plant location.

5. I can see no effect moralewise on personnel under this new policy.

Plain Talk

1. *Newscaster:* "Sorry, folks, but the weekend is going to be damp and humid."

2. I think the new plan will result in bigger profits.

3. We can cut our costs by working only those territories where we can expect volume sales.

4. Colfax and Denton are about the same distance away, so mileage is not a factor in picking one over the other.

5. I doubt that employee morale will be affected by this new policy.

Finally, there are the folks who have an uncontrollable urge to add *uate* to certain words to indicate action. There are hundreds of good *uate* words—*perpetuate, evaluate, fluctuate,* and *evacuate,* for example—but among these are not *actuate, effectuate, eventuate,* and others of that ilk. Don't, for example, say, "We expect to actuate the revised retirement plan early next year." This is better: "The revised retirement plan goes into effect early next year." And *not:* "It is our hope that the results of the study will eventuate in substantial savings." *But:* "We hope our study will result in substantial savings."

Vogue Words

Like teenage fads, words come and go. It would seem that the minute some government official throws out a sophisticated sounding word at a press conference, every respectable bureaucrat immediately picks it up as his or her own. Several years ago, the word *parameter* mysteriously appeared in print as a synonym for *perimeter* or boundary, and hundreds of thousands of speakers and writers picked it up. Today it is a vogue word. Unfortunately, *parameter* does not mean the same thing as *perimeter,* which is an indication of how gullible we are when it comes to word selection.

Today, there seem to be no alternatives but *viable* ones. People who have a personal appeal are *charismatic* (or have *charisma*). When positions of people conflict or contrast on a particular issue, there is *polarization.* When we struggle to make a decision, we *interface* with the problem. When we offer an opinion, we take a *posture* or *stance.* And when different groups disagree on something, there is a *dichotomy.* And so on.

Just as serious is the tendency to use nouns as verbs, as in "How will the move impact on turnover" (instead of "What impact will the move have on turnover?") and "Please critique the attached report" (instead of "Please let me have your critique [for assessment] of the attached report.")

If you are one of those who believe there is nothing wrong with going along with the crowd in using federalese language, that's up to you. We urge you, however, to use plain English in your letters, for it is the simple word, the natural word, the conversational word, the everyday word that will do the most to make your writing readable, interesting, and persuasive.

Stereotyped Writing

Almost as bad as federalese is writing that is lifeless and stale. In the days of celluloid collars and spats, almost every letter began with "Yours of the fifth inst. and contents duly noted," which really meant, "I read with interest your letter of June 5." And the same letter usually ended something like this: "Begging your kind indulgence, I remain, sir, your most obedient servant." Probably you've never seen such phrases and wonder why we even call attention to them. It's because letter writers tend to fall into a rut, using the same words and phrases over and over without thinking. Even today, if you could examine one day's worth of correspondence that emanates from a typical large company, you would find stereotyped writing such as the following:

Stereotyped: I am in receipt of your letter of the 15th. (This is a throat-clearing phrase that says absolutely nothing, the slow windup before the pitch.)
Lively: The 25,000 mailing labels you asked about in your letter of May 15 left here yesterday.

Stereotyped: The terms of the contract are not clear to me. *Please advise.*
Lively: Please explain paragraph 7 on page 2 of the contract.

Stereotyped: As per your instructions, the hood ornaments are being sent air express.
Lively: I've sent the hood ornaments by air express, and you should have them by now.

Stereotyped: Please let me hear from you *at your earliest convenience.*
Lively: I really need this information by May 16—please.

Stereotyped: Attached herewith is the information you requested on Marple Brothers.
Lively: Here is the information you requested on Marple Brothers.

Stereotyped: I hope you will *avail yourself of the opportunity* to save 20 percent on all your cardboard containers.
Lively: I think you'll agree that a 20-percent saving on your cardboard containers represents big money. Why not order now?

Stereotyped: Hoping for your concurrence in this matter, I remain …
Lively: I hope you will agree that this is a good arrangement.

Stereotyped: Due to the fact that we've had trouble getting the parts …
Lively: We've had trouble getting parts. Therefore …

Stereotyped: *According to our records,* there is an *outstanding balance* of $322.76 in your account.
Lively: Your check for $322.76 will clear your account.

Stereotyped: *Kindly* let me know if this date *meets with your approval.*
Lively: Is December 14 a good time for us to meet?

Other stereotyped expressions include the following:

Along this line
At hand (your letter)
Attached (or enclosed) please find
I wish to state
I hereby advise
I solicit your kind indulgence
In due course
Your order has gone forward
Under separate cover
Up to this writing
With your kind permission
Pursuant to your request
This is to inform you that
We wish to call your attention to
Above-mentioned (person, invoice, letter, etc.)
We are writing to tell you that

Section 5

Personalize Your Letters

Letters are written by people to people. Even though you use a company letterhead and represent an organization when you write letters, it's still you who delivers the message. Generally, you will have complete freedom to write as you please.

We hope this means that you will treat people as live human beings and not as "to whom it may concerns." Earlier we mentioned that people are very much alike in certain respects. Most are reasonable, civilized, thoughtful, and friendly. All have an ego, which means they like to be treated as though they have better-than-average intelligence and are important to the company they work for.

Knowing these things about people, how could a sales manager dictate this message to a new customer whose business the company has sought for many months?

Dear Sir:

This will acknowledge your order for 16 Multi-Craft belt sanders and 8 disc grinders. This order will be shipped promptly. Thank you for your business.

Yours truly,

It's not a bad letter. All the "necessary" ingredients are there: order acknowledged, shipment will go forth promptly, and thank you. But there's something missing: the from-me-to-you personal touch. Depending on the circumstances, several different, friendlier approaches might be used. In the following, we've focused on the sales representative who calls on this customer.

Dear Mr. Rosetti:

Just last month Hal Milsap and I were talking about how we might persuade you to carry our Multi-Craft line of power tools at Four Corners

Building Supplies. Then this morning Hal strode in and handed me your order for 16 belt sanders and 8 disc grinders. I didn't get to keep it very long because Hal grabbed it, saying something about "getting these items on the truck this afternoon."

We're mighty happy, Mr. Rosetti, that a reputable store like yours has chosen Multi-Craft tools. I admit prejudice when I say that they're in a class by themselves, but I'm predicting that you'll have such success with them that you'll think I've been modest!

Hal will be in touch with you soon to see how he can help you with your display and promotion. And if I can do anything, just pick up the phone and call me.

Thank you—and good luck!

Sincerely yours,

The second letter should leave no doubt in Mr. Rosetti's mind that he is not looked upon as just another new customer, but a person who is somewhat special. Note that we've used Mr. Rosetti's name in the body of the letter, which adds a personal touch. This is a good idea for many, if not most, of your letters; just be careful not to overdo it.

Following is another example of a to-whom-it-may-concern letter. It was written by a town tax supervisor in response to a property owner's note that her property tax was paid twice.

Madam:

Enclosed check for $378.88 is due you because of the duplicate payment of taxes on your property.

Yours truly,

The letter above will not make the taxpayer cranky. She wanted a refund and she got it. But why treat her as just another anonymous taxpayer? Why not something like this?

Dear Mrs. Guilford:

You're entirely right—there was a duplication of payment of your property taxes. Both you and Oakdale Savings and Loan sent checks, and the enclosed $378.88 is your refund.

This situation arises every now and then, Mrs. Guilford. Eventually, we discover the duplicate payment and mail a refund, but you speeded things up by calling the matter to our attention.

Sincerely yours,

Form Letters

Certainly, the second letter in either of the preceding examples takes a little more time to write, and this is the excuse many people give for not exerting extra effort in answering routine letters. But in many instances, the time problem can be solved by writing a model letter for each frequently recurring situation, then adapting it slightly to fit the circumstances.

For example, let's say you are a personnel supervisor, and you receive dozens of applications for positions for which there are no vacancies. Your model letter might look something like this:

Dear _____:

I appreciate your letter in which you inquire about a position in our _____ department.

Unfortunately, (name), we have no vacancies in this department now, and I cannot predict when there will be one. Certainly, I will be pleased to hold your application and get in touch with you if the situation changes. However, I suggest that you continue your search for a position in other companies, rather than wait to hear from me.

I'm very grateful for your interest in Hutchinson-McGee, and I wish I could be more optimistic about employment opportunities. In any event, I hope you are successful in locating precisely the job you want in the _____ field.

Sincerely yours,

You might wind up with a dozen or more model letters, in which case you can instruct the typist on the incoming letter, "Send #5." Or, "Send #5 with this PS: 'The latest issue of our employee magazine, which you requested, is being mailed separately.'"

Additional Examples of Personalized and Nonpersonalized Letters

On the following pages are four additional examples of personalized and nonpersonalized letters.

Example 1

Nonpersonalized

Dear Friend:

We have your request for a trial copy of *Cooking with the Experts*, which we recently published.

We regret to say that this book is temporarily out of stock. A copy will, however, go forward promptly when a new supply is available. This should be approximately April 10.

DIAMOND PUBLISHERS

Personalized

Dear Mrs. Morley:

Thanks a lot for your interest in *Cooking with the Experts*.

It seems that this exciting new book is attracting a good deal more attention than we predicted, and at the moment there isn't a single copy left. Naturally, we ordered a new printing before we ran out, and we expect to receive copies by April 10. To speed delivery, I'm having your book sent directly from the printer, so you should have it by the time (or before) we get ours.

Bon appetite!

Sincerely,

Martha Mallon

Martha Mallon
Editor in Chief

Example 2

Nonpersonalized

Dear Sir:

Regrettably, this organization is no longer supplying free tote bags to business show visitors, although Scribe ballpoint pens are still being made available for such events.

Upon receipt of an estimate of your requirements, shipment will be made.

Yours truly,

Personalized

Dear Mr. Dunn:

I wish we could supply tote bags for your visitors to the Phoenix Business Show. However, we discontinued this practice a few months ago because the demand dropped to a trickle, leading us to believe that so many other organizations were supplying bags that ours weren't needed.

I'm pleased to say, however, that Scribe ballpoint pens are still being distributed without cost for affairs such as yours. If you'll let me know about how many you need, Mr. Dunn, I'll get them to you well before your opening on October 9.

I have hopes of attending the Phoenix Business Show; certainly, several of our people will be there. In any event, I hope it's the best ever.

Sincerely,

Example 3

Nonpersonalized   Dear Ms. Osberg:

The button-tufted swivel chair (Naugahyde with chrome base) you inquired about is not available in sunset yellow, and it is regretted that your preference cannot be satisfied.

Yours truly,

Personalized   Dear Ms. Osberg:

Thank you for your interest in our button-tufted swivel chair in Naugahyde with chrome base.

Although we do not have this chair in sunset yellow, there are four other colors that you might choose from: chestnut brown, black, moss green, and gold. I'm enclosing the sheet from our catalog on which all these colors are shown.

I'm hoping, Ms. Osberg, that the gold Naugahyde is near enough to sunset yellow to please you. Incidentally, the most popular color with our customers is black—very smart-looking in any office environment.

Please let me know if I can supply you with one of the colors mentioned. The price is $169.95, with a discount of 10 percent on cash orders.

Sincerely,

Example 4

Nonpersonalized   Sirs:

Please return the Merlin compact copier that you claim arrived in a damaged condition. All shipping charges will be paid by us.

The damaged copier is being replaced by another one.

Very truly yours,

Personalized   Gentlemen:

This afternoon I sent you a replacement of the Merlin copier by UPS, and you should have it by the time you receive this letter. I'm sorry the first shipment was damaged.

One of our representatives will drop by in a day or two to pick up the first copier you received. Thanks for your patience.

                              Yours very sincerely,

"I" and "You" Business Letters

Somewhere along the line you may have had instructions to avoid the pronoun *I* in business letters and, wherever possible, use the pronoun *you*. Scores of textbooks emphasize that good writers should always employ the "you approach," which means playing down *I* (the writer) and playing up *you* (the reader). Some authors harp especially on the sin of starting a paragraph with *I*.

These rules are sheer nonsense. Nothing in a letter is more personal than *I*, and you should use it just as naturally as though you were carrying on a conversation with a friend. *You* is also a good word that should show up frequently in your letters, but if you force its use, you can sound patronizing. For example:

You approach: You will be pleased to learn that your application for credit has been approved.

Natural: I'm pleased to tell you that your application for credit has been approved.

We think the "you" approach is a bit condescending (lucky you; our great company has approved you for credit). "I'm pleased to tell you" gives the message an entirely different meaning (we're glad to have you as a credit customer).

Compare:

1. *Your presentation at the workshop was very enjoyable, provocative, and valuable.*

2. *I certainly enjoyed your presentation at the workshop. I found it very provocative and valuable.*

Compare:

---

1. *You are to be congratulated on your promotion to product manager.*
2. *I'm delighted to learn about your promotion to product manager. Congratulations!*

The point is that you should not struggle for ways to use *you* and avoid *I*. Use both pronouns, along with *your*, *me*, and *my*, when it seems natural to do so.

"We" and "I"

It is sometimes difficult to choose between I and *we* in letters concerning business matters. In a few companies, *we* is often preferred on the theory that the writer speaks for the company and not just for himself or herself. In most cases, however, the choice is left to the individual. Our advice is this: Use *I*, *me*, and *my* when you want your letters to have a from-me-to-you flavor; use *we*, *us*, and *our* when you want your reader to feel that others share the message you are conveying. For example:

---

1. *I very much enjoyed your visit to my office last Tuesday. Enclosed are the materials I promised to send you.*
2. *Thank you for calling this situation to our attention, Mr. Culver. We appreciate your patience with us.*

Often, you will use both *I* and *we* in the same letter.

Dear Mr. Rambeau:

All of us at Lazarus Brothers have been highly pleased with the excellent service you gave us during the trucking strike. The situation called for great inventiveness on your part to see that we got the materials we needed. I really believe that we were the only contractors in this area who didn't have to shut down because of lack of materials.

For the whole crew here, I want to express sincere thanks for your performance during this difficult period. Thank you.

Sincerely yours,

The Letter Writer's Craft

Here is another.

Dear Professor Strachan:

I enjoyed immensely your talk on supplemental benefit plans at AMA's Symposium on Life Insurance in San Francisco last week.

We are evaluating our voluntary benefits program here at Beckwith Corporation, and I know our group would find your ideas not only stimulating but extremely helpful in our planning. Is a copy of your paper available? If so, may we borrow it and reproduce it for distribution here? We'd be extremely grateful.

Sincerely,

The following letter was written in response to a viewer of a television program who commented on the excellence of the show.

Dear Mrs. Guilford:

Thank you for your letter commenting favorably on our new television series, *America in Transition*. It is viewers like you that give us confidence that we are on the right track. Thank you also for your suggestions for future programs.

Sincerely yours,

Again, the foregoing letter is not bad. Indeed it has all the earmarks of a successful communication. However, we think it doesn't go far enough. Compare the letter just illustrated with the following.

Dear Mrs. Guilford:

How thoughtful you were to write us in praise of our new television series, *America in Transition*. Naturally I'm delighted to hear that you have enjoyed these programs—especially that you found them "provocative and stimulating."

Your suggestion that we include programs on the arts in very appropriate. We have developed six new shows devoted to music, painting, photography, theater, dance, and cinematography. Beginning with "Music in America" these new shows will be aired on six consecutive Thursdays starting October 16 at 9 o'clock (EST).

We certainly hope you find these new shows equally entertaining and informative. In any case, we thank you for writing. Letters like yours always boost our spirits!

Very cordially yours,

Section 6

Emphasize the Positive

We've said it several times, but it's worth repeating: Most of the letters you write will have some sales content. You don't have to be selling a product—a relatively small percentage of business letters are written for this specific purpose. But if you're an effective writer, you try to make or keep friends and customers, persuade readers to accept an idea (whether it's an apology or a proposal), or build a favorable image for your company. Call it what you will—tact, warmth, friendliness, enthusiasm—any method you use to persuade people to think well of you is still salesmanship.

The first thing a salesperson learns is to be positive. You wouldn't make many sales if you approached each prospect saying something like this: "You wouldn't like to join our Books-on-Tape Club, would you, Mrs. Wimple?" You've made it too easy for her to say, "You're certainly right. I wouldn't like to join your Books-on-Tape Club. Good day!"

You'll have a lot better chance making a sale if you say something like this: "I expect that, like most people, Mrs. Wimple, you love to read but simply can't find the time...." Then, when Mrs. Wimple nods in agreement, you proceed to show how your Books-on-Tape Club can solve her problem.

You can emphasize the positive in your letters in several ways, four of which are:

---

1. *Stress what you can do—not what you can't.*

2. *Stay away from negative words and phrases.*

3. *Do more than you have to.*

4. *Time your letters for best results.*

Stress What You Can Do

Some people just naturally think negatively. Following are examples.

Example 1   In a national magazine, a mail order firm advertises a flight bag for $24.95 in brown, tan, and black. The black bags quickly sold out, but a new shipment is expected within ten days. What response should be given to those who order black flight bags?

Negative   Dear Mr. Dillon:

I'm sorry that we are presently out of stock of black Nova flight bags and will be unable to fill your order at this time.

An order has been placed with the manufacturer in the color you want, but it will be at least ten days before we will receive shipment.

I trust this delay will not inconvenience you.

Yours very sincerely,

Observe the negative words and phrases in the example above: "I'm sorry" (a poor beginning for almost any letter), "unable," "will be at least ten days," "delay," and "inconvenience."

Positive   Dear Mr. Dillon:

Thank you for ordering a black Nova flight bag.

The color you chose proved to be very popular, and we quickly sold all we had in stock. However, we've placed a rush order for more and are promised delivery within ten days. Yours will be shipped the same day our new supply arrives.

I know you'll be delighted with this unique carry-on flight bag, Mr. Dillon. It's not only very handsome, but incredibly rugged.

Yours very sincerely,

Example 2   A well-known university president has been invited to give the keynote address at the annual Delaware Education Association convention in Dover on April 11. The theme is "The Impact of New Technologies on Education." The president can't accept the invitation since he will be in Europe at that time. He suggests another speaker from the university staff.

Dear Professor Kinkaid:

I regret that I will be unable to accept your invitation to speak at the Delaware Education Association convention on April 11. Unfortunately, I will be in Europe at that time.

If you would be willing to accept a substitute, I'm quite certain that Dr. Adele Josephson, vice president of administration, would be available. If this proves to be an unsuitable recommendation, I'm sorry.

Cordially yours,

Dear Professor Kinkaid:

Nothing would please me more than to give the keynote address at the Delaware Education Association convention on April 11. Not only are educators my favorite audience, but your theme is of special interest to me.

Several months ago, however, I made arrangements to attend the International Education Congress in Stockholm and will be out of the country the first two weeks in April.

May I suggest an alternate? Dr. Adele Josephson, our vice president of administration, is not only a well-known authority on new educational technologies (you may have seen her recent series of articles on this subject in the *Journal of Higher Education*) but an excellent speaker as well. I have discussed this assignment with her, and she showed much enthusiasm for it. You may write her directly if you wish.

In any event, I wish for you the best convention the DEA has ever had. I'm really sorry to miss it.

Cordially yours,

Stay Away from Negatives

Be especially careful in your letters not to attach labels to people or intentions or actions that will be offensive to them. Following are examples.

Negative: In your October 3 order, you *neglected* to specify the color of vinyl sheeting you require.
Better: Just let me know the color of vinyl sheeting you prefer, and I'll send the materials immediately.

Negative: Your *complaint* about the quality of paper used in the forms we supplied you is regrettable.

Better: I'm sorry that the quality of paper in the forms we supplied you *was not up to your expectations.*

Negative: You *claim* that you did not understand our discount terms.
Better: The terms of sale are described on the invoice we sent you, and perhaps you overlooked them.

Negative: You *obviously ignored* the assembly instructions accompanying the equipment.
Better: The assembly instructions accompanying the equipment are very specific about proper installation. Did you not receive them?

Negative: Quite frankly, I am surprised at your insinuation.
Better: Of course, I can't claim that we're infallible, but let me explain how this problem came about.

Negative: Your alibi for skipping the March payment on your promissory note ...
Better: Thank you for explaining why you did not make payment in March on your promissory note ...

Negative: I dispute your assertion that the merchandise we sent was inferior.
Better: Please look at the specifications on page 321 of our catalog. I think you'll agree that the shirts you received match them.

Negative: Surely you don't expect us to violate company policy by extending six-month credit terms to you.
Better: You will remember that we allowed you four months to pay for your October 23 order, which is the maximum permitted under our standard policy.

Negative: You should know by now that we need at least two weeks' lead time in filling orders for imported articles.
Better: As indicated in our catalog, we need at least two weeks' lead time in filing orders for imported articles.

Negative: If you had read our advertisement carefully, you would have seen that at least a year's field experience is required for sales representatives.
Better: As noted in our ad, at least a year's field experience is necessary for sales representatives.

Negative: You *failed* to enclose the check you referred to in your letter of May 10. *Obviously,* we can't credit your account until we receive payment.

Better: By the time you receive this, you will probably have discovered that the check you meant to enclose in your letter of May 10 was missing. No doubt, you have already placed it in the mail.

Do More Than You Have To

It costs very little to do a bit more than you actually have to when answering letters. Not only will this extra effort make friends, it will make you feel better. The following illustrate what we mean.

Example 1

The Creighton Academy of Art is a private art museum. Because its name suggests a school, many young people write asking for information about the curriculum, tuition, and so on.

Grudging

Dear Miss Douglass:

The Creighton Academy of Art is not a school—it is a private art museum. Therefore, I'm afraid we can't help you.

Sincerely yours,

Helpful

Dear Miss Douglass:

I appreciate your letter asking about art education at the Creighton Academy of Art.

Although our name does suggest that we offer art education courses, we are actually a private art museum. There are, however, several reputable art schools in the Philadelphia area that are accredited by the state. A photocopy of the art schools section from the state directory is enclosed.

Sincerely yours,

Example 2

Robert Rheinhold, 70, is retiring as an engineer in a firm where he worked for 48 years. during this time, he often spoke about a book of mathematical tables he used in college and to which he referred frequently later on the job. Unfortunately, it was lost, and he failed to try to replace it, even though he often talked about doing so. His friends want to try to find a copy to present at the retirement party, but no one is sure (not even Rheinhold) of the exact name of the author (Schultz?), the date of publication (about 1920?), or the publisher. One of the Rheinhold's friends writes a dealer in rare and out-of-print books. Following are two responses.

Grudging   Dear Ms. Lomax:

I am sorry we cannot identify the book about which you wrote and therefore cannot help you. Certainly we have nothing that fits your sketchy description.

Yours sincerely,

Helpful   Dear Ms. Lomax:

I have scoured our lists of out-of-print books very carefully, and I think I have a clue to the identity of the one you asked for. A book entitled *Practical Handbook of Mathematical Tables*, by J. W. Shurz, was published in 1919 by Eureka Publishing Company. It went our of print in 1932, and the publisher is no longer in business. At one time we had a few copies, but unfortunately we have had none for several years.

There are many dealers throughout the country who specialize in rare books, and you may wish to write some of them. I suggest that you visit a good library and ask for such publications as *The Atlantic* and *Publisher's Weekly*, which often contain back-of-the-magazine ads of rare book dealers.

Good luck!

Yours sincerely,

Timing for Positive Reaction

Promptness in attending to your correspondence nearly always reveals a positive attitude. It shows you're eager to be of service, you respect your correspondents' time, and you want them to be impressed with your level of efficiency. Certainly a lot of friends have been lost by writers who are too slow in answering their mail.

When you receive a letter to which you cannot respond fully in less than a week or so, acknowledge it immediately and say when you will have the information asked for. Here is an example:

Dear Mr. Ireland:

Thanks for sending the sample cartons we are so eager to make a decision on.

Three of my colleagues who must see the samples before a final decision can be reached are attending a materials-handling seminar in Aspen this week. Then they plan to spend a couple of days at our Denver subsidiary.

I expect them back by November 14, and I hope we can get a decision that same day. I'll relay it to you by phone—I know you're just as eager to have this thing settled as we are.

Sincerely,

And another:

Dear Ms. Rosmund:

Your proposal of Stroud as a site for our new Tulsa area distribution center caught me in the midst of a series of long-range planning meetings which will require my participation for the next several days—perhaps as long as two weeks.

Just as soon as I have a chance to study your proposal and share it with others here, I will write you.

Sincerely yours,

Yet, there are times when promptness in answering letters may not be wise, even though you are prepared to make a full response immediately. Let's say you've received a proposal from a new ad agency that wants to represent you, or a manufacturer who offers you an exclusive dealership in a new product, or a designer who submits what she thinks is an ingenious packaging idea for your product. In each case, you know the answer is "no." So you could dictate a response at once and put it in the mail. Those who write might be impressed with your fast answer, but they are likely to think you gave them short shrift—that your mind was closed (as it was).

When you have to say "no" to people who offer what you can't use or ask for a hefty favor you can't grant, it's usually best to let the correspondence age a bit before responding. If you want to, you can write a quick note something like this: "Thanks for your letter about ... . This matter deserves careful study, and I will be in touch with you about it later." Then after a decent interval—perhaps a week—you can dictate your "no" response.

Overpromptness is especially dangerous if you're dealing with long-time customers who ask for special favors that you are not in a position to grant. Letting the incoming letter age a bit—but not too long—is likely to lead the customer to believe that you're at least considering the request.

The same is true when you're dealing with job applicants. A same-day "no" to qualified applicants may tell them that you didn't think enough of them to even look at their résumés, and it won't hurt to delay a reply for a couple of days. But not much longer, since turned-down applicants will want to get letters out to other companies quickly.

One more thing about timing: Don't be too quick about putting letters in the mail that deal with matters of extraordinary importance and are quite lengthy. Prepare a rough draft and let it age for a spell, returning to it from time to time to make sure you have written exactly what is appropriate under the circumstances. It is not unusual for executives to rewrite an important letter three or four times before they are ready to release it.

Section 7

Use the Correct Letter Form

Readers get their first impression of a business letter even before they read it. The quality of paper, letterhead design, placement of the message on the page, and letter style all have something to say about an organization. A weakness in any of these elements can detract from the effectiveness of the message, even though it is expertly written.

Paper

Paper quality is based on weight and what the paper is made of. In many companies, letterhead paper that most correspondents use is a 20-pound bond with a 25 percent cotton-fiber (rag) content. In others, a 16-pound bond of the same rag content is standard. Top executives often choose a 24-pound bond with from 50 to 100 percent rag content for personal and social correspondence. A few firms to whom very high quality is enormously important choose this more expensive paper for all their correspondence.

Bond paper comes in a wide variety of finishes—smooth, fluorescent, ripple, and many others. You can select one of the standard finishes available, or you can have paper made with your own watermark.

The least expensive stationery is made of sulfite, and a 16- or 20-pound weight is commonly used for mass mailings, routine announcements (a price change, for example), and interoffice memoranda.

Of course, envelopes and second sheets should always match the letterhead in quality and finish.

Color	White is by far the most widely used color of stationery, but light tints—gray, blue, antique ivory, green, and so on—are also popular. Organizations may also choose such tints as pink, peach, lavender, or aqua if they believe their clientele will be receptive to those colors.

Size
The standard size of letterhead paper is 8½ by 11 inches. For personal and social use, however, some managers and executives often choose a smaller size, such as Monarch (7¼ by 10½ inches) or Baronial (5½ by 8½ inches). Envelopes should, of course, be chosen expressly for the size of letterhead used. The envelope ordinarily used for the standard letterhead is 4⅛ by 9½ inches (called a No. 10).

Letter Style

You can choose from a half dozen letter styles (by style, we mean general layout). A few companies select a style and insist that everyone use it, but in most cases the choice is up to the writer. The three most popular styles are semiblocked, blocked, and full-blocked.

Semiblocked Style
In the semiblocked style, the dateline starts at the middle of the page, as does the complimentary close. Each paragraph is indented five spaces. (See page 46.)

Blocked Style
The only difference between the semiblocked style and the blocked style is that in the block style the paragraphs are not indented.

Full-Blocked Style
Here, everything in the message is placed flush with the left margin: dateline, inside address, salutation, paragraph openings, complimentary close, writer's name, and so on.

Comparison
Each style has its own devotees, and we won't point out the advantages or disadvantages of each. They are all good-looking, assuming the letter has good balance, as does the one illustrated.

Stateport Chamber of Commerce

Crystal Beach Road, Stateport, North Carolina 28461

February 19, 19--

Mr. Charles A. Greenlund
1806 Devon Drive
Clarinda, Iowa 51632

Dear Mr. Greenlund:

I'm delighted to learn that you and your family are thinking about spending your vacation this summer in Stateport.

Located at the southeastern tip of North Carolina, Stateport is the northernmost subtropical region on the East Coast--"where the pines meet the palms." Its stately live oaks and scenic waterfront give Stateport a small-town charm rarely to be found these days.

You won't find high-rise hotels or neon amusements here, but you will find opportunities galore to enjoy yourself. The town itself is right in the lap of the historic Cape Fear River and the Intracoastal Waterway, and just down the road a piece is the beautiful Atlantic with 14 miles of wide, sandy beaches that are never crowded--a great place for swimming, surfing, collecting seashells, or just basking.

There are oceanside golf and tennis courts, and the fishing is unsurpassed--whether you prefer the surf, pier fishing, or angling from your own boat or one of the many charter boats for hire. and there are protected waters for sailing, fishing, and water skiing. Bike trails, miniature golf, water clides, and a dozen other fun things to keep the youngsters amused; and for the less adventuresome, there are historic sites and beautiful gardens nearby and museums only a short ferry ride away.

You'll find many places to stay in and around Stateport--from beach-front cottages to apartments to mobile homes in the piney woods. A directory is enclosed.

Really, the only way to truly appreciate what Stateport has to offer the vacationer is to come see for yourself. You'll receive a warm welcome!

Sincerely yours,

Ross T. Jessup
Executive Director

fcd
Enclosure

The Letter Writer's Craft

Margins and Placement

There should be at least a 1-inch margin at the left side of the letter, and the right margin should be roughly the same (some say a little wider). If the letter is short—say, half the length of the one ilustrated—you can increase your side margins to 2 inches or more.

The margin at the bottom of the page is usually at least one and one-half times that of the side margins; the same is true of the top margin when you are using plain paper instead of a letterhead. (When you are using a letterhead, of course, the top margin is established for you.)

Regarding placement, secretarial reference manuals provide formulas for centering a letter on the page. Most experienced secretaries, however, can tell from the quantity of their shorthand notes how to place the transcribed message so that it has the desired symmetry—like a picture in a frame.

Spacing

Most business letters are single-spaced, as shown in the model. However, there is one blank line between paragraphs, between the inside address and the salutation ("Dear Mr. Greenlund:"), and between the salutation and the first line of the message. The complimentary close ("Sincerely yours,") is two spaces below the last line of the letter. Four spaces are generally allowed for the signature, although some people think three are enough.

For relatively short letters, say, a couple of brief paragraphs you can achieve good effect by double-spacing the entire message (though not the inside address). In this case, there is no additional space between paragraphs.

The Salutation

When writing to individuals, always use their name if you know it.

Dear Andy: (personal friend or close business associate)
Dear Mrs. Gibbs:
Dear Dr. Breedlove:
Dear Professor Quinlan:
Dear Miss Diaz:

Dear Ms. Williams: (when you are addressing a woman whose marital status is not known or when you think this is her preference)

If you are addressing an individual whose name you do not know—the purchasing manager, director of personnel, president, and so on—use the following:

Director of Personnel
Leverett Products Corporation
1112 N.W. Lovejoy
Portland, Oregon 97209

Dear Sir or Madam:

When you are writing to an organization rather than to an individual, the following is appropriate:

Windsor Knitting Mills, Inc.
295 Magnolia Avenue
Spartanburg, South Carolina 29301

Ladies and Gentlemen:

Note: The salutation "Gentlemen" was widely used for many years. Today, however, it is considered sexist by some, and there is a growing tendency to use "Ladies and Gentlemen."

The Complimentary Close

A complimentary close is nearly always used in business letters. The wording you choose depends on you.

Personal	Sincerely, Cordially,	Sincerely yours, Cordially yours,	Very sincerely yours, Very cordially yours,
Formal	Yours very truly, Very truly yours, Respectfully yours, (to one whose stature is awesome)		
Highly Informal	Best wishes, Warmest regards,	Cheers! See you in Phoenix!	

For the typical business letter, our preferences are "Sincerely yours" and "Cordially yours."

Writing on Plain Paper

If you are writing a personal letter on plain paper, you will include your address and the date at the top of the letter. For a semiblocked or blocked style, this information will begin at the center of the page. For example:

> 708 West Pine Street
> Midland, Texas 79701
> June 30, 19—

(*Mr. Newton's address here*)

Dear Mr. Newton:

If you're using the full-blocked style, this information is flush with the left margin, thus:

Cambridge Court, Apt. 9-B
4719 McPherson Avenue
St. Louis, Missouri 63108

February 16, 19—

(*Ms. Young's name and address here*)

Dear Ms. Young:

Other Elements

Some people prefer to address the company rather than an individual so that, if the person addressed is not the one who would handle the letter or has left the company, the company will not return the letter to the sender. (This practice is not as common as it once was. Unless a letter to a former employee is marked "Personal," it is assumed to pertain to company business and is opened without hesitation and sent to the appropriate person.)

The Attention Line	Following is the placement of a typical attention line:

Plymouth Rock Manufacturing Company
412 Atlantic Avenue
Boston, Massachusetts 02110

Attention: J. P. Scovill, Chief Engineer

Ladies and Gentlemen:

Note that the salutation is "Ladies and Gentlemen" (not "Dear Mr. Scovill"), since the letter is addressed to the company.

The Subject Line	To speed up handling of mail, it is sometimes wise to indicate the subject of the letter. The following are typical:

Ms. Olivia Moreno, Claims Supervisor
Pacific Marine Insurance Company
643 Powell Street
San Francisco, California 94108

Dear Ms. Moreno:

Subject: Claim No. MA—457972

I have just received your report concerning the ...

Signatures	Unless a man's given name might be confused with that of a woman, he need only sign his name without a title. Compare:

Cordially yours,   Cordially yours,,

Daniel A. Speaker   (Mr.) *Loyce O'Donohue*

Daniel A. Speaker,   Loyce O'Donohue

Incidentally, many people sign letters with initials only or fail to indicate a courtesy title when their name could be either masculine or feminine. This presents a special problem when you respond to these individuals. The following are recommended:

M. G. Kroeger,   Loyce O'Donohue
XYZ Corporation ...   ABC Company ...
Dear M. G. Kroeger: Dear Loyce O'Donohue:

A woman may sign her name in a variety of ways:

1. *If she wants to indicate that she is unmarried:*

   Sincerely,   Sincerely,

   (Miss) Melanie C. Prudhomme   *Melanie C. Prudhomme*

   Melanie C. Prudhomme   Miss Melanie C. Prudhomme

2. *A woman who does not wish to reveal her marital status may use one of the following:*

   Very sincerely yours,   Very sincerely yours,

   (Ms.) Judith Moscowitz   *Judith Moscowitz*

   Judith Moscowitz   Ms. Judith Moscowitz

3. *A married woman or widow who wants to be addressed as Mrs. may use one of the following:*

   Yours very cordially   Yours very cordially,

   (Mrs.) Sadie Watts Browne   *Sadie Watts Browne*

   Sadie Watts Browne   Mrs. Sadie Watts Browne

Part 2

REQUEST LETTERS AND RESPONSES TO REQUEST LETTERS

Among the most frequent letters business people write are those that ask for something. Often a request represents a golden opportunity to make a sale. Perhaps the recipient invited readers, viewers, or listeners to send for free samples or literature, or maybe the recipient's advertisements simply provoked enough interest to trigger an inquiry. Some requests may benefit the person who makes them as much as or more than the person who receives them.

Response letters answer questions, supply information and/or materials, offer special help, and attempt to satisfy the needs of those who make the requests.

This part contains letters making various types of requests and the responses to these requests.

Section 8

Asking for Information About Materials, Prices, and Discounts

8-1 Asking for a Free Catalog

Situation

To generate interest in its business gifts, a company takes an ad in the July issue of *Personnel International*, inviting readers to send for a free color brochure entitled "Premium Products."

The Letter

Ladies and Gentlemen:

Please send me six copies of your free catalog, "Premium Products," which was advertised in the July issue of *Personnel International*. I plan to keep a copy and send the remaining five to our regional managers.

Thank you!

Yours very truly,

Alternate Letter

Ladies and Gentlemen:

I am intrigued by your advertisement in the July issue of *Personnel International* concerning your free brochure, "Premium Products." This sounds like the answer to the eternal question, "What shall we give our outstanding employees when we want to reward them?"

I'd like six copies—one for myself and one for each of our regional managers in Hartford, Dallas, San Francisco, Miami, and Atlanta.

Thanks very much.

Sincerely yours,

8-2

Responding to a Request for a Free Catalog

Situation

See Letter 8–1 on the preceding page.

The Letter

Dear Miss Crandall:

In a separate first-class mailing, I am sending you six copies of our catalog, "Gifts Galore." I am very pleased that you want a copy for each of your regional managers.

The catalog "tells it all," so I do not need to expand on the gifts in this letter. I do want to say, however, that for quantities of 20 or more gifts we offer an attractive discount.

Please let me know if I can be of help in other ways.

Yours cordially,

8-3   Requesting Free Products

Situation

The National Association of School Superintendents is holding its national convention in Atlantic City in August. The Executive Secretary of NASS, Patricia Keating, wants to prepare 500 kits that will be given to all the people attending. The kit will include such things as ballpoint pens, pocket calendars, toilet articles, and other items. Following is her request, sent to Ward Foster, President of The American School Supply Company, asking for ballpoint pens and pocket calendars. The response to this letter is on the next page.

The Letter

Dear Ward:

As you know, the National Association of School Superintendents is holding its annual convention at the Ambassador Hotel in Atlantic City (I know you always have an exhibit at these conventions). We are assembling products for a kit to be given to everyone attending. Last year you supplied 500 ballpoint pens and 500 pocket calendars.

Will you do the same this year? Our members prize these kits each year and look favorably on those who furnish the articles.

Please send the materials to me at the Ambassador Hotel in Atlantic City, Zip Code 08402. Thanks a lot!

Sincerely,

8–4

Responding to a Request for Free Products

Situation   See Letter 8–3 on the preceding page.

The Letter   Dear Patricia:

Within the next two weeks, I'll send you 500 ballpoint pens and 500 pocket calendars to the Ambassador Hotel in Atlantic City. Thank you for giving us this opportunity to help your organization which we very much respect.

As you know, we have an exhibit at the NASS convention each year, and I plan to attend the one in Atlantic City. I hope to see you there as well as many of my other friends.

With very best wishes, I am

Very sincerely yours,

8–5 Asking About a New Product

Situation

Jeanette Hines, Marketing Manager of Century Publishers, receives the following letter from a retail customer, Rita Barnes, Owner of Downtown Bookstore, about books on tape.

The Letter

Dear Ms. Barnes:

Please send me information about books on tape as well as information you have on playback equipment.

Thank you.

Very truly yours,

Alternate Letter

Dear Ms. Barnes:

Many of my customers have been asking recently about books on tape, and I know almost nothing about this relatively new product. I have an idea, though, that taped books may be a splendid item for my store.

I'll be grateful if you would send me literature concerning this exciting new (for me) market. I'd like not only to know which books are available on tape, but also want to inquire about tape-playback equipment that either you carry or know about.

Cordially yours,

8–6

Responding to a Request for Information About a New Product

Situation   See Letter 8–5 on the preceding page.

The Letter   Dear Ms. Barnes:

I am delighted to have your letter in which you ask about books on tape.

Today I am sending you a special brochure that we've just had printed, "Books on Tape," which contains an up-to-date listing and description of all our taped books. The number of tapes is expanding at an accelerating pace, and the market increases daily. I'll see to it that you are kept up-to-date on new arrivals.

I'm sorry I'm out of stock on the booklet describing the play-back equipment, but I'll get a copy to you right away—next week for sure.

Sincerely yours,

8–7

Asking About a Product and the Name of a Dealer

Situation   Carefree Mobile Homes, Inc. placed an ad in *Mobile Homes Monthly* in which readers are invited to write for a free catalog. Richard Vannoy has been thinking about going into the mobile home business and writes asking for the free catalog and the name of a local dealer.

The Letter   Ladies and Gentlemen:

Please send me your free catalog, "Luxury Living," as advertised in *Mobile Homes Monthly*.

I am considering entering the mobile home market, and I would like to know the name and address of a wholesale distributor in the Visalia, California area.

Thank you.

Cordially yours,

8–8   Supplying Information About a Product and the Name of a Dealer

Situation   See Letter 8–7 on the preceding page.

The Letter   Dear Mr. Vannoy:

Thanks very much for your letter requesting the catalog that we advertised in *Mobile Homes Monthly*. I placed the catalog in the mail this morning, first-class postage.

The nearest location of a Carefree Mobile Home outlet is Fresno, California. The owner of this outlet is Mrs. Muriel Overton, and I am certain she would be delighted to see you.

Enclosed is a copy of an article, "Are Mobile Homes the Answer to America's Housing Problem?" which appeared in *Business Week*. I think you'll enjoy it.

Very truly yours,

8-9

Asking About Prices and Discounts

Situation

As Sales Manager for a company that does door-to-door selling, Donna Rowe wants to provide each sales representative with an eight-digit electronic calculator. Rowe saw one that she likes and wants to know about discounts on large orders and other details. See the response to this letter on the next page.

The Letter

Dear Mr. Wolfenberger:

We are considering providing each of our sales representatives with an eight-digit electronic calculator. Last week I saw a demonstration of your Model GH Wizard at the Boise Business Show, and I think it would fill our needs very nicely.

I understand that the Wizard retails for $33.95. Is there a trade discount for companies that buy in fairly large quantities? Our initial order would be for about 80 units and reorders in perhaps lots of 20.

Not only do I need price information, but I also want complete details about service, warranties, carrying case—any information you think will assist me in making a decision.

Cordially,

8-10

Responding to an Inquiry About Prices and Discounts

Situation   See Letter 8–9 on the preceding page.

The Letter   Dear Miss Rowe:

Your high opinion of our Model GH Wizard pleases me very much.

We offer a discount of 10 percent on orders of 40 or more calculators. I have enclosed an order blank if you wish to take advantage of this offer.

The enclosed booklet gives complete details about service, warranties, and the like. Actually, a carrying case is not necessary with the Model GH Wizard; the handsome, leather-like exterior of the Wizard not only makes carrying it convenient but gives it full protection.

Thank you for allowing me to supply you with this information, Miss Rowe. If I have left anything out, just call me collect at (415) 547-1060.

Cordially,

8–11 Requesting Advice and Product Inspection

Situation

The Administrative Services Manager of Faultless Insurance Company, David Morgan, faces a serious problem of inadequate office space. Morgan has seen an impressive office setup in which modular units have been installed. He now wants to visit the manufacturer of these units in Syracuse to see a display of different types of modules and to get advice from experts. Morgan will be accompanied by two other people. See the response to this letter on the next page.

The Letter

Dear Mr. Phillips:

The rapid growth of our company has made office space a real problem in recent months. Rather than buy or lease additional space, we believe our immediate problem might be alleviated by making more efficient use of the space we now occupy.

On a visit to one of our suppliers in Rochester (Landover Data Systems), I saw how well that company utilizes every available square foot without sacrificing privacy or efficiency. Mrs. Robbins, the Administrative Vice President, told me that the modular units installed there were purchased from you. She also said that you have many different types of modular equipment and suggested that I make a trip to Syracuse and talk with you.

Two of my associates and I would like to visit you and discuss our special problem. Would Wednesday, April 18, at 9:30 a.m. be a suitable time for you? If not, please suggest another date during the week of the 16th, and we'll arrange our plans accordingly.

We will bring with us the dimensions and layouts of three floors in our building. If there is any other information you need, please let me know.

Yours very sincerely,

8–12

Responding to a Request for Advice and Product Inspection

Situation   See Letter 8–11 on the preceding page.

The Letter   Dear Mr. Morgan:

By all means plan to visit us. April 18 at 9:30 a.m. is ideal. Several members of the customer relations section will join us for discussions and demonstrations. We'll be happy to have your people, of course.

As you suggested, it will be helpful if you bring the dimensions and layouts of the three floors you are interested in refurbishing. We have a variety of acetate overlays that will be useful in deciding on your exact needs.

If you are flying, give us your flight number, airline, and time of arrival in Syracuse. I'd gladly meet you at the airport and drive you to our building.

Very Cordially yours,

PS: I am happy to know that Mrs. Robbins is so pleased with her new setup. We really enjoyed working with her.

8-13   Asking About Training Materials

Situation   Leonard Ducey, Training Director of a large company, has been asked to arrange a series of communication seminars on listening, writing, and speaking for top executives. At a recent professional meeting, Ducey heard a speaker refer favorably to a new multimedia program on listening. He decides to write the publisher (specifically, the editor in chief) to obtain information on the listening program and to find out whether other communication materials are also available. See the response to this letter on the next page.

The Letter   Dear Sir or Madam:

Our speaker at this month's Society for the Advancement of Management meeting mentioned that you have developed an excellent program of instruction on listening.

I am arranging a series of communication seminars for our top executives, which will include instruction in writing, speaking, and listening. I am especially interested in your materials on listening, but would welcome information about programs you may have on writing and speaking as well.

The seminars will begin October 16, so I don't have a lot of time to choose the materials. Would you therefore rush this information to me? I would be very grateful.

Sincerely yours,

8–14

Supplying Information About Training Materials

Situation   See Letter 8–13 on the preceding page.

The Letter   Dear Mr. Ducey:

I'm sending you immediately a copy of "A Guide to Effective Listening," along with an instructor's manual, a sample tape, and a booklet describing other aids for the instructor.

You'll see that the basic textbook is programmed—that is, it can easily be used for individual instruction with immediate feedback and reinforcement. In addition to the textbook, there is a set of tapes on which conversations, directions, speeches, discussions (meetings), and other oral communication situations are recorded. Although this program can be used without an instructor, many companies prefer group instruction under the leadership of a teacher. The instructor's manual provides day-by-day classroom procedures and methods of evaluating performance.

I think this program may be just right for the listening segment of your communication seminars, Mr. Ducey. It is being used by hundreds of business firms and government agencies, and the reactions we've received have been most enthusiastic.

We're in the process now of putting together a similar program on writing. Publication is scheduled for March of next year—a bit late for your first seminar, but perhaps in time for the second or third. I've made a note to send you a set of these materials just as soon as they are released. A prepublication flyer is enclosed.

At the moment, we have no publishing plans in the area of speaking, Mr. Ducey. Have you seen *Speaking Out*, which is published by New Dimensions Press? I understand it is a multimedia program and is being favorably received by users. The address of New Dimensions is 2000 Sheridan Road, Evanston, Illinois 62201.

Thank you for writing.

Cordially,

8–15

Asking for Detailed Information on a Service

Situation Ads in recent issues of *Fortune* invite readers to join a publisher's Executive Book Club. You are interested in learning how well your field of personnel administration is represented or whether there is a special club for personnel executives. See the response to this letter on the next page.

The Letter Ladies and Gentlemen:

I have two questions about the Executive Book Club that you are advertising in *Fortune* magazine.

1. What proportion of the books published by the club are in the personnel field?

2. Do you have book clubs especially for those in personnel administration? Thank you for your help.

Sincerely yours,

Alternate Letter Ladies and Gentlemen:

I notice that Executive Book Club advertisements in *Fortune* feature books over a wide spectrum of management. I am considering joining the club, but I'd like some information.

My area of special interest and responsibility is personnel administration. Generally, what portion of the books that members may choose from is in the personnel field? Or do you perhaps have other book clubs in specific management disciplines, including personnel management?

I would be very grateful for answers to these questions and any other information you can provide.

Very truly yours,

8–16   Supplying Detailed Information on a Service

Situation   See Letter 8–15 on the preceding page.

The Letter   Dear Mr. von Hoffritz:

I am delighted to know that you are interested in our Executive Book Club and am happy to answer your questions about it.

Between 30 and 40 new books in the field of management are made available each year to the members of the Executive Book Club. And, as you have mentioned, the topics treated vary widely. From four to six of these pertain specifically to personnel administration; in addition, a similar number of general management books embrace some aspects of personnel management.

Although we have several specialized book clubs—for example, accounting, computer sciences, and marketing—there isn't yet one in personnel administration. The decision to set up a specialized book club, is, of course, based entirely on demand, and it is possible that we will one day establish a club in personnel. Certainly, there is a growing interest in this field.

The circular enclosed contains complete information about the Executive Book Club. Please note that the average price of books distributed by the club, if purchased separately, is about $35. However, as a member you would pay only about three-fourths that amount.

I do hope you will want to become a member of the Executive Book Club, Mr. von Hoffritz. You can do so by filling out the coupon on the back of the circular. If you join now, you'll receive absolutely free one of the popular handbooks on page 3.

Yours very truly,

Section 9

Requests to Reproduce Printed Materials

9–1   Requesting Magazine Reprints or Permission to Reproduce

Situation

Charles Maloney, Marketing Director of Pinnacle Products Corporation, is planning the company's national sales conference, which all sales personnel attend. Maloney is very impressed with the article, "The Sale Doesn't Stop with the Order," which appeared in the May issue of *Marketing Horizons*. He decides to write to the editor of the magazine asking if reprints are available and, if not, permission to reproduce the article. See the response to this letter on the next page.

The Letter

Dear Mr. Taylor:

We are having our national sales conference in Birmingham on August 10, and the theme this year is "Winning Sales Through Service." I was much impressed with the article, "The Sale Doesn't End with the Order" by Cynthia O'Brien, which appeared in the May issue of *Marketing Horizons*.

Are reprints of this article available? If so, I would like 90 copies at your regular reprint rate. If reprints have not been made, may I have your permission to reproduce the article? I would, of course, include the author's and publisher's name and other information you require.

Cordially yours,

9–2

Responding to a Request for Reprints or Permission to Reproduce

Situation   See Letter 9–1 on the preceding page.

The Letter   Dear Mr. Maloney:

Thank you for telling me how much you enjoyed the article, "The Sale Doesn't End with the Order." Reprints aren't available, but you have our permission to reproduce 90 copies of the article at 15 cents per copy.

Just make sure that credit is given: Reproduced with permission of *Marketing Horizons*, by Cynthia O'Brien.

I like the theme of your upcoming sales conference and extend my best wishes for a successful event.

Sincerely yours,

9–3 Requesting Free Reproduction Privileges of a Book Illustration

Situation
Madalene Strong has been asked to present a paper at a national convention on the preparation of annual reports—a paper that she plans to distribute to those attending. Strong wants to include in her paper a chart from a handbook, and she writes for permission to do so. See the response to this letter on the next page.

The Letter
Ladies and Gentlemen:

I have been asked to present a paper on the preparation of annual corporate reports at the annual convention of the Financial Executives Association in Salt Lake City on March 5.

I plan to make copies of my paper and distribute them to those present—about 50. May I have permission to include the chart on page 425 of *Handbook of Public Relations*, Second Edition, by Frank L. Selden? It's the best structure for an annual report that I have seen.

The paper in which the chart would appear will, of course, be distributed without cost and only to those attending my meeting. Certainly, I would make sure that full credit is given to the author and publisher. If you have a standard credit line that you require, I will be pleased to use it.

I'd be grateful for your approval of this request. If you would like a copy of my paper when it is reproduced, I'll be happy to send it to you.

Yours very cordially,

9–4

Responding to a Request for Free Reproduction Privileges

Situation   See Letter 9–3 on the preceding page.

The Letter   Dear Mrs. Wrisley:

I appreciate your request to reproduce 50 copies of the chart that appears on page 425 of *Handbook of Public Relations*, Second Edition.

As soon as I received your request I talked with Mr. Selden. He has enthusiastically given us the go-ahead, feeling that the Financial Executives Association is the ideal group for this material.

Here is the credit line that you should use at the top or bottom of your reproduction: "From *Handbook of Public Relations*, Second Edition, by Frank L. Selden, published by HarperCollins."

Would you please send me a copy of your reproduction? Thank you.

Very sincerely yours,

9–5   Requesting Reproduction Privileges for Commercial Use

Situation

As Assistant to the Director Of Merchandising for a large franchiser, you are preparing a sales training manual for employees, which will be sold to the franchise stores. You write to the publisher asking for permission to reproduce one chapter from a book this company publishes, offering a royalty fee on each copy of the training manual that is sold. See the response to this letter on the next page.

The Letter

Dear Mr. Kauffman:

I am preparing a special training manual for retail sales employees in our 1620 franchised stores throughout the country. The manual, which will contain 256 pages, will be sold to the franchises at $2.50, which is about half the actual production and distribution cost.

I would like very much to include in the manual the excellent chapter, "The Last Three Feet," from your book, *Practical Selling Techniques*, Third Edition, by C. A. Dowling. We expect to distribute about 12,000 copies a year and propose a royalty of 2½ cents on each copy sold. This would amount to about $300 a year in royalties.

If this proposal is satisfactory to you, please let me have your concurrence in writing, along with information you require for copyright identification. We would not, of course, use your material in any other manner without your permission.

Cordially yours,

9-6

Responding to a Request for Reproduction Privileges for Commercial Use

Situation   See Letter 9–5 on the preceding page.

The Letter   Dear Miss Christie:

The arrangements you suggested in your recent letter concerning "The Last Three Feet," from C. A. Dowling's book, *Practical Selling Techniques*, appear to be satisfactory.

The credit line on this section of your manual should appear as follows: "Reprinted by permission of C. A. Dowling, from *Practical Selling Techniques*, published by Vanguard Press. Further reproduction is prohibited."

Please send me two copies of your training manual when it is published, one of which I will forward to Mr. Dowling.

Very truly yours,

9-7 Requesting Permission to Reproduce Noncopyrighted Materials

Situation

Dr. C. B. Ogden is a chemical engineer. He heard a paper presented by Katherine C. Mangum on dry storage of nuclear reactor fuel at a recent convention of the American Society of Chemical Engineers. He'd like a copy from which additional copies can be made and distributed to the company's engineers, who are debating the pros and cons of wet and dry storage of nuclear wastes. See the response to this letter on the next page.

The Letter

Dear Mrs. Mangum:

I was greatly impressed with your remarks at the recent ASChE convention in Baton Rouge. Certainly, your experience in the TVA project encourages me to suggest that we at Bolling Chemical take a closer look at dry storage. I'm afraid some of our people are not aware of the advantages you described.

Is it possible to obtain a copy of your report and reproduce, say, a dozen copies for our internal use? We're involved right now in discussions of waste control, and I think your report would provide valuable guidelines in our deliberations. We would not distribute the material outside the company without permission from you.

Perhaps you have plans to publish your paper in one of the trade magazines. If so, you may be reluctant to release it for our use. If that is the case, would you let me know where and when it is to be published? I'll want to order reprints as soon as possible.

Thank you for your excellent presentation and for your consideration of this request.

Yours sincerely,

9–8

Responding to a Request for Permission to Reproduce Noncopyrighted Materials

Situation   See Letter 9–7 on the preceding page.

The Letter   Dear Dr. Ogden:

I have no objections to your using my paper delivered at the recent ASChE convention in Baton Rouge. Indeed, I am flattered that you think this material will be useful to your engineers. I have no publication plans for the paper.

Although not absolutely essential, I would appreciate your indicating on your copy the source of the material, such as: "From a presentation at the 1994 ASChE convention in Baton Rouge, delivered by Katherine C. Mangum."

May I have a copy of your reproduction when it is ready for distribution?

Cordially yours,

9-9

Requesting a Copy of a Speech for Distribution

Situation   Carmen Gomez, Vice President and Personnel Director of Bardoff Corporation, recently spoke to the Phoenix NOMA Chapter on the topic, "A New Look at Incentive Compensation." The speech was enthusiastically received by the audience, and the President of the Phoenix NOMA chapter decides to write Gomez asking for a copy of the speech to be distributed to all the Arizona members of NOMA.

The Letter   Dear Dr. Gomez:

Judging by the fine reception our NOMA members gave you, I believe your presentation at our October 7 meeting was nothing short of spectacular. I thought they would never let you go in time to make your 11 o'clock flight!

Do you by any chance have a copy of your presentation that I can reproduce and send to all our members and other NOMA chapters in Arizona? I am confident that all these people will enjoy and profit by your remarks.

Thank you!

Sincerely,

9-10

Responding to a Request for a Copy of a Speech for Distribution

Situation   See Letter 9–9 above.

The Letter   Dear Crom:

Here is a copy of my speech at the Phoenix NOMA Chapter on October 7. Make as many copies as you like.

I only wish that all my speeches would draw such favorable attention! Please extend my greetings to your NOMA members.

Best of everything,

Section 10

Letters Asking for an Appointment

Generally, when you want to visit an out-of-town person or business to obtain information that you need, it is usually wise to ask for an appointment in writing, even though it may be more of a benefit to the host than it is to you. It is hard to see who you want, if you simply pop in without advance warning. Besides, asking for a specific appointment for your visit saves time for both of you. Follow these guidelines:

1. *If you're unknown to the recipient of your request, tell who you are and the purpose of your visit.*

2. *If you're the primary beneficiary of the meeting, try to convince the recipient that your mission is worthy.*

3. *Suggest a specific date and time, but leave the matter open in case the recipient wants another date.*

4. *Be courteous—no matter what the situation is.*

10–1

Asking to Visit Showrooms

Situation

The Director of Planning for a medium-sized corporation in Dayton visits a friend in a large downtown building, and is impressed with the intelligent use of space. She was told that there is a company that specializes in modular furniture. The firm has a special building in which modular furniture of various types is displayed. The Director of Planning decides to write the Tulsa firm, asking about visiting the company for more information.

The Letter

Gentlemen:

May I visit your building in Tulsa in which various office layouts, using modular equipment, are displayed? My schedule is very flexible, and I can come any time that is most convenient for you.

Thank you.

Yours very truly,

Alternate Letter

Ladies and Gentlemen:

A few days ago I visited the office of a large corporation in Dayton, and was much impressed with the layout of their various departments in which modular furniture is displayed. During my visit, I inquired about manufacturers of such equipment and was told that you have an entire building in Tulsa in which various modular fixtures and equipment are displayed.

I would like very much to visit your Exhibit Building. I can come to Tulsa any time that is convenient for you. If I do not hear from you to the contrary, I will plan to visit you on Thursday, March 8.

Cordially yours,

10–2

Responding to a Request to Visit Showrooms

Situation   See Letter 10–1 on the preceding page.

The Letter   Dear Dr. Lomax:

I am delighted to know that you are planning to visit us on Tuesday, March 8. While I'm not sure about your arrival time, it doesn't really matter—the Exhibit Building is open at 8:00 a.m., so we'll be looking for you.

I hope you will be with us all morning because we're planning a special luncheon for you at the Omaha Club.

Sincerely yours,

10-3　Asking for an Appointment to See a Computer Operation

Situation

George Kyme is a public accountant, and among his clients is a chain of six pharmacy stores. Kyme is alarmed at the increasing costs of record keeping in operating a pharmacy and is looking for a way to lower them. A magazine article calls attention to the growing popularity of computers in drugstores, and Kyme decides to write the author, requesting an appointment with her to learn firsthand about the applications of computers to small businesses.

The Letter

Dear Dr. Ruyle:

One of my clients is a chain of six pharmacies in the Greater Portland area. I was much impressed with your article, "Drugstores Control the Paper Blizzard," in the May issue of *The American Druggist*. You are right on target in saying that in some pharmacies about one-fourth of the owner's time is spent on paperwork.

I was especially interested to learn that drugstores are turning to computers for help. This may be the answer to my client's problem, and I would like to know more.

I will be in Seattle the week of June 18 on other business. Would it be convenient for you to see me on that day? If so, would it be possible for me to see a computer operation in one of your client's places of business? If you are free for a couple of hours on the 18th, please suggest a time and I'll be there. Please call me collect at (806) 257-1818.

Thanks!

Cordially yours,

10–4

Responding to a Request for an Appointment to See a Computer Operation

Situation   See Letter 10–3 on the preceding page.

The Letter   Dear Mr. Kyme:

I'll be pleased to see you when you are in Seattle. It happens that June 18 is ideal, and I'll mark my calendar "10:00–12:00—Kyme."

I plan to take you to two pharmacies here in Seattle that have a computer setup, as well as a real estate firm. I think you'll be amazed how the flow of papers has decreased dramatically in these businesses.

I'm scheduling an informal luncheon at 12:30, and I have invited Ms. Sharon Tibbets, Executive Secretary of NOMA, to talk with us about how computers have simplified the role of office managers.

Have a good trip!

Sincerely,

Section 11

Other "Asking" Letters

Other "asking" letters include asking about conference accommodations, housing, residence, and vacation property.

11-1   Asking About Conference Accommodations

Situation

Gold Medal Insurance Company is planning a sales conference in October, and a suitable meeting place is under discussion. Outer Banks Conference Center in North Carolina has been recommended, but specific information about accommodations is required. You are asked to write for details concerning rates, facilities, services, and so on. See the response to this letter on the next page.

The Letter

Ladies and Gentlemen:

Several people have recommended Outer Banks Conference Center as a first-rate place for our regional sales conference in October.

Would you please send me full details on rates, meeting rooms, recreational facilities, food services, and so on. The following information will help you.

Dates: October 22 (evening) to October 27—five nights and five days

Numbers: 40 men, double occupancy
8 men, single occupancy
16 women, double occupancy
9 women, single occupancy

Food Services: Three group luncheons—73 people
Four dinners—80 people—with guest speakers

Meeting Rooms: One room large enough to accommodate 80 people
Three smaller rooms, each to accommodate 30 to 40 people

Equipment: One 16 mm film projector, screen, one overhead projector, four chalkboards, four easels

I also want information on sports and other recreational activities, entertainment, tours, and so on.

Shortly after I receive this information, I will be in touch with you. May I hear from you no later than February 7?

Cordially yours,

11–2

Supplying Information About Conference Accommodations

Situation   See Letter 11–1 on the preceding page.

The Letter   Dear Mr. Watson:

We'd like very much to be the headquarters for your annual sales management conference October 22 to 27. You've chosen the ideal time, not only because of our ability to offer you all the accommodations you require, but also because of weather. It's a glorious time of year in the Outer Banks of North Carolina!

Complete information about Outer Banks Conference Center is given in the booklets I'm enclosing: "So You're Having a Meeting," "Getting to Know Us," and "Recreation Unlimited." When you look these materials over, I think you'll agree that Outer Banks Conference Center has it all.

Another advantage of the date you selected is that summer rates are still in effect. This means that all rooms are just a little less than half the winter rates that take effect December 1. (For rates, see the back page of "Getting to Know Us.")

We've had the privilege, Mr. Watson, of hosting meetings and conferences for hundreds of organizations such as yours; some of these are listed on page 2 of "So You're Having a Meeting." I'd like to share with you some of the letters I've received praising our excellent accommodations and our know-how in looking after our guests. You'll find us just as eager as you are to make your October conference the best you have ever had.

Please let me know just as soon as you can whether I should reserve accommodations for you. While the October date is open now, the situation could quickly change. In the meantime, if there's anything you would like to know that isn't covered in the booklets, please telephone me collect at (919) 453-9562.

Sincerely yours,

11-3 Asking About Housing

Situation

Harold and Beth Robinson are moving to Lexington, Kentucky from Enid, Oklahoma (Harold is being transferred to Lexington by his company). From a local realtor, the couple learned the name and address of a large real estate firm in Lexington (Century 21) and decide to write the firm a letter.

The Letter

Ladies and Gentlemen:

In October the company I work for is transferring me to Lexington (I learned about your agency from a local realtor).

Do you have literature on housing in the Lexington area? Beth (my wife) and I prefer suburban living—but not more than 40 minutes or so by train or bus from downtown Lexington. We'd like something in the $100,000 range if that figure is not too low for prestigous housing. Also, we hope to live in an area where there is an excellent grade school and high school. We'd also be interested in shopping malls nearby and golf and tennis facilities.

I eagerly await your response.

Very truly yours,

11–4

Responding to a Letter About Housing

Situation   See Letter 11–3 on the preceding page.

The Letter   Dear Mr. Robinson:

Thank you for asking about housing in the Lexington area.

I'm sending you today a special catalog, which describes some of the housing in this community. I must, however, tell you that it's nearly impossible to describe available houses with any degree of accuracy; houses come on the market daily, and our catalogs can't keep up with the changes.

After studying your letter, I selected four possibilities, and I'm enclosing leaflets, which I have prepared especially for you. Of course, the information is sketchy at best. To really appreciate the houses described in the leaflets, you have to visit them.

I hope you and Mrs. Robinson will have an opportunity to come to Lexington soon. Please call on me when you arrive in Lexington. You may be sure that I'll take all the time necessary to acquaint you with the many possibilities.

Sincerely yours,

11–5

Asking About Residence and Vacation Property

Situation   John Warren, from Minneapolis, is retiring at age 70. He has heard a good deal about the Coastal Georgia area as a place to retire. He saw an ad in *Travel* magazine placed by Coldwell-Banker describing the Coastal Georgia area and inviting readers to write for more specific information.

The Letter   Gentlemen:

I was intrigued by your ad in the September issue of *Travel* about the Coastal Georgia area, and I would like to have a copy of "So You're Planning to Retire."

Thank you for whatever additional information you would care to send me about this appealing area.

Yours very truly,

11–6 Responding to an Inquiry About Residence and Vacation Property

Situation

See Letter 11–5 on the preceding page.

The Letter

Dear Mr. Warren:

I certainly appreciate your interest in the Savannah area of Coastal Georgia. Enclosed is a copy of our booklet describing this area entitled "So You're Planning to Retire."

The Coastal Georgia area is finally being discovered by the rest of the world. Not long ago, development was concentrated both north and south of us. These areas are considerably higher in density and property prices. Interest in this area, however, has been extremely high of late, and I can't resist saying that our time has come.

We are fortunate that we have a mild climate, which permits outdoor activity year round. Golf and tennis are very popular here—there are eight highly rated golf courses within less than half-hour away (three are located in the Coastal Georgia area) and many, many public tennis courts. Our waters offer some of the best fishing to be found; so enjoy the sport or the culinary delight of fish that someone else caught! The growing season is long, and gardeners delight in growing a wide variety of flowers and vegetables. While ours is not a subtropical climate, palmettos grow naturally here. We do have changes in seasons, but not in the extreme.

I have the feeling that this may be the ideal place for you. Property values are still reasonable, the tax rates low. You can expect the investment you make in the Coastal Georgia area to appreciate over the long term, as demands continue to increase for both retirement and vacation homes.

Coldwell Banker is the largest full-service real estate firm in southern Georgia; so I can assure you that you will receive outstanding professional services.

After you've read "So You're Planning to Retire," please write me. I'd like very much to hear from you.

Oceanic wishes!

Part 3

TRANSMITTAL, CONFIRMATION, AND "ANNOUNCING" LETTERS

Section 12

Transmittal Letters

When you send something important in the mail, such as a check, contract, purchase order, invoice, statement, or promissory note, it's often a good idea to cover what you're sending with a letter. This gives you a chance to explain what is being sent and why, but equally important, a copy of your letter provides a valuable record. Thus you won't have to wonder later, "Did I send that service contract to Nicholls? If so, when did I send it?"

12-1 Transmitting Payment on Account

Situation

Marilyn Beck recently opened a hospital supply business and has arranged credit terms with Haywood-Kirby, a wholesaler. Beck has agreed to pay for her purchases in four equal installments of $2416.40, and is now transmitting a check for the second payment.

The Letter

Dear Mr. Gussow:

Here is my check for $2416.40, which represents my second payment. According to my calculations, the new balance on my account is $7249.20. If your records don't agree, will you please let me know?

I'm having great success with two of your products—the Deluxe Breatholizer and the Travel-Ease walker. The Pender three-prong cane is just beginning to catch on.

Best wishes.

Very truly yours,

12-2 Transmitting Final Payment on Account

Situation

As a new business owner, you have arranged 60-day credit terms with a supplier on a large order, the payments to be made in two equal installments. You have made the first payment on schedule and are now ready to transmit the second.

The Letter

Dear Miss Fogel:

Here is my check for $1100.40, which is the final payment on my order of March 5.

Thank you for the courtesy extended me.

Cordially yours,

12-3

**Transmitting Payment—
Discrepancy Explained**

Situation

You receive a statement from the Credit Manager (Irene Harlow) of Benson Corporation in the amount of $1059.51. According to your records, however, you owe only $979.74. Obviously, Harlow did not give you credit for merchandise you returned amounting to $79.77; indeed, you were issued a credit memorandum for that amount.

The Letter

Dear Irene:

Enclosed is our check for $979.74 in payment of the statement I received from you on December 11.

You'll see, Irene, that this amount doesn't jibe with your statement, which indicates that I owe $1059.51. The reason for the difference, I'm sure, is that the credit memo issued to me on December 2 for $79.77 had not been posted to my account at the time the statement was prepared.

If there is any question, Irene, please let me know. Otherwise, I'll assume that our records agree.

Best regards,

12–4   Transmitting a Contract

Situation   Brad Crandall works for an automobile leasing firm. He has met with a customer, Margaret Fisher, who is treasurer of Penobscot Corporation, to draw up a contract between the two businesses. After all the kinks have been ironed out, Crandall sends the agreed-upon contract to Fisher.

The Letter   Dear Margaret:

The original and one copy of our leasing agreement are enclosed. I think this contract encompasses all the changes we talked about last week in Indianapolis. If you agree, please sign both copies and return the original to me. (An addressed, stamped envelope is enclosed.)

We look forward to a very cordial relationship between our two organizations. If you get to Indianapolis, Margaret, be sure to give me a ring. Maybe we can celebrate a mite at lunch or dinner which, I assure you, will be my pleasure.

Sincerely,

12–5 Transmitting a Program Draft for Approval

Situation   Pamela Voiles is Executive Secretary of the Association of Life Underwriters, which is having its annual convention in Orlando on February 16—three months hence. Pamela has finished the rough draft of the program and wants the approval of the Association's President, Carl Martin, before releasing the program to the printer.

The Letter   Dear Carl:

At last all the pieces of the program for the February ALU convention are fitted into place, and I'm ready to turn it over to the printer when I have your blessings. The draft is enclosed.

I am especially pleased with the layout and typeface selection, and I hope you will like them too. Also enclosed is a sample of the paper (called antique gold), and I have picked a rich brown ink for the printing. Of course, the Association's logo will go at the top center of the cover page.

All the speakers and panelists have okayed my use of their names, titles, and topics assigned. I plan to print 500, more than enough for the number of people we expect, but the cost of an additional 150 is very little once we go on press.

If you want changes, just say the word. I've promised the printer that he will have the copy by February 3.

Cheers!

12–6   Transmitting Materials Separately

Situation   See Letters 9–5 and 9–6 on pages 75-76. The training manual has been published and two copies are being sent separately to the publisher of the book from which a chapter was taken.

The Letter   Dear Mr. Kauffman:

Our *Training Manual for Salespeople* has just been published, and I am mailing you two copies in a separate package.

We are quite pleased with the result and hope you will like the way we handled the chapter from *Practical Selling Techniques*. Thanks again for your cooperation.

Very cordially yours,

Section 13

Confirmation Letters

Confirming an agreement by letter is critical when the discussion involves a serious commitment, such as offering special prices or services, making appointments or reservations, or changing procedures and policies.

In the models that follow, some of the letters are from the person receiving the services (such as a customer), and others are from the person providing the services.

There are three guidelines for writing confirmation letters:

1. *Make it entirely clear what you are confirming.*

2. *Leave room for debate if there is any likelihood that the recipient has an interpretation of the agreement different from yours.*

3. *Since you will probably be acquainted with the person to whom you write a confirmation (you've had some previous contact), personalize the message.*

13–1   Confirming Oral Instructions

Situation

Several retail customers of Woodmore Paint Company have recently complained about defective spray nozzles on Velvetcoat, a popular brand of enamel. Helen Gilbert, one retail customer, telephoned Woodmore's adjustment manager, Louis Leslie, saying it was too much trouble to return the paint—that credit should be granted solely on the retailer's word. Leslie agrees with Gilbert and follows up the telephone conversation with a letter.

The Letter

Dear Helen:

Thank you for your suggestion about not returning the Velvetcoat paint cans to me. I agree with you completely, and I'm writing all our customers, telling them we'll take their word for the faulty cans and just to tell us how many.

Needless to say, I'm very sorry you've had so much trouble with the Velvetcoat brand. It's never happened before. But you can be sure we'll ride the manufacturer until this thing is settled. No solution, no more Velvetcoat!

Sincerely yours,

13-2   Confirming Prices and Discounts

Situation   Ronald Rietzke is a Sales Supervisor for National Builders Supply Corporation. On July 21 he received a telephone call from Joseph Minor, a retailer, asking about prices on Modu-Screen acoustical partitions. Rietzke quoted the prices on the telephone, and promised to confirm them in writing.

The Letter   Dear Mr. Minor:

Thank you for calling me on July 20. This will confirm our telephone talk about prices on Modu-Screen acoustical partitions. Here is the information I gave you during our discussion.

Partition dimensions	Regular price each	Special price each (12 or more)
4×4-foot straight	$122.75	$ 98.20
4×5-foot straight	$132.00	$115.50
5×5-foot straight	$152.75	$129.85
5×5-foot curved	$191.00	$152.80

The prices indicated apply to all four colors available in modacrylic partitions. All frames (clear and anodized aluminum) and hardware (end legs and top caps to match frames) are provided at no extra cost. These prices will be slightly higher after July 31.

I am prepared to send you the partitions you need upon receipt of your order, and I look forward to hearing from you.

Yours very cordially,

13-3 Confirming an Appointment

Situation Ray Jordan, Vice President of Landover Chemicals, notices an advertisement in *Board Room* magazine for the Luxury XII helicopter and writes for the name of a dealer near Louisville. He receives in response the name of the dealer in Memphis, Kenneth Malone, and his telephone number. Jordan telephones Malone and is invited to Memphis to see the Luxury XII in person. Jordan is planning to visit Malone on August 8, and writes him regarding the visit.

The Letter Dear Mr. Malone:

I enjoyed talking with you today about the Luxury XII helicopter. I plan to take you up on your invitation to visit Memphis, and your suggested date of August 8 is fine. I'm driving up on the 7th, and will stay at the Best Western Lakeland Inn. I plan to see you at 9:00 a.m. on Tuesday, the 8th.

The Luxury XII sounds very exiciting. I hope someone on your staff will take me for a spin!

                                          Cordially yours,

13–4 Confirming Travel Arrangements

Situation

J. D. Folsom, who owns four music stores in Wilmington, North Carolina, has just returned home after attending a convention of the Music Educators National Conference. It was there that Folsom met Cynthia Clinton, President of Worldwide Musical Instruments. Clinton extended an invitation to Folsom to visit Worldwide's plant in Shreveport, Louisiana, offering to pay for travel and other expenses. Folsom accepted the invitation, and the date for the visit was set for July 14. Later, Clinton plans the itinerary and confirms the arrangements.

The Letter

Dear Mr. Folsom:

I've made travel arrangements for your visit on July 14, and I'm enclosing your airline tickets. In brief, you leave Wilmington on US Air's Flight 220 at 11:30 a.m. for Atlanta, and arrive there at 1:30 p.m. You then take Delta's Flight 416, which departs at 2:00, arriving in Shreveport at 4:15 p.m.

I will meet your plane and take you to the Best Western Chez Vous Motor Inn, where you have a reservation. Our purchasing manager, Harold DiGarmo, and I will join you for dinner at the Chez Vous if this is convenient for you.

We'll be glad to see you and give you the grand tour of our plant.

Sincerely yours,

Section 14

"Announcing" Letters

In every business there are constant changes, and these changes are frequently acknowledged by letters announcing them. In this section we cover three "announcing" situations: announcing a new product, announcing an acquisition, and announcing an anniversary.

14–1   Announcing a New Product

Situation

Lowe's, a wholesaler of building supplies, has just signed a contract with Monarch Paint Company, Inc., authorizing Lowe's exclusive distribution of the Monarch line of paints and varnishes in northern Utah. Martin Lowe, President of Lowe's, writes his better customers announcing the event.

The Letter

Dear Mr. White:

I am proud to announce that Lowe's has just signed a contract with Monarch Paint Company, giving us exclusive distribution of the Monarch line in northern Utah.

For years we have experienced tough going in paint and varnish sales because we were competing with Monarch products. Now it's a different story—why compete when there's a better way? This is indeed a happy occasion for us!

I've enclosed a color brochure, "Meet Monarch—the World's Best Paint." Please read it carefully, for it tells the story of Monarch's success much better than I could.

I am also enclosing an order blank for your convenience. Don't forget, your credit is unlimited at Lowe's, and we invite you to try out some of the Monarch brands. You won't be sorry!

Sincerely,

14-2 Announcing an Acquisition

Situation Payne-Wyatt recently purchased Rodeheaver Medical Publishing Company, a relatively small but prestigious publisher of both textbooks and professional publications in the medical field. Payne-Wyatt sends the announcement to all employees of both companies, to medical schools, and to medical libraries.

The Letter Ladies and Gentlemen:

Payne-Wyatt is pleased to announce the acquisition of Rodeheaver Publishing Company, a long-time publisher of medical textbooks and books for practicing physicians.

We are immensely proud of this marriage of two important publishing houses—Payne-Wyatt and Rodeheaver. Rodeheaver was founded in 1932 by Douglas H. Rodeheaver, a distinguished medical professional who felt the need for modern textbooks for medical schools, as well as books for practicing medical men and women. For over 60 years, Rodeheaver has been the most successful medical publisher in the country. Its current president, Michael L. Rodeheaver, is the grandson of Douglas Rodeheaver and has continued to publish outstanding medical publications. It was Michael who launched the publishing of *Medical Innovations*, a sophisticated monthly magazine with a circulation of over 50,000 medical professionals, libraries, and hospitals.

We welcome Rodeheaver into the Payne-Wyatt family. Michael Rodeheaver will continue as President, bringing with him 22 editors and production specialists. The Editor in Chief is Samantha Wilcox, and the Manager of Production is Peter Alsop. Rodeheaver will continue in its location in Denver, but is expected to occupy our headquarters at 1246 Avenue of the Americas, New York City.

Sincerely yours,

14–3   Announcing an Anniversary

Situation

TimePlus Watch Company will celebrate its fiftieth anniversary on May 16. To commemorate the occasion, the president writes to a list of retail customers offering a special bonus.

The Letter

Dear Mrs. Fisher:

On May 16, TimePlus will celebrate its fiftieth anniversary, an occasion we think deserves some sort of celebration. At least, we're taking note of the event!

It all began in May 1944 in Ithaca, New York when the founder of TimePlus, Morton Reed, decided to take his "invention" to a prestigious clock maker. Thus began a revolution in watches. Mort Reed is now retired, but his name will forever be revered as the father of the country's most coveted watch. He was among the first to graduate from pocket watches to wrist and pendant watches for men and women, young and old.

As one of our valued customers, you are to be congratulated on helping America to identify the finest timepiece that money can buy. In recognition of this anniversary, we're offering a discount to our customers: Order one of our TimePlus watches at $60 for just $45! This special discount is good only through June, so act now.

Best regards,

Part 4

SALES COMMUNICATIONS

It's no secret, of course, that in every profit-making organization the sale (to paraphrase Shakespeare) is the *thing*. No subject occupies the thoughts of top executives so consistently. No question is asked more often by management than "How are sales?" Even those not directly involved in selling the company's products or services have learned that the answer to that question is critical. When sales are soft over a prolonged period, gloom prevails and sooner or later there are cutbacks in personnel, in costs, in employee benefits, and in plans for growth. When sales are on the upswing, the organization hums with excitement.

There are many facets to selling. In many organizations, sales representatives who call on prospects and customers are largely responsible for sales, and a lot of money is spent in recruiting, training, and motivating these people. In such companies, there are really no effective substitutes for face-to-face, personal selling.

Sales representatives, however, need support: through effective advertising, exhibits and displays, PR efforts, efficient service from the home office, and various promotional devices.

Letters can play an important role in the sales process—responding to inquiries about the organization's products or services, following up on sales representatives' calls, acknowledging orders, supplying information to customers about a product, and ironing out problems that arise between customer and supplier.

A great many companies make extensive use of the sales letter—one written specifically to obtain an order—even though they employ a large field force for personal selling. Enterprises that do no personal selling, such as magazine publishers and mail-order concerns, depend almost entirely on letters to do their selling.

Section 15

Writing Sales Letters

According to the basic rules of selling, you first have to get the prospect's attention. Once you do that, you must build his or her interest to the extent that the prospect has a strong desire for the product. Assuming you've succeeded so far, the battle is still not won. You have to close the sale—that is, get the prospect to say, "I'll take it—where do I sign?"

The elements just described—attention, interest, desire, and action—are often referred to as the AIDA formula, which is just as applicable to sales-letter writing as to personal selling. Thus, in planning your letters, you should concentrate on these four questions:

1. *What's the best way of getting the reader's attention so that she or he will want to read on?*

2. *When I have the reader's attention, how can I create genuine interest in my product?*

3. *Once I have created interest, how can I persuade the reader that he or she really should buy what I have to sell?*

4. *Finally, how can I get the reader to take action—that is, respond in some way?*

Although each of these considerations is essential in a good sales presentation, they are not always separate and distinct elements. Thus, you might open your letter like this:

Just fill out the enclosed card to receive—absolutely free—a box of four of our Super Write pens.

Here you not only have gained attention in the first paragraph, but have triggered action. And the elements of building interest and creating desire are not necessarily separate entities; they may be intertwined throughout the message.

Guidelines in Writing Sales Letters

We offer four general guidelines for writing sales letters:

1. *Keep the letter of reasonable length, say, a maximum of 1½ pages.*
2. *Make sure you have skillfully covered the four elements of AIDA, but avoid huckstering.*
3. *Use language that your reader will understand and relate to.*
4. *Make it as easy as possible for the reader to take action.*

15-1   Selling a Product

Situation   A manufacturer of portable electronic refrigerators obtains a mailing list of members of an organization of camping enthusiasts, and decides to write a letter to obtain orders or requests for a catalog.

The Letter   Dear Fellow Camper:

It's a great day to start your vacation. The sun is ablaze, the van or wagon is humming nicely down the Interstate, and the family is settled comfortably in anticipation of what lies ahead. Even the dog is amiable.

Can you guess what happens next? Suddenly there are echoed demands for a rest stop and something to eat. The rest stop idea you take in stride, but the "something to eat" shakes you a little—you have visions of hauling out the old billfold and plunking down fifteen bucks or so for snacks at a fast food place.

BUT NOT IF YOU HAVE LEKTRON KOOL WITH YOU!

The Lektron Kool is the greatest little portable fridge you've ever seen. Pack it with sandwiches, drinks, fried chicken, fruit, whatever, and you'll have at your fingertips really cold food and drink day and night.

The Lektron Kool is not an ice box. It's a lightweight but roomy electronic refrigerator that you can plug into your car or a 110-volt adaptor that we make available, assuring you of fresh edibles for days and days. The secret is in Lektron Kool's thermoelectric solid-state module, which replaces all the bulky piping coils, compressors, and motors you find in conventional portable refrigerators.

One enthusiastic owner of Lektron Kool writes: "Last summer our family took a camping trip to Canada. It was one of those 'perfect' vacations; everything went just as we had planned. But when we got back to Atlanta all of us agreed that, aside from our new Caprice Diesel wagon, the most indispensable item of equipment we carried was our Lektron Kool. Not only was it a convenience, it saved us a bundle!"

Now you can own the Lektron Kool for $40 to $50 less than the regular price. That's right. Our three models ordinarily priced at $139, $179, and $199 can now be had for $99, $139, and $149. But you must hurry because this offer will be withdrawn April 1.

Call us toll-free at 1-800-622-0391 to place your order, or mail us your check or credit card number. But if you want more information before you order, the enclosed postage-paid card will bring you a complete catalog of our three Lektron Kool models.

Yours very sincerely,

15–2   Selling an Educational Course

Situation

Cameron Career Institute offers home-study courses in various trade occupations. The sales promotion director has obtained a list of subscribers to a practical mechanics magazine, who are often good candidates for home-study training. He writes a sales letter, the purpose of which is to persuade readers to send for a free catalog, which describes a course in small-engine repair.

The Letter

CAMERON CAREER INSTITUTE
766 HIGHLAND AVENUE
ORLANDO, FLORIDA 32802

WOULDN'T YOU LIKE TO OWN YOUR OWN BUSINESS?

If you're looking for the chance to be your own boss ... or earn extra income in your spare time ... or a way to achieve independence when you retire ... SMALL-ENGINE REPAIR could be the answer.

CCI can quickly train you—in your spare time at home—to service and repair mowers, tillers, chain saws, outboards, garden tractors, mopeds, motorcycles, snowmobiles, and dozens of other types of small-engine equipment. It's a great way to get your own business, full- or part-time, with a minimum investment. And it's a field with growing opportunities for qualified people.

CCI's Small-Engine Course contains forty-five lessons, each easy to read and understand. Every lesson is short and fully illustrated with step-by-step diagrams and photographs. It's "hands-on" training—you actually build a 3½-horsepower four-cycle engine. You also perform experiments that show you how every part of an engine works. And we supply you with professional tools—a complete set of wrenches, electrical system tools, inductive tachometer, engine overhaul tools, volt-ohm-milliam-meter, and others. Everything you need!

Our big catalog tells you all you need to know. It describes the content of each lesson (and there are sample pages of the actual study materials), and contains illustrations and descriptions of the equipment you will use. The instructor you will be assigned to has been a professional small-engine mechanic. He will be your "partner" in your studies.

Just fill in and mail the enclosed post card for your free catalog today. It needs no postage.

Sincerely,

Director of Studies

P.S.: No sales representative will call you!

15-3   Selling a Book

Situation   The First American Library writes to college and university professors to whet their interest in purchasing a just-published book.

The Letter

THE FIRST AMERICAN LIBRARY
2100 Rose Road
Schenectady, New York 12340

Dear Friend:

The most comprehensive selection of Abraham Lincoln's speeches, public writings, and private letters ever published!

YOURS FOR JUST $3.95!

Abraham Lincoln was not only one of our greatest presidents; he was also the greatest writer ever to occupy the White House.

Here are all of Lincoln's speeches, from the early days in Illinois to his profoundly moving presidential speeches, including the inaugural addresses, the Gettysburg Address, and his annual message to Congress.

Here, too, are the full texts of the stormy Lincoln-Douglas debates, including Douglas's own speeches.

Here is Lincoln's personal and political correspondence, including his satirical—and hilarous—"Rebecca" letter that nearly led to a duel, and his poignant letter to Mrs. Lydia Bixby upon hearing she had lost five sons in battle.

Here are Lincoln's war dispatches, his presidential messages and proclamations, poems, and private reflections on democracy, salvery, and the meaning of the Civil War's immense suffering.

Above all, here is Lincoln's absolutely distinctive language, resonant with dignity, wit, and the uniquely American flavor—with the bark on—of his frontier origins.

Write today for your copy of the writings of Abraham Lincoln. You'll be awfully glad you did.

Sincerely yours,

15–4   Selling Conference Accommodations

Situation   A conference center manager writes to subscribers of *The Sales Executive*, asking them to choose *Whispering Pines Conference Center* for their next meeting.

The Letter   Dear Mr. Edwards:

"Thank you—for helping us put on the best conference we've ever had. Your superb facilities, service, know-how, and helpful attitude all add up to one word: *professionalism*."

Pardon me for crowing just a bit, but the statement above was received a few days ago from the vice president of one of the country's largest manufacturing companies. And it's typical of many we get from top executives who chose Whispering Pines in Myrtle Beach, South Carolina as their host for meetings, conferences, seminars, and get-togethers.

At Whispering Pines we know how to help you make your meetings really successful. It's what we were designed to do, what we're in business for, the reason we like to think we're the ideal convention headquarters. Whispering Pines is not just another magnificent resort center that offers everything any meeting goer could ask for—outstanding cuisine ... big name entertainers ... elegant nearby shopping malls ... all sports, including a championship golf course and tennis courts ... and a stunning view of the Atlantic Ocean. We're all those things, of course, and we are more.

By "more" we mean that we really are professionals when it comes to arranging space for your specific needs and providing every service you require to make outstanding meetings and conferences. At Whispering Pines you'll find a staff that is dedicated to personal and friendly hospitality.

Skeptical? Let me prove what I have said. Please look over the enclosed colorful booklet, which shows our spectacular setting and elegant facilities. Then, to learn about our professional side, mail the enclosed card for your free copy of *Organizing, Planning, and Running a Meeting*.

Hopefully yours,

15–5 Selling a "Retirement Concept" of Living

Situation Sunset Harbor Village, a retirement community under construction, purchased a mailing list of retired people in the state of Texas, and endeavors to sell them on signing up for special housing.

The Letter Mr. F. C. Logan
3606 Hillside Drive
Beaumont, Texas 77704

Happy birthday, Crom!

How do we know about your birthday and your age? Let's just call it "research" with a little help from your friends.

Now that you've joined the over-60 crowd—the golden years, some say—I'd like to talk to you about something that may enrich the many years you have left beyond your dreams—Sunset Harbor Village.

Sunset Harbor Village offers you the best life-care retirement living, in a gracious new community being developed just outside Brownsville. You'll enjoy a private apartment, one provided meal each day, social and recreational activities, and personal services such as laundry, housekeeping, scheduled transportation, and health care should you ever need it. Entrance fees start in the mid-$90,000's and up to 90 percent of this payment is returnable to you or your estate.

I personally invite you to visit me at our Information Center so that I can show you the rich, rewarding lifestyle that can be yours at Sunset Harbor Village. We're open from 9 to 5, Monday through Friday, at 1400 Bellevue Road. Please call me at 686-7181.

Sincerely,

Helena Draper
Marketing Director

PS: For more information by mail, please complete and mail the enclosed postage-paid card.

Section 16

Writing Sales Promotion Communications

Letters written expressly to sell a product or service, such as those illustrated in this section, represent only one method of generating business by mail. Any communication that attempts to attract favorable public attention, make new friends, generate additional business, keep present customers buying, or reawaken interest from old customers who have strayed comes under the broad heading of "promotion."

There is virtually no limit to the promotional methods that can be employed. In this section, we illustrate several different promotional letters that have been used successfully.

16-1   Invitation to an Open House

Situation

The National Association of Teachers of Homemaking is having its annual convention in Minneapolis on June 4 to 7. Sterling Mills, manufacturer of flour and other food products, has its main headquarters in Minneapolis. The director of educational relations invites each member of the association to an open house during the convention.

The Letter

Dear Friend:

I hope you are planning to attend the annual convention of the National Association of Teachers of Homemaking in Minneapolis June 4 through 7. Perhaps you know that Sterling Mills calls Minneapolis home, and I consider it a rare opportunity for our city to host such a distinguished group.

While you're here, we'd like you to visit us, so we have arranged a special Open House for all members of NATH on Thursday, June 6, at our main plant from 5:30 until 8:30 p.m. (This is a free evening, according to the officers of your organization.) We'll have refreshments and a buffet, followed by a guided tour of the sections of our plant that we think will interest you most, including our famous recipe testing center.

We're only about twenty minutes from the Radisson, your convention headquarters, and will have courtesy limousines to pick you up there and return you to the hotel at the end of the tour. Full details will be provided at the registration desk.

If you are planning to attend the convention, would you please indicate on the enclosed card whether you are likely to attend the Open House? I certainly hope you will be with us!

Sincerely,

16–2 Formalized Invitation to a Special Exhibit

Situation

Excello Illumination Corporation plans to exhibit at a convention of the American Institute of Architects at the Cow Palace in San Francisco. The sales manager reserves space for the exhibit plus a conference room adjoining it. The conference room will be converted into a "little theater," where a promotional movie will be shown continuously. A formal invitation is sent to all members of AIA.

The Invitation

EXCELLO ILLUMINATION CORPORATION

cordially invites you to

visit its exhibit at the American Institute of Architects at

THE COW PALACE, SAN FRANCISCO

March 6 to 9, 19—

and to view an exciting new film

"LET THERE BE LIGHT"

at the "Little Theatre" that adjoins the exhibit.

The film briefly traces the history of artificial
illumination and presents startling new developments
and innovations in the science of lighting.
It will be shown every hour from 9 a.m. to 5 p.m.

16–3   Follow-Up to an Exhibit Visitor

Situation

Excello Illumination Corporation has kept a guest log of the visitors to its exhibit in San Francisco. (See the invitation on the preceding page.) Later the sales manager writes each guest and encloses a promotion brochure prepared especially for the occasion. The letter and enclosure will reestablish contact with the visitor and keep the company's name and products up front.

The Letter

Dear Mrs. Ramos:

Thank you for visiting our exhibit at the AIA convention in San Francisco. I hope you enjoyed the film, "Let There Be Light," and that you helped yourself to the free materials on display.

Since the convention ended, Excello has published a colorful booklet, "Low-Energy Lighting," a copy of which is enclosed. The 24-volt lighting system described draws only 2½ watts per lamp with a life expectancy of fifty years. We think this is one of the most exciting developments to come along in recent years.

Please let me know if you would like additional copies of this booklet and any of the materials that were handed out at the convention.

Sincerely yours,

16–4 Announcing New Products and Services

Situation

Holliman's, a leading office supply store in Cheyenne, Wyoming, recently acquired Foley's Business Machines. The following announcement is sent to the store's regular mailing list, as well as to members of NOMA, SAM, Personnel Director's Association, Kiwanis, Lion's, Optimists, and other groups to attract new customers.

The Announcement

> Holliman's—for over 50 years,
> Cheyenne's leading office supply store—
> is proud to announce the acquisition of
> Foley's Business Machines,
> featuring the following:
>
> - Imaging Systems
> - Xerox Copiers
> - Barnes Laser Printers
> - IBM Electric and Electronic Typewriters
> - Fiske Desk-Top Computers
> - Morgan Electronic Billing and Accounting
> - Plus a thoroughly modern service department
>   with factory-trained technicians
>
>
>
> Same location: 1400 Terhune Drive, Cheyenne
> Same telephone number: 457-8500

16–5   Announcing a New Location

Situation

M&N Equipment Rentals, in Baltimore, Maryland, has occupied rental space in Baltimore proper for nearly ten years. Recently the firm constructed its own building in Glen Burnie, a suburb of Baltimore. Lauren Martin, President, announces the change of location to its many customers and to suppliers in the vicinity.

The Announcement

M&N EQUIPMENT RENTALS, INC.
Sales and Service

On May 21 M&N will occupy its new building at 323 Eastwood Road in Glen Burnie, Maryland. Come visit us in our new home—same excellent equipment and great service.

Air Compressors, Welding Machines
Masonry Saws, Vibrators, Pumps,
Scaffolds, Forklifts, Mortar Mixers,
Electric Hand Tools, and Concrete
Accessories

Telephone 555-3529

16-6   Welcoming a Newcomer to the Community

Situation

In small towns and suburban areas surrounding large cities, it's fairly easy to keep track of local events by means of the newspaper. New residents are of special interest to local retail stores, and often these people are welcomed to the community by a personal letter. Mr. and Mrs. George Bryson and their three young children have recently moved to Springdale (he will be the new high school principal) and receive a welcome letter from a clothing store.

The Letter

Dear Mr. and Mrs. Bryson:

We may not be the first to welcome you to Springdale, but count us among those who are genuinely glad you chose our community to live and work in. As the new principal of Springdale High School, Mr. Bryson will, we are confident, bring a new standard of excellence to that institution.

For over twenty-five years, Walton Family Clothiers has been Springdale's favorite shopping place for women's, men's, and children's wear, featuring such well-known brands as Botany, Kingsridge, Palm Beach, Cardin, LaCoste, Levi, Florsheim, Buster Brown, Red Cross, Arrow, and Sero. You can charge your purchases with one of our convenient charge accounts; we also accept major credit cards.

But whether you need anything now or not, please come to see us. We'd like to meet you and present each member of the family with a special gift. Just bring this letter with you.

We hope you'll like living in Springdale. We do. What we lack in size we make up for in down-home friendliness!

Sincerely,

Part 5

LETTERS FROM CUSTOMERS TO SUPPLIERS

All too often, business executives and others take their suppliers for granted. "We're valuable customers," they say, "and the people we buy from should be made constantly aware of our importance." Then they proceed to make unreasonable demands, fuss about inconsequential errors and delays, and exert their "authority" in numerous other ways.

Yet some suppliers are every bit as important as loyal customers. When you find an organization that provides you with competitive merchandise or services at competitive prices, gives you unfailingly good service, and bends over backwards to help you in times of crisis, then you should reciprocate by treating that supplier with courtesy and respect.

At the same time, there are occasions, when customers have reason to be dissatisfied with a supplier's service, merchandise, policies, or treatment. And, of course, they should not hesitate to call attention to these problems and insist on a fair solution to them.

Section 17

General Letters from Customers to Suppliers

All to often, business executives and others take their suppliers for granted. "We're valuable customers," they say, "and the people we buy from should be made constantly aware of our importance." Then they proceed to make unreasonable demands, fuss about inconsequential errors and delays, and exert their "authority" in numerous other ways.

Yet some suppliers are every bit as important as loyal customers. When you find an organization that provides you with competitive merchandise or services at competitive prices, gives you unfailingly good service, and bends over backwards to help you in times of crisis, then you should reciprocate by treating that supplier with courtesy and respect.

At the same time, there are occasions when customers have reason to be dissatisfied with a supplier's service, merchandise, policies, or treatment. And, of course, they should not hesitate to call attention to these problems and insist on a fair solution to them.

17-1 Placing a Cash Order

Situation Price Boone, owner of a retail stationery store, places an order for supplies from Mid-Continent Stationers. There is a 10-percent discount for cash orders, and Mid-Continent pays mailing costs.

The Letter Ladies and Gentlemen:

Enclosed is my check for $246.94 for the following:

15	Liquid Paper	$2.80	$ 42.00
18	Desk calendars	3.20	57.60
12	Ace correction tape	2.99	35.88
18	Scotch tape	2.88	34.56
10	Ko-Rec-Type	3.72	37.20
6	WD-40	1.99	11.94
80	Tru-Point pens	.69	55.20
			$274.38
	Less 10% discount		27.44
	Net amount		$246.94

I'm getting low on the above items, and I would appreciate your giving my order high priority.

Very truly yours,

17–2 Placing a COD Order

Situation   Gretchen Crowley, a retail florist, orders items from a supplier with whom credit has not been established.

The Letter   Gentlemen:

Please send me the following items COD:

Stock number	Item	Quantity	Price	Extension
S–2	Staplers	2	$14.10	$ 28.20
S–7	Staples	6 boxes	$ 3.22	19.32
S–T	Masking tape	12 spools	$ 2.72	32.64
B–2	Binders	5	$ 3.84	19.20
P–5	Plastic rolls	3	$ 9.75	29.25
			Total	$128.61

I would like to establish credit with your organization, and I am enclosing a current income statement and balance sheet. May I hear from you soon?

Yours very truly,

17–3   Placing a Credit Card Order

Situation

Theodore Wood sees an ad in the July issue of *Atlantic* magazine for a Czech Tractor/Wagon. Wood wants to order the miniature for his grandson's birthday on July 27, to be sent directly to him, the amount to be charged to Wood's credit card.

The Letter

    This is my order for the Czech Tractor/Wagon, which was advertised in the July issue of *Atlantic*. This miniature is to be a birthday gift and should be sent to:

Mr. Keith Wood
115 South Williams Street
Holder, Florida 32645

    Please charge the gift ($39.50) to my Discover credit card as follows:

Theodore Wood
Number 0000 0000 0000 0000
Expiration date: 9–96

    Is it possible to schedule this mailing so that the gift arrives no earlier than August 15 and no later than August 20? I would greatly appreciate it if you could. Thank you!

                                  Sincerely,

17–4 Praising a Supplier's Sales Representative

Situation

Gulf Cove Marina, a new facility that provides services, equipment, and supplies to boat owners and would-be owners, recently held its Grand Opening. The sales representative for a nautical supply house has been so helpful prior to and on that occasion that the owner decides to write the supplier's sales manager, Gordon Swayne, a letter of appreciation.

The Letter

Dear Mr. Swayne:

Last Saturday, Gulf Cove Marina had its Grand Opening. I'm happy to report that it was a great success—the attendance was about twice our expectations. So I think we're off to a fine start.

As I look back on the event and the magnificent confusion that one expects on such an occasion, I think of the wonderful help your representative, Victor Jacobs, was to me and my associates. Not only did Vic show up a couple of days before the opening to help us with displays and other preparations. He also remained on the "big day" to perform numerous chores whenever he was needed—from talking with visitors and demonstrating equipment, to serving cold drinks and sea food. He was a godsend.

I'm enormously grateful to you, Mr. Swayne, for "lending" Vic to us on this important occasion. As far as I am concerned, he'll be accorded a warm welcome here every time his travels take him in our direction.

Yours very cordially,

17–5

Thanking a Supplier for Service and Support

Situation

Ranier Wholesale Hardware is celebrating its fiftieth anniversary in business. On the occasion, the president writes many of the company's loyal customers to thank them for their support. About a month later it occurs to the president that several of his suppliers also deserve recognition, and he decides to write them to express appreciation for high-quality merchandise and services.

The Letter

Dear George:

Generally, it's the customer who gets all the attention.

When we held our Golden Jubilee Anniversary last month, we had a wonderful celebration. One of the things we thought of first was to write a couple of hundred of our retail hardware customers to thank them for their loyal support over the years. Without them, we said, we couldn't possibly have become what we are; in fact, we wouldn't even be around to celebrate those fifty years. Of course, we meant it; you know the importance of loyal friends as well as we do.

But later I got to thinking: What about those people who kept us supplied most of those years with quality hardware products that dealers wanted to buy and did buy time and time again? Don't they deserve some credit, too? Of course, they do. We've been buying hammers, saws, blades, wrenches, and a couple of dozen other Mikkelson-brand products from you for how long—thirty-five years? And you've always given us genuine quality at a fair price, plus outstanding service. What more can a wholesaler ask from a manufacturer? Sure, we've had our minor squabbles from time to time, and your attitude was that the customer is always right (in our case, he often wasn't!). Whatever the problems were—I forget—they haven't detracted one bit from our high opinion of your company, your products, and your people.

So, on at least one occasion, I want to direct my full attention not to my important customers, but to my important suppliers. Mikkelson stands very high on our list of those to whom we owe a great big thank you. Thank you!

Sincerely,

PS: When a small crisis arises between us—and it will!—you won't hold over my head the nice things I've said, will you?

Section 18

Problem Letters from Customers to Suppliers

Problem letters to suppliers are of an almost infinite variety. In this section, we deal with poor service on a special order, poor performance on a service contract, receipt of unsatisfactory merchandise, suspected error on an invoice, and complaint about a supplier's sales representatives.

Guidelines for writing such letters follow:

---

1. *Describe clearly, tactfully, but firmly the situation that triggered your letter.*

2. *Explain what you expect the supplier to do—improve service, change a policy, send a new shipment, offer an adjustment, or whatever.*

3. *Avoid showing anger (unless, of course, the problem you're writing about has occurred repeatedly and previous letters have produced no results).*

4. *If you expect some kind of adjustment, your letter falls in the sales category, and you're more likely to get what you want if your message is persuasive rather than threatening.*

18-1 Receipt of a Low-Quality Office Product

Situation

Among the dozens of products sold by Paramount Office Supplies, a retail outlet, is typewriter correction tape. The brand featured by the store for many years is Pendant, and customers have been happy with their purchase. Recently, however, there has been a change for the worse in the quality of Pendant. It does not satisfactorily cover the typewriter type. The owner of Paramount, Katherine Lewis, writes the wholesaler (Bruce Owens) the following letter.

The Letter

Dear Bruce:

For the first time in memory, I have a complaint about one of your products—Pendant Correction Tape. The quality of the last order I received from you is very bad, and my customers are driving me to distraction with their complaints and returns.

Are you aware of this situation, Bruce? If not, just try the "new" Pendant, and you'll find out what I'm saying is true. I've been so besieged with returns by customers that I'm now considering stocking another brand.

I've done business with you too long, Bruce, not to give you another chance with Pendant. If you can do something about this, fine; I'll order from you. If not, I'll try another correction tape.

Sincerely,

18-2

Response to Letter About Receipt of a Low-Quality Office Product

Situation   See Letter 18–1 on the preceding page.

The Letter   Dear Katherine:

I couldn't agree with you more when you say that the Pendant Correction Tapes you received from me are not satisfactory. I have telephoned the Pendant people. Their attitude is that this correction tape is of the highest quality, and they see nothing wrong with it.

I am sending you in a separate mailing (Priority Mail) a couple of rolls of Cover-All correction tape, and I think when you use this tape you will be delighted with it. This is the brand we'll be distributing from now on, and I hope I will receive an order from you. I predict that there will be no more complaints from your customers.

Sincerely,

18–3   Error in an Invoice

Situation   Sutton, Inc. is a manufacturer of Plymouth electric stoves. The sales representative for Sutton calls upon a retailer, Mark Willoughby, and sells him six Plymouth DeLuxe stoves. There is a sale on these stoves at the price of $177.75, compared with $215.35, which is the regular price. However, when the invoice arrived, the amount was $1292.10—a difference of $225.60 more than the anticipated amount. Willoughby writes the manufacturer about the mistake.

The Letter   Ladies and Gentlemen:

When your representative, Alan Powers, called on me in late April, he told me that you were offering a special price of $177.75 on the Plymouth DeLuxe stove. I ordered six. However, the invoice I received showed the amount due as $1292.10—a difference of $225.60.

I'm enclosing a check for $1066.50. Unless I hear from you to the contrary, I will assume that this is the correct amount. If this is not the case, I would like to cancel three of the stoves.

Very truly yours,

18–4   Response Regarding Error in an Invoice

Situation   See Letter 18–3 above.

The Letter   Dear Mr. Jennings:

Mea culpa (or, I'm sorry) about the mistake we made in our January 17 invoice. You are right, and the fault is mine. I have entered the amount on your ledger sheet as $1066.50 (thank goodness, the $1292.10 had not been posted).

I can't really account for this mistake, Mr. Jennings, and I am delighted that you caught it. Thank you for writing.

Cordially yours,

18–5

Complaint About a Supplier's Sales Representative

Situation

Bennington High School, like other schools all over the country, is frequently visited by sales representatives of publishers and other firms. At Bennington, each teacher selects the textbooks for his or her classes; thus, this is the individual a book representative likes to talk with. The principal, Frances Morelli, welcomes sales representatives, but she insists that they check in at her office before visiting teachers. One company representative consistently violates this rule, and Morelli decides to write the regional manager about the problem and tactfully request a change in the sales representative's conduct.

The Letter

Dear Mr. Engels:

Although I find it an unpleasant task, I feel that I must bring to your attention a problem I am having with your representative, Graham Hardy.

I am, of course, delighted to have sales representatives call on our teachers. I firmly believe that teachers should keep up to date on everything new in textbooks and other educational products and that no one is in a better position to inform them than the people who sell them.

Concerning sales representatives, I have a rule that I feel that I must enforce. Every representative is to check in at my office for clearance before proceeding to the classrooms. The reason is understandable to you, I am sure. I want to be certain that each visitor is one that teachers will want to see and, equally important, I think it is unwise for me to allow teachers to be interrupted while their classes are in session.

Mr. Hardy was informed of this rule when he first began to call on us in September. However, he has repeatedly ignored it. I know only because the teachers themselves have complained to me about his frequent interruptions, often at extremely awkward times.

Naturally, I do not want to cause trouble for this young man. He seems very personable, and I know the teachers he sees have great respect for his knowledge and the company he represents. I am sure you will understand my position, and I hope that you will pass the word on to him.

Very truly yours,

18-6

Response to Complaint About a Supplier's Sales Representative

Situation   See Letter 18–5 on the preceding page.

The Letter   Dear Ms. Morelli:

I appreciate your letter concerning Graham Hardy and his attitude toward the teachers on your staff.

Graham is a new representative and was probably not aware that he was causing difficulty in your school. I have talked with him at some length, and he thoroughly understands that when he visits a school he must get the principal's permission to visit teachers. Also, I'm making note of this matter to be discussed again at our next sales conference on October 16.

Thank you for writing. According to his schedule, Graham's next visit to Bennington High School is early March. If the situation you describe occurs again, I would like very much to hear from you.

Gratefully yours,

18–7   Poor Service on a Special Order

Situation

Lomack's, a retail gift shop, places a special order with a long-time supplier for monogrammed crystal stemware. The stemware is to be a widding gift, and delivery is promised by May 15. Not only does the order arrive after the wedding; the monogram is wrong and two pieces are cracked. The owner of Lomack's, Mrs. Lydia Lomack, writes the supplier about the problem.

The Letter

Dear John:

I'm enclosing a copy of my order, dated February 17, for Prestige crystal stemware: eight 11-ounce goblets, eight 5½-ounce wine glasses, and eight 7-ounce champagne glasses. As you will see, these pieces were to be monogrammed "G" in Old English lettering, and delivery was requested not later than May 15.

Well, John, here is what happened:

1. The stemware was finally received May 28. Because I became anxious about delivery before the wedding (for which the stemware was to be a gift), I telephoned your customer service department twice—May 4 and May 11—and in each case was assured that delivery would positively be made by May 15.

2. The monogram on the stemware was "C" in block lettering.

3. Two of the wine glasses were cracked.

I think you will understand, John, why I am upset at the manner in which this order was handled. My excuses and apologies to the customer (an aunt of the groom) are of no comfort; to her, the incident was "terribly embarrassing—unforgivable," and I confess that I agree with her. I did persuade her not to cancel the order simply because there were no other gifts of this nature, but I had to promise very fast delivery.

Obviously, you know what must be done: Get the *right* stemware to me as fast as you can. I'd like to save this good customer, and if you don't turn handsprings to expedite delivery, I don't have a prayer. But let me know so that, if necessary, I can make other arrangements.

Incidentally, John, the Colonial ironstone is going very well. If you're bringout out new patterns, be sure to let me know.

Cordially yours,

18-8

Response to a Letter Regarding Poor Service on a Special Order

Situation   See Letter 18–7 on the preceding page.

The Letter   Dear Lydia:

When Willoughby's goofs an order, they do a bang-up job of it! Under the awful circumstances involved, I think your letter was a classic indication of patience and understanding. I'm afraid I would have been more put out about this experience.

Let me summarize the errors:

1. You were promised a delivery date of May 15, but received the order on May 28. Result: an unhappy donor and a pair of disappointed newlyweds.

2. There were two mistakes on the monogram on the stemware—"C" instead of "G," and block lettering rather than Old English.

3. Two of the wine glasses were cracked.

Pardon the repetition, but I needed to see the "picture" as it has developed.

I have difficulty understanding how even *one* of those errors occurred. Three serious errors is almost beyond belief, and the President of Willoughby's is as embarrassed as I am. While I had the President on the phone, I extracted a promise of a June 9 delivery date on your order, insisting that if there were more errors we would go elsewhere for our future orders.

Hopefully yours,

18–9   Poor Performance on a Service Contract

Situation   Severn and Kearns, an architectual firm that occupies its own one-story building, has a two-year contract with Universal Maintenance Service to provide complete janitorial services. During the eight months the contract has been in effect, the firm has been frequently dissatisfied with the service given, and the Administrative Services Manager, Kathleen Malette, has discussed the problem numerous times with the manager of Universal. The situation has not improved to Malette's satisfaction, and she puts her case in writing, describing explicitly the reasons for dissatisfaction with the service given and putting Universal on notice that the contract is in jeopardy.

The Letter   Dear Mr. Weidner:

You will recall that you and I have discussed at least four times during the past eight months the low quality of service provided by your company. After each conversation, service improved for a short time, only to revert back to the old standard that brought about my original complaint.

I will summarize in this letter my previous discussions about your performance. You may wish to refer to our contract as you read my comments.

1. *Windows.* According to the contract, all windows are to be cleaned once a month. This is not being done. Often from six to eight weeks elapse between cleanings. Even when the windows are cleaned, the job is less than satisfactory. But you are aware of this—you've seen the results on several occasions and always promised a better job "next time." It has not happened.

2. *Floors.* The floors throughout the building are to be cleaned after each workday—the carpeting is to be vacuumed and tile and wood floors cleaned with special solvents. Although your service people do show up each day, their efforts can only be described as careless.

3. *Furniture and Equipment.* Furniture and equipment are to be dusted or vacuumed daily, and once a month desks, chairs, tables, and other furniture are to be cleaned and polished. Neither of these two contract stipulations is being met to my satisfaction.

4. *Walls and Drapes.* Walls and drapes are to be vacuumed every week. I'm convinced that this is not being done in several offices.

5. *Miscellaneous.* I could mention a dozen other cleaning responsibilities that are not being met satisfactorily—pictures, glass-front cabinets, lavatories, and ash trays, for example.

I call your attention to paragraph 7c in the contract, Mr. Weidner, in which the provisions for revocation of the contract are described. I do not like to consider such a possibility, but I must unless I have your written assurance that all provisions of the contract will be met.

I will be pleased to meet with you once more to discuss this situation and again point out to you why we are not satisfied with the present arrangement. I assure you that this is a matter of some urgency to me.

Yours very truly,

18–10   Responding to a Letter About Poor Performance on a Service Contract

Situation   See Letter 18–9 on the preceding page.

The Letter   Dear Miss Malette:

I don't blame you for being upset about the poor performance on our service contract. If I were in your position, I would be more than un-happy—I would be outraged.

This morning I talked at length with the people providing the service. Unfortunately, they disagree with much of what you had to say about their performance. But this makes no difference to me; the customer's word is my bond. So I will not quarrel with your objections. All I can do is inspect the premises each time they visit your building. If I find any lack of attention to the list of "no-no's," I will make certain that their shortcomings are corrected.

Will you do me a favor? I'd like to hear from you soon after the next services have been rendered. I believe this sad showing can be corrected, and I am determined to make it happen.

Apologetically yours,

18–11 Receipt of an Unacceptable Substitute

Situation

Harbor Light Press, a book publisher, has had great success with *The Handy Desk Companion*, a style manual for secretaries. Long published as a traditional hard-bound book, the publisher, because of customer demand, has also recently made it available in a spiral binding. Laughlin's Book Nook has placed two orders for *The Handy Desk Companion* in spiral binding over the past three months, and each time received the hard-bound book with the note on the shipping ticket, "Please accept this substitute; we're temporarily out of stock on the spiral binding." The owner of the Book Nook, Mary Beth Laughlin, writes the publisher to call attention to the recurrent out-of-stock situation and receive assurance that in the future no substitutions will be sent.

The Letter

Ladies and Gentlemen:

During the past three months I have placed two sizable orders for *The Handy Desk Companion*, by Mauck, specifying the new spiral binding that you are advertising in *Publisher's Weekly*. Both times you sent me the hard-cover binding because you were out of stock on the spiral.

Fortunately, I am still selling quite a few of the hard covers, but more and more customers ask for the new spiral-bound book (at least two of your competitors have similar reference books in this easy-to-use binding).

I'm frankly concerned that unless you solve this out-of-stock problem, we're both going to be hurt. Up to now I have stocked only the Mauck book—my customers tell me it is the best of its kind on the market—but I may have to change my policy in self-defense. It may sound a little foolish that people will choose a book because it's easier to use rather than on the merits of the content, but it really seems to be happening.

Enclosed is my order for 75 copies of *The Handy Desk Companion* in spiral binding. Please do not, under any circumstances, send me anything else. I have plenty of the hard-cover copies in stock.

The new *Recipe Date Book* is a winner. I sold 162 of them in April and will soon have to place another order. Please don't be out of stock!

Sincerely yours,

18–12 Response to Letter About an Unacceptable Substitute

Situation   See Letter 18–11 on the preceding page.

The Letter   Dear Mrs. Laughlin:

I agree with you. I would be very upset, too, about not receiving spiral binding on your latest order for *The Handy Desk Companion*, by Mauck.

As soon as I received your letter, I called the book manufacturer and was told by the production manager that they have difficulty keeping up with the demand for the spiral-bound book. He said that, because he is not equipped to handle spiral-bound books, he has to farm out the binding to another manufacturer. He realizes that buyers are not happy, and swore that we would have no further difficulty in getting orders filled.

Thank you for your patience, Mrs. Laughlin. I assure you (and I base my opinion on what I was told by the bindery) that you will have no further trouble in getting what you want.

Cordially,

18–13   Customer Receives a "Pay-or-Else" Letter in Error

Situation

DuVall Wholesalers purchases hardware from Minnesota Supply Corporation. DuVall receives a warning that if the company does not pay the amount owed ($6440) within ten days, their account will be turned over to a collection agency. The fact is that DuVall has always paid for purchases promptly on receipt of the statement, and the company owes nothing. The letter was obviously sent in error. DuVall writes an irate letter. See the response to this letter on the next page.

The Letter

Gentlemen:

I am very annoyed with you for sending me a threatening collection letter when we owe your company nothing. The amount you referred to ($6440) was paid six weeks ago!

Obviously, you have our account mixed up with someone else's; you'll discover it when you take another look at the records. I have my cancelled check, which you endorsed, in the amount of $6440. Please give me some explanation for your insulting letter. For five years I have been a customer of Minnesota Supply Company and have always paid for my purchases within four or five days upon receipt of your statement.

Don't you think you owe me an apology?

Very truly yours,

18–14

Response to a Complaint About "Pay-or-Else" Letter

Situation   See Letter 18–13 on the preceding page.

The Letter   Dear Harry:

I deserve the thrashing you gave me and more. This error is just one of those flukes that, fortunately, are very rare but which cause great discomfort.

Our computer that spews out bills to our customers obviously had a "glitch," which has now been fixed. Needless to say, I find it hard to understand how we could insult such a valuable customer as you, and there are several people who are chafing even more than I am because I made them aware of the seriousness of the error!

Obviously, your account has a zero balance, but I'm hoping that will change—we like having you owe us because we're always certain that we will be paid on time and in the right amount.

Apologetically yours,

18–15

Irate Customer Accuses Supplier of Sloppy Record Keeping

Situation

Mrs. Sara Patton, owner of Rexway Distributors Corporation, is a fairly new customer of Reliable Supply Company. She has reason, she believes, to write an irate letter to the Vice President of Reliable, questioning the accuracy of their accounting records. According to her ledger, she has a zero balance with the supplier. The supplier indicated in a second statement that Patton still owes $971.80—quite a discrepancy. Patton writes the following letter to the Vice President of Reliable Supply Company.

The Letter

Dear Mr. Marshall:

When I received your second statement, showing our account in arrears in the amount of $971.80, I was astonished—no, I was very angry. My records show that we have a zero balance at Reliable Supply Company! And I got nowhere with your accountants when I questioned the first statement I received.

I'd like a letter from you showing me how you arrived at your preposterous figure. Immediately, please. Apparently you're guilty of sloppy record keeping.

Yours very truly,

18–16 Response to Customer About Sloppy Record Keeping

Situation   See Letter 18–15 on the preceding page.

The Letter   Dear Mrs. Patton:

Thank you for writing about your account balance. I can understand why you could be so angry about our "sloppy record keeping." Yet I must agree with our accountant; according to your ledger sheet, you still owe us $971.80.

Would you please examine your records again, Mrs. Patton? I dislike asking you to do so, but I can't account for the difference in our records—both yours and mine. We have checked our credit entries for Rexway Distributors for the past three months and can find no entry of $971.80.

I understand it's asking a lot of you to recheck your records, but I have no alternative. Thank you for your patience.

Cordially yours,

18–17 Response by an Irate Customer Who Discovers an Error

Situation   See Letter 18–15 on the preceding page and Letter 18–16 above.

The Letter   Dear Mr. Marshall

You said I would be embarrassed about the discrepancy in my account, and I must confess that you are right and I am wrong. The check for $971.80 was made out but never mailed. It is enclosed.

I can't imagine what caused this foul-up, but it is a beauty! I'm embarrassed most by the wording of my letter to you. Forgive me, please.

Sincerely yours,

18–18 Complaint About Loss of Conference Materials

Situation

Frances Weller is Assistant Manager of Western Motor Hotel, which counts among its customers individuals as well as groups of people attending conventions and meetings. A few days ago Weller receives the following letter from Bryant Skinner, President of Pocono Realty Association, whose members recently completed a five-day stay at the hotel.

The Letter

Ladies and Gentlemen:

Thanks to the inefficiency of your staff, the fall meeting of the Pocono Realty Association was a big disappointment.

As you very well know, the materials that were shipped to your hotel two weeks in advance for use in our group sessions were misplaced by someone there and were never found (they arrived here today from your hotel). The entire program had been built around these materials, and as a result of their being misplaced, we had to improvise. This was both awkward and unproductive.

Your statement for $2178.95 arrived today, and I am tempted not to pay it. In any event, it would seem that we are entitled to some kind of discount for the inconvenience we suffered at your hands.

I expect an explanation from you before I authorize payment.

Very truly yours,

18–19   Response to Complaint About Loss of Conference Materials

Situation   See Letter 18–18 on the preceding page.

The Letter   Dear Mr. Skinner:

Everyone here at Western Motor Hotel is terribly embarrassed about the misplacement of your conference materials. Permit me to tell you exactly what happened.

Our investigation reveals the accuracy of what you said about the missing materials. They were indeed received several days before your meeting. The part-time custodian who signed for the materials (they arrived late in the evening) did not know what to do with them, so he locked them up in the Lost and Found Room. He left the hotel to go on vacation the following day, and his whereabouts were unknown. Later, someone piled several pieces of luggage on top of the carton so that it was hidden from sight. Although the Lost and Found Room was searched at the time, no one thought to lift the luggage to see if there was anything underneath.

I expect you'll have trouble understanding all this. I certainly do! If it's any comfort to you, this is the first time in our history that such a mistake was made—and it was a corker!

Please give us another chance, Mr. Skinner. I'd like to prove to you that we're really top-notch in the hostelry business.

Sincerely yours,

18–20 Customer Not Given an Expected Discount

Situation

Timothy Kelly is a sales representative of Hearthstones, a manufacturer of sporting goods. He calls frequently on Twin Cities Mart in Minneapolis.

On his last visit, Kelly said that the popular Partner golf bag will be on sale during August at 20 percent off the regular price of $45 to retailers, for a net price of $36. Twin Cities Mart ordered six bags.

Heathstones also offers retailers a discount of 5 percent on cash orders. So the accountant for Twin Cities, Beryl Kendrick, assumes the net amount owed is $210.90 rather than $220.00.

When Kendrick's check is received, Hearthstones objects to the amount, saying that Twin Cities still owes $11.10. Following is the letter that Kendrick wrote to Hearthstones.

The Letter

Ladies and Gentlemen:

When I placed my order for six Partner golf bags on the basis of your announced 20-percent discount, I assumed that your regular 5-percent discount on cash orders would apply. I can find nothing in your catalog on this matter.

I will do whatever seems fair to you. I don't want to be an exception, but I do think my logic is sound, don't you? Incidentally, I'm having quite a run on Comet golf club covers, and I will probably be placing an order soon.

Cordially,

18–21 Response to a Customer Who Is Not Given an Expected Discount

Situation   See Letter 18–20 on the preceding page.

The Letter   Dear Beryl:

You are absolutely right—you owe us nothing. Of course, we did mark down Partner golf bags 20 percent and, of course, we do offer a 5-percent discount for cash. My apologies to you—you owe us nothing. I can't account for this—I was about to say *stupid*—error. Well, I said it and I'm glad.

Sincerely,

Part 6

LETTERS FROM SUPPLIERS TO CUSTOMERS

One of the odd things about some business organizations is that they spend so much money to lure new customers and spend so little to keep them after they've been landed. It just doesn't make sense. Taking customers for granted is routine in some larger organizations, where mere bigness generates an attitude of indifference.

Loyal customers are an organization's only protection against bankruptcy, and losing them because of neglect or indifference is downright sinful. Not only do satisfied customers continue to fatten the till, they often encourage others to buy. This is advertising that doesn't cost a penny. And although there are always problems in giving good service to customers, maintaining their patronage isn't all that difficult. It's a matter of attitude, of believing that everyone who buys from you is entitled to the best treatment you can deliver. Plus giving just a little more than you have to.

We said there are always problems in giving good service to customers. The reason, of course, is that no organization is perfect, and there's many a slip 'twixt the cup and the lip: unreasonable delays in filling orders, shipping the wrong merchandise, making errors in invoices and statements, writing cranky letters to customers for no good reason, failing to answers letters promptly, and so on.

Sometimes these errors or failures can't be helped. For example, if you can't get parts because of material shortages or a transportation strike, customers may be denied the goods they've ordered. And not infrequently the customer is to blame—for example, by failing to clearly identify the article or service required.

Yet no matter who is at fault, customers whom you value highly should generally be given the benefit of any doubt. Note that we said "customers whom you value highly." The old saying that all customers should be treated alike is a myth. Customers who repeatedly place large orders and pay for them will naturally get more attention than those who buy infrequently and have to be badgered to pay what they owe. However, you have to make the assumption that all customers are good unless proved otherwise.

Still, you should not get the impression that you always have to turn the other cheek. Some customers—even highly valued ones—may make demands that are impossible to accommodate or ask for exceptions to standard company policy. So there will be instances when you have to say no. Yet there are ways of doing so without creating animosity.

Section 19

General Letters from Suppliers to Customers

Many suppliers go out of their way to find legitimate opportunities to write letters to their customers, thanking their customers for friendly and cooperative treatment of a sales representative or other visitors who call upon the customers; expressing appreciation for prompt payment of an account or for an unusually large order; congratulating a customer who has been cited for professional achievement on a local, regional, or national basis; telling customers how much their past support has meant—these are examples of letters that don't really have to be written, but are in the interest of good customer relations.

Take note, however, of the word *legitimate* in the first paragraph. When thank-you and appreciation letters are written on a "formula" basis, "soft soap" will be recognized as that and will have very little meaning.

In this section, we present four examples of goodwill letters that we think will have a positive effect on customer-supplier relations.

19–1   Introducing a New Sales Representative

Situation   Price Brownles, Sales Manager of Revere Food Products, Inc., has accepted the resignation of Rebecca Wittstein from the sales staff. Wittstein's father recently had a heart attack, and Rebecca prefers an inside job so that she can look after him. She was given the position of Manager of Customer Services.

The traveling position has been filled by Milton Tarter, and Brownles decides to write each of the customers Wittstein has been calling on to announce the change.

The Letter   Dear Jeff:

May I introduce Milton Tarter to you?

Milt replaces Rebecca Wittstein, who has been given the job of Manager of Customer Services. This change developed when Rebecca's father suffered a heart attack, and she found it necessary to stay closer to home.

I'm certain you will like Milton Tarter. He is a graduate of DePaul University, in Chicago, majoring in sales management. He is a real go-getter and his "people IQ" is very near 100 percent. Milt was our representative in Arkansas and Missouri, and did an outstanding job. Our files are bulging with letters of appreciation from the customers he called on, and I'm confident you will also be praising him—he knows his products and his customers. He is very touchy when he thinks one of his customers is "put upon".

I would be delighted if, after you've spent some time with Milt, you would jot down your impressions of him. I predict your reactions will be highly favorable.

Sincerely yours,

19–2   Follow-Up of a Sales Representative's Call

Situation   William Bell is Marketing Director for Maryland Wholesale Hardware. One of Maryland's sales representatives, Keith Nixon, has just paid his first visit to Myra Bolton, owner of Bolton Hardware, in Patuxent. Bell follows up each salesperson's call, thanking the firm for its kindness in receiving the sales representative.

The Letter   Dear Myra:

Keith Nixon has just returned from his Maryland territory, and spoke very highly of you and your people. Of course, I have known you folks for several years (12?) and was not surprised with his report.

I want you to know, however, that I really appreciate your receiving Keith and helping him understand your business. Keith is new with us, but he has already made a remarkable showing in his territory. Apparently his visit with you was one of the highlights of his trip.

Very cordially yours,

19–3

Thanking a Customer for Courtesies to a Sales Representative

Situation

As the District Manager of a textile firm, Jan Campbell supervises several sales representatives who travel the assigned territories to call on buyers and purchasing directors. Each time she receives the report of a representative's successful visit with a customer or prospect, she follows up with a letter of appreciation.

The Letter

Dear Mr. Lewis:

Thank you for the courtesies you extended Jack Raglan when he called on you last week.

Jack is one of our most effective representatives, and he was delighted to have the chance to meet and talk with a person of your background and experience. From his report, I gather that you were very generous with your time, and he came away, in his words, "far more knowledgeable about our own products than when I went in."

The swatches of our new Fashion Sheen drapery fabric that Jack promised are being sent to you today, along with a special brochure that contains complete descriptive information. I hope you will let me—or Jack—know how we can be of service.

Cordially,

19–4 Acknowledging a First Order

Situation

Alex Kissinger, Sales Promotion Manager for Rhodes Furniture and Fixtures, Inc., has just learned that Ethel Bailey, owner of Nevada Interiors, has placed a big order. This is Rhode's first order from Nevada Interiors, and Kissinger decides to write Bailey a special welcome letter.

The Letter

Dear Ms. Bailey:

Thank you for your order for furniture and the check that accompanied it. Welcome to our ever-growing list of satisfied customers. The furniture is being shipped today—by special instructions from me.

Our sales representative in Western Nevada, Norman Archer, will call on you within the next couple of weeks to thank you in person. I think you'll like Norm. He is extremely knowledgeable about our line of furniture and fixtures, and he will be anxious to learn how he can be of help to you.

In a separate mailing, I'm sending you our just released pamphlet on our new line of patio furniture, "Outside Living at its Very Best."

Sincerely yours,

19–5

Follow-Up After Services Have Been Rendered

Situation   Shortly after Gold Medal Insurance Company ends its conference at Outer Banks Conference Center (see Letter 11–2, page 87), the Director writes a follow-up letter to the conference leader. Its purpose, of course, is to build goodwill and encourage Gold Medal to return for another stay at Outer Banks.

The Letter   Dear Mr. Watson:

I hope you were pleased with your experience at Outer Banks Conference Center and that all the participants returned to work with pleasant memories of their stay here. We certainly enjoyed having you and look forward to seeing you again.

Meanwhile, we're enlarging our accommodations. Soon you will see the addition of an Olympic-size indoor pool, stables for horses to ride, three new tennis courts, and a sauna. Incidentally, if you plan a winter conference, you'll find this area outstanding for all outdoor sports. The Kitty Hawk area (where the fabled Wright Brothers launched their first flight) is only a half-hour's drive away.

If there is anything you can suggest that will help us improve our accommodations or services, Mr. Watson, I hope you will write me.

Yours very sincerely,

19–6　Follow-Up on a Previous Order

Situation　Lomax, Inc., a mail-order distributor of sporting goods, receives a large number of orders for "junior" golf clubs (for golfers, ages 7 to 11) that are often sent to an address other than the buyer's. Thus it can be assumed that the clubs are a gift for a grandson, niece, nephew, or other young friend. After five years, the Sales Manager writes each customer a letter encouraging him or her to invest in standard-size clubs.

The Letter　Dear Mr. Heath:

Five years ago I had the pleasure of filling your order for a set of Pinnacle junior golf clubs, which I presume was a gift for a nephew, niece, grandchild, or other young friend.

Years have a way of slipping away from us, and perhaps you haven't thought much about this gift, but I have not forgotten! It occurred to me that that young person has reached the age of 16 or 18 and graduated to regular clubs. Is this not so? What a wonderful way to acknowledge this youngster's grown-upness, as well as a certain mastery of the game, to purchase an elegant set of adult-size clubs for this special person in your life.

Christmas isn't far away, and I think you may be interested in the handsome catalog I'm sending you, which features some of the greatest names in golf—Wilson, Spaulding, Nelson, and Hogan, to name a few. Incidentally, the Wilson clubs that were selling for $495 are now priced at $399.95. And there are great savings on other golfing needs—gloves, head covers, balls, and weekend bags.

Just indicate your needs on the order blank/envelope and put it in the mail. If you do it now, I absolutely guarantee delivery no later than December 15.

Very truly yours,

19-7 Thanking a Customer for a Referral

Situation Ralph Miller is the owner of a wholesale business called Centennial Automotive Parts, Inc. One of Centennial's long-time customers is Ithaca Auto Parts, and Miller has just learned that Paul Harmon, owner, has recommended Centennial products to a friend at Binghamton Auto Supply. Miller writes Harmon, thanking him for the referral.

The Letter Dear Paul:

Yesterday I received a large order from Binghamton Auto Supply and was told by the owner, Janet Rosenberg, that you were responsible for my getting the business.

I was mighty pleased to have the new business, Paul, but even more pleased that you thought well enough of me to recommend my company to Janet Rosenberg. That's the highest recommendation I can imagine, and I'm grateful for it. Thank you!

Cordially,

19–8

Thanking a Customer for Payment and for an Order

Situation

A good customer and personal friend, Andrew Hallock, of Midwest Supplies, Inc., has sent a sizable check in payment of an invoice and, in the same letter, placed a large order. It is the policy of Midwest to acknowledge all orders received as well as all payments.

The Letter

Dear Mr. Hallock:

I really appreciate your order for 200 Gem-Con Plastique motorcycle tanks. These will be shipped at once. Thanks, too, for the check!

Beginning in June, we're offering a special discount on the Gem-Con line. In addition to the trade discount of 33⅓ percent, we're giving a cash discount with terms of 10/EOM. This means you have an extra month to make payment and still receive the cash discount.

A lot of our customers are switching to the Plastique tank as a replacement for original metal equipment. They report hearty endorsements from participants in motorcross competition—that the tanks are very lightweight, but extremely tough. We predict you'll have a similar endorsement!

Sincerely yours,

19-9 Expressing Appreciation for Past Support

Situation Tyler Warbucks, President of Warbucks, Inc., in Decatur, Georgia, has been in business for only a short time. On the third anniversary of the company's founding, Warbucks writes a letter to loyal customers to thank them for their support.

The Letter Dear Mr. Vargas:

On March 16 Warbucks, Inc. will celebrate its third anniversary. It's a wonderful occasion for us, and we're not so quietly strutting a bit about the progress we've made.

Yet we're fully aware that our accomplishments are not simply attributable to "genius" leadership or hard-working employees. We grew and prospered only because we found some great friends like you who gave us loyal support along the way.

So this is a thank-you note—for buying and pushing our products, putting up with occasional errors due to "growing pains," and just helping to put Warbucks on the map. The future looks bright, and we want to acknowledge your contribution to this rosy outlook. As we say in Georgia, "'Preciate it!"

Very sincerely yours,

19–10   Acknowledging a Large Order

Situation   The Sales Manager of Revere Publishing Company, Vernon Brown-lee, has just received a big order fromMrs. Cynthia Eulan for accounting textbooks. Brownlee writes to Mrs. Eulan about the order.

The Letter   Dear Mrs. Eulan:

Gary Trout and I were both excited about your large order for Kahn's *Accounting 10/12*. Although the Kahn instruction books have been very popular, I don't believe we've had an order like yours—215 copies!

I think you will find Kahn's materials very easy to teach from, and I predict that you will receive outstanding results—better than any of those of its competitors.

We are now in the process of developing a film for the Kahn program, and I'll see that you get advance information on it. I'm sending you an advance copy of an article which will appear in the October issue of *Business Teacher*, "Bookkeeping and Accounting Are Not the Same." I hope you enjoy it.

Cordially yours,

19–11   Congratulating a Customer on a Professional Achievement

Situation   A food wholesaler learns that one of her long-time customers has just been elected president of a state retail food association. Like many business owners and executives, the wholesaler keeps track of such things by reading the trade journals, and writes contratulatory messages to customers and friends who have received recognition.

The Letter   Dear Curtis:

I was delighted to see in the September issue of *Food Retailer* that you have been named president of the Missouri Association of Independent Grocers. This pleases me for two reasons: first, because I think you will bring dynamic leadership to this important organization, and second, because the honor was bestowed on a longtime friend and customer.

I extend hearty good wishes and, at the same time, an offer of any help our company can give to the MAIG. We're behind you all the way!

Very sincerely yours,

19–12 Writing to a Customer Who Has Stopped Buying

Situation

Marvin Talese is Sales Promotion Manager of Fenwick Carpet Company. Talese makes it his business to keep track of customers—not only those who are active buyers but those who have stopped buying from him. He really believes the axiom, "Once a customer, always a customer." Every two or three months, he writes to the people who have not placed an order in recent months.

The Letter

Dear Mr. Black:

I've just talked with our sales representative, Louise Maynard, who visited you last week. While she was received cordially and had a good chat with you, she wasn't successful in persuading you to place an order.

Louise reported that you said you have a new supplier of industrial carpeting and that you are satisfied with the company's products and service. I recall that for many years you and Fenwick had a highly satisfactory relationship. You liked our product, our prices, and our salespeople. Something apparently went wrong, and I'd like to know what happened.

Would you do me the favor of telephoning me (collect) to tell me what happened between us? Or, if you prefer, complete the enclosed sheet headed, "Why I Stopped Buying from Fenwick Carpet Company." I will be most interested in your response.

Most sincerely,

19–13 Winning Back an Inactive Customer

Situation

Hoffstedder Sporting Goods has in the past received sizable orders annually from certain customers who, for some reason, have ordered nothing for the last two years. The president sends each of these customers a printed, personalized letter, along with an announcement of a special sale.

The Letter

Dear Friend:

We've had the happy experience of receiving one or more orders from you every year for several years. But, as I study our list of faithful customers, I note that you haven't bought anything from us for the past two years.

This set me to wondering: Did we goof on a shipment? Was the merchandise you last ordered not exactly what you wanted? Maybe you've been too busy lately to indulge in your favorite sport? Or is it simply because you haven't needed anything?

Whatever the reason, I'd really like to know it, and I hope you'll tell me on the enclosed form, which you can mail in the postage-paid enveloped.

In the meantime, I'm sending you a flier describing our special "rock-bottom prices" sale on all Tru-Flight Golf equipment and Grand Prize tennis gear. Maybe when you see the bargains offered, you won't even need to fill out that form I referred to—just the order blank that's on the flier.

Sincerely,

19–14 Thank-You Letter for Sending a Friend

Situation Pelican Building Supply Center writes a letter to one of its new customers, Peter Ryan, thanking him for sending a friend.

The Letter Dear Pete:

I am really grateful for your visit to Pelican Building Supply on Tuesday. It was a real treat for me to meet you and discuss our mutual interests. So thank you for dropping in.

This letter, however, is about another important matter: your recommending Pelican Building Supply Center to Frank Donnelly. I have tried a number of times to get Donnelly to give me his business without success, and you, in one conversation with him, succeeded where I failed. I'm as pleased with this as I was when you "adopted us."

Thank you, Pete. If you'll drop in around noon one day, come in and I'll take you to The Fish Place for some of the finest seafood you've ever eaten.

Sincerely yours,

19–15   Congratulations on Opening a New Store

Situation

Troy Conley is President of the Brigham City, Utah Chamber of Commerce. Recently Conley saw a piece in the paper about the opening of a new business, Far Western Office Supplies. Although Conley had heard rumors about such a store, it had not been confirmed until today's paper arrived. He decides to congratulate the owner, Elizabeth Lemmon.

The Letter

Dear Ms. Lemmon:

Congratulations on the opening of your store, Far Western Office Supplies. I have heard people say that such a new enterprise was in the offing, and I was mighty pleased to have the deed accomplished.

I'm sure you already know how enthusiastically local merchants and citizens will be about this new store. I've personally resented having to go to Ogden or Salt Lake City when I needed typewriter ribbons, correction tape, pens, stationery, and the like. How much more convenient to buy these and other office supplies right across the street, so to speak: Congratulations.

I'll be in touch with you about joining the Brigham City Chamber of Commerce—but that can wait. Right now I only want to welcome you to our bustling town and express the hope (and conviction) that you'll suceed handsomely.

Sincerely yours,

19–16   Thanking a Customer for Receiving a Sales Representative

Situation   Charles Zoubek, Marketing Director for Dennison Carpet Company, writes a letter thanking a customer for receiving a sales representative.

The Letter   Dear Mr. Woodson:

Janice Hurley returned to the office today and told me about her visit with you. She said you gave her a lot of time and were very responsive to her "sales spiel" about our new line of Oriental-type carpets.

I'm very grateful to you for receiving Janice so warmly. I had told her about your thorough knowledge of the carpet business and, just as I expected, she verified my opinion.

As you know, Janice is a new representative and, thanks to customers like you, she is fast learning the business from all angles. Although she wasn't successful in selling you anything, her hopes were not dashed at all. "Just give me one more visit," Janice said, "and I'll guarantee you an order from Woodson Carpets." With my fingers crossed, I hope she's right!

Most cordially yours,

19–17

Thanking a Person Who Has Been a Satisfied Customer for 20 Years

Situation Emily Fawcett, owner of Northfield Audio-Video Center, has been a satisfied customer of National Electronics for 20 years. The Vice President of National Electronics decides to write to Emily Fawcett a warm letter of thanks.

The Letter Dear Emily:

When Harold Crosley returned to the office after visitng you last week, he said to me, "I always enjoy my visits to Mrs. Fawcett. She is so nice!" Then Harold went on to say, "Mrs. Fawcett treats me just like family."

This remark prompted me to haul out my records on the Northfield Audio-Video Center. Do you realize, Emily, that you've been a good customer of ours for 20 years? I know we have done business with you long before I entered the picture, but, with 15 years on the job, I'm a relative newcomer.

Anyhow, it set me to thinking about our stalwart customers, wondering what would have happened to us if there had not been a Northfield Audio-Video Center. I'd rather not think about it. I'm just basking in the realization that it truly happened. Need I say more—except you sound like family to Harold Crosley because you really *are family!*

Thanks a heap,

19–18 Letter to a Customer About the Illness of a Sales Representative

Situation

Dewey Hill, a sales representative for Acacia Foods, Inc., was recently admitted to a hospital with a heart attack. The attack was serious, and the doctor has ordered bed rest for Hill "for the next month or two." The Sales Manager of Acacia Foods, Inc., writes to all of Hill's customers, explaining the situation.

The Letter

Dear Mr. Hines:

I have the sad duty of telling you that Dewey Hill, our sales representative in your territory, recently suffered a heart attack and is now hospitalized. The doctor feels that it is important for Dewey to have bed rest for the "next month or two." You can be sure that Dewey is getting the best of care and, although he is worried about his customers, I've assured him that his territory will be well covered for the next few months.

Which brings me to Diana Whitson, who will be calling on you while Hill is recuperating. She is a fine young lady who has been on our sales staff for the past 18 months. She is thoroughly familiar with all our products and will be of great help to you during Dewey's absence. I hope you will give her the same splendid treatment that you accorded to Dewey Hill. Thank you.

Very sincerely yours,

19–19 Inviting a Cash Customer to Use Credit

Situation   Bayside Building Supply in Patchogue, New York has just sold a large order for lumber and other materials to Ernest Lacy, a new contractor in Patchogue. The owner of Bayside Building Supply, Ed Casler, writes Lacy a letter inviting him to purchase building materials on credit.

The Letter   Dear Mr. Lacy:

Thank you for your check for $455.90 for lumber and other materials. I appreciate your business and your check too!

Let's get acquainted. The next time you visit Bayside Building Supply, let me know you're in the building. I want to meet you and encourage you to join our large family of charge customers.

We've been suppliers for many contractors for over 60 years and, with the "building boom" in progress, the future looks bright for all of us. I hear you've bought the old Willard place on Shamrock Road. That's great. It's a genuine landmark in these parts—one of the finest buildings on Long Island.

Cordially yours,

Section 20

Problem Letters from Suppliers to Customers

As mentioned earlier, the customer is not always right. He or she may be responsible for having received the wrong merchandise, returning damaged products that cannot be resold, making an error on checks sent in payment of an account, abusing the supplier's rigid company policy, and many, many other slip-ups. Although the supplier will do everything possible to avoid clashes with customers, often it simply can't be helped and the supplier must "tell it like it is."

In this section, we present a variety of letters from suppliers to customers, each written as tactfully as possible yet framed in such a way that they will achieve the desired result.

20–1 Delayed Shipment

Situation

The manufacturer of institutional uniforms and supplies received an order on July 14 from Wichita General Hospital for 20 nurse's uniforms. Fifteen days later, the hospital writes that the uniforms did not arrive. The uniforms were sent to another hospital in Iowa City. In the response, the manufacturer tries to set things right and retain the hospital's goodwill.

The Letter

Dear Mr. Barrett:

The 20 nurse's uniforms you ordered July 14 are being sent to you today (UPS) and should be at your place by Friday of this week.

When I investigated the original shipment, I was astounded to learn that your uniforms were sent to another hospital (in Iowa City!). It's hard to account for such an error, and the only excuse I can offer is that we've had several part-time warehouse people this month to fill in for some of the regular crew who are on vacation.

I hope, Mr. Barrett, that this special shipment will compensate in part for the trouble I know we have caused you. Please let me know how things turn out. It would be unthinkable for you to be penalized on account of our poor performance.

Best personal wishes.

Sincerely yours,

20–2 Unexpectedly Out of Stock

Situation

Charles Weaver, a sales representative for Five Star Publishers, has just visited the Downtown Bookstore in Chicago (Mrs. Cleda Maggard, owner) and promised Mrs. Maggard that she would receive 16 copies of *Handbook of Electrical Engineering*. Upon arriving at company headquarters, Weaver learned that there are no copies left due to the unexpected purchase of the entire inventory by a foreign publisher. The Vice President of Five Star Publishers writes to Mrs. Maggard to apologize for Weaver's unfulfilled promise.

The Letter

Dear Mrs. Maggard:

When you placed an order with Charles Weaver last week for 16 copies of the *Handbook of Electrical Engineering*, he promised immediate shipment.

I would have made that promise, too, Mrs. Maggard, because our inventory of this handbook seemed adequate for at least six months. However, neither of us was prepared for the news that, just three days ago, a European distributor cleaned us out of stock.

Of course, we immediately put in a large order for the handbook, and have been promised copies by October 22. The same day we get our copies we will send yours to you, and if everything goes right (!) you should have your copies by October 24.

We're feeling very good about our professional handbook series. I'm mailing you today a booklet describing the books in this series. In the meantime, Charles Weaver joins me in wishing you a smashing fall season at Downtown Bookstore.

Sincerely yours,

20–3   Mistake in Filling an Order

Situation   Clifford Sanford, owner of the Trophy House, sells, among other things, trophies and awards. A customer and personal friend, Harlan Kallous, orders 12 watches with a tennis motif, and receives instead watches with a golf motif. The watches are to be presented to the winners of a tournament conducted by Lakeside Tennis Club. Sanford writes Kallous to relieve Harlan's anxiety and seek to win his continued friendship and patronage.

The Letter   Dear Harlan:

Twelve Gemset wrist watches with a tennis motif were sent today by Priority Mail to replace the watches you received with a golf motif.

You know, Harlan, one would think it would be imposible to make an error like this one. You clearly specified in your order that these watches were to be awarded to winners of the Annual Lakeside Tennis Tournament on August 18. The stock number you supplied was correct. There was no reason for a slip-up at this end, and I can't even guess how it happened.

I am much relieved, however, that you will have the right watches in time for the awards dinner. I really don't know what a tennis player's reaction would be to having a classic golf swing in bas relief on his prize!

When you get around to it, would you please send the golf watches to me? I'll pay the postage.

Yours very sincerely,

20–4 Wrong Size Shipped Twice

Situation

Sidney Reeb is Asistant Sales Manager for Mid-Continent Distributors, Inc. A building supply dealer, Beth Silver, is a longtime customer of the firm. She places an order for six 48-inch ceiling fans with globes. The fans she receives are 36 inches. When the mistake is discovered, another shipment is made—this time it's 56-inch fans. She writes an angry letter to Reeb with an edge to it—she has customers waiting. Reeb answers the letter that he hopes will pacify the customer and retain her as a loyal customer.

The Letter

Dear Mrs. Silver:

Six 48-inch Victory fans are on their way to you. I know because I saw them loaded on the truck.

By this time you must think we take special delight in mixing up your orders—two careless errors in a row. I suppose, judging from these mistakes, if we had had a fourth sweep dimension we would have sent that before getting your order right!

It's embarrassing to inconvenience any customer, but unforgivable when that customer is so highly valued as you. Red-faced and contrite, I ask your forgiveness and offer you my personal assurance of better service in the future.

Thank you for your patience, and best personal regards.

Sincerely,

20–5 Error in an Invoice

Situation

Amelia Harper, owner of Harper Lighting Fixtures, sends a special announcement to customers, telling them that, in addition to the usual 15-percent trade discount on lighting fixtures, they will receive an additional 10 percent on certain fixtures. When customers who took advantage of this offer received their invoices, they discovered that the additional discount promised was not deducted. Harper writes each customer a letter of explanation and an apology.

The Letter

Dear Mr. McDougle:

You're entirely right. In our January 16 statement that you requested, we neglected to deduct the extra discount of 10 percent to which you are entitled.

As sometimes happens, the folks who prepare the statements don't always get the message. And this time for good reason: I simply didn't get the word to them about the additional discount; so I'm the guilty party.

Please deduct $462 from the statement you received. The net amount due is $4158 instead of $4620.

I want you to know that I'm very sorry about this oversight and that I'm grateful to you for pointing the error out to me. I appreciate your business!

Cordially yours,

20-6

Wrong Merchandise Sent— Customer Primarily to Blame

Situation

David Fitzhugh, owner of Southport Marina, places an order with Northeast Boating Supplies, Inc., for eight outboard motors. A number of errors were made in writing up the order, and as a result the dealer is shipped motors that he doesn't really want. The customer is primarily to blame, but the manufacturer must also share some of it. Northeast Boating Supplies writes Fitzhugh a letter of explanation and apology.

The Letter

Dear Mr. Fitzhugh:

I am very sorry you did not receive the eight 6-hp Sea Serpent outboards you wanted, and I guess both of us share the blame.

Your order (photocopy enclosed) lists the 7.5-hp motor along with its stock number, yet the price indicated is for the 6-hp motor. Since you've regularly ordered the 7.5, we assumed that this one was what you really wanted, and we went ahead and shipped it. We should have checked with you, and I'm sorry we didn't.

We will, of course, ship the eight 6-hp motors immediately. Do you think you might sell the 7.5s? If so, you may wish to keep them awhile, and if they don't move you can return them to us. In any event, we'll pay all shipping charges.

I'm delighted you're having such a good season with the Sea Serpent line. We'll be ready for your next order; I promise no mix-ups!

Very cordially yours,

20–7　Customer Takes an Unearned Discount

Situation David Saunders, Vice President of Northwestern Housewares, Inc., sends a check to Regal Plastics Corporation in payment of an order. However, a cash discount has been deducted from the amount shown on the invoice—a discount to which Saunders is not entitled. Regal Plastics writes Saunders to accept the check, pointing out tactfully that money is still due on the invoice and at the same time retaining Saunders' friendship.

The Letter Dear Mr. Saunders:

Thank you for your check dated September 7 for $927.96. Your check has been credited to your account, leaving a balance of $48.84.

The terms of sale, you will recall, were 5/10 ROG. Since you received the lamps August 12, you would be entitled to a 5-percent discount only if the invoice were paid within ten days of that date. Unfortunately, these terms were not met.

Although I would like to make an exception in your case, Mr. Saunders, such an action would penalize those who are given the same privilege. I suspect you enforce such a policy in your organization, even though—as in this instance—it isn't a pleasant thing to do.

I think you might be interested in the enclosed reprint of an article written by our own Syna Lee Glasser, which appeared in the September issue of *Scientific Research*.

Sincerely yours,

20-8 Unauthorized Return of Merchandise

Situation

The customer relations manager of a paint manufacting firm receives a report from the receiving department that 34 gallons of paint have been returned by Cabrizzi's Building Supply. There has been no advance warning, but it is assumed that the customer wants full credit for the returned paint. This particular brand was discontinued many months ago, and all dealers were notified, and there is no satisfactory way to dispose of it. The customer must be told that full credit for the returned paint cannot be allowed and a compromise must be suggested that is fair to both parties.

The Letter

Dear Mr. Cabrizzi:

Early this week we received 34 one-gallon cans of exterior white Dura-Perm paint from you. I assume that you wish us to issue a credit memorandum for $261.12 (34 gallons @ $7.68).

I am very sorry, Mr. Cabrizzi, that we cannot allow you full credit on this paint, which you purchased over eighteen months ago. As announced to all our customers, we discontinued the Dura-Perm brand last April, at which time we cleared out our entire inventory. We are now handling only Luxor Sheen house paints.

I have a suggestion that may save time and effort for both of us. At the time we discontinued Dura-Perm, we marked it down to our actual cost of $5.76 a gallon. We are willing to give you credit for the difference between $7.68 and $5.76—or a total of $65.28. Or, if you prefer, we can return the paint to you for disposal at the price you choose.

Please let me know your decision right away, Mr. Cabrizzi, and I will take immediate steps to handle the matter accordingly.

We've had wonderful success with the new Luxor Sheen line. Dealers are delighted with consumer acceptance—some reporting up to 40 percent increase in paint sales since they took on Luxor Sheen. We'd be mighty happy to have an order from you!

Best wishes,

20-9 Damaged Stock Returned for Credit

Situation

Edgewater Interiors has a policy of accepting returns of products within six months of the date of purchase. Customers, however, receive credit only if the product is in salable condition. Ardell Lawrence, a decorating consultant, returns 16 framed art reproductions so badly damaged that they cannot be resold. Ken Murphy, of Edgewater Interiors, writes Ms. Lawrence, refusing to accept the damaged prints for credit, while salvaging as much goodwill as possible.

The Letter

Dear Ms. Lawrence:

When I talked with you on the telephone about returning the 16 reproductions in our Art Master Series, I said that our policy is to accept for full credit all items returned in *salable* condition.

The reproductions arrived today, and I was shocked at their condition. Apparently, they were stored in a damp place. The pictures are faded and the canvas warped; what's more, the finish on the frames is blistered.

Would you like me to return the reproductions to you? Perhaps you can dispose of them at a special reduction in price. Since we can't sell them to our customers, the only thing we can do is donate them to local hospitals and charitable organizations.

I'm sorry to disappoint you, Ms. Lawrence, but under the circumstances I am confident that you will fully appreciate my position.

Very truly yours,

20–10 Unauthorized Use of Service Personnel

Situation   Dykstron Computers, Inc. has service contracts with many of the firms that use the company's equipment. These contracts stipulate that the company will provide service on Dykstron computers only. It comes to the Service Manager's attention that at one customer's place of business, Kykstron technicians are being asked to service other brands. The Service Manager wants to put a stop to it and writes the Administrative Services Manager, a personal friend, to tactfully explain the situation and have the practice stopped.

The Letter   Dear Linda:

I have a knotty little problem that I want to unload on you. As you know, our contract with Great Western Insurance stipulates that we will provide services to all Dykstron equipment over a three-year period. I hope you feel that our service so far has been prompt and professional in every respect; certainly, we have been happy with the arrangement.

Until now. Our service personnel report that lately they have been asked by some of your supervisors to service equipment other than our own. In some cases, our technicians have actually done the work merely to be as helpful as possible. I have asked them to politely decline these requests in the future for two reasons:

1. They are already hard-put to keep up with the job of fulfilling other service contracts.

2. I think those who produce competing computers are in a better position than our people to provide the professional service you require.

I suspect, Linda, that you have known nothing about this, and I bring the matter to your attention only because I believe you, too, will feel it is not a satisfactory arrangement for either of us.

Okay?

Sincerely,

20–11

Damaged Shipment— Carrier Perhaps to Blame

Situation

Clark Amend, Director of the Claremont Public Library in Lincoln, Nebraska, placed an order with Wonderbuilt Interiors for six carrels. According to Amend, the carrels arrived in a damaged condition; the finish on four of the panels is badly scratched and there are numerous dents in two of them. Amend telephones Hazel Forbes, Vice President of Wonderbuilt Interiors, and Forbes agrees to investigate the matter. In the meantime, Forbes writes Amend a letter.

The Letter

Dear Clark:

Thank you for telephoning me this morning about the damaged carrels you received from us. As I told you, I will thoroughly investigate the matter and get in touch with you when I have some answers. The first thing I will do is talk with the Blue Dart Transport people. I suspect, as you do, that the damage to the carrels was the work of their servicepeople.

I'm very sorry about this incident, Clark, especially because I know how eager you are to complete the library renovation. I really hope the delay will be a short one.

Sincerely,

20-12 Damaged Shipment—
Customer Definitely to Blame

Situation Wonderbuilt Interiors (see Letter 20–11 on the preceding page) receives a copy of the shipper's waybill, signed by a responsible employee of the Claremont Public Library, showing that the carrels arrived in excellent condition. Forbes writes to Amend, giving him a status report.

The Letter Dear Clark:

I have finished my study of the "damaged carrels" situation, and what I have to say will not please you, I'm afraid. I talked with the Blue Dart servicepeople, and they are certain that the carrels were in excellent condition when they were unpacked. Therefore, I cannot put in a claim against them.

I have a suggestion: Suppose you hire someone locally to put a new finish on the carrels and repair the dents, and send me a bill. I have no other recourse.

As I mentioned in my previous letter, I am bothered most by the delay in your library renovation. I hope within the next few days this problem will be solved to everyone's satisfaction.

Cordially yours,

20–13 Suggesting a Substitute

Situation

Vivian Keller, Manager of the Text-Film Division in a large publishing house, orders six copies of the film "Filing and Finding" from Show-Voelker, a leading manufacturer of office equipment, systems, and related products. Although there are several copies of the film, it is badly out of date. Ernest Dorr, Product Manager for Show-Voelker, writes Keller, asking her if she would accept a new film, "Modern Records Management," since it is more modern and a more complete treatment of the subject of filing.

The Letter

Dear Mrs. Keller:

The film you asked for, "Filing and Finding," is certainly available, and I'll be happy to send you six copies immediately.

However, you might like to know that we have just released a new 16-mm color film, "Modern Records Management." The new film covers the traditional methods of "paper" filing—alphabetic, subject, numeric, and geographic—along with the procedures and equipment accompanying these methods. But it also presents the many new aspects of records management that have emerged in recent years—in short, "electronic record keeping." As you know, records management has undergone a dramatic revolution, triggered, of course, by the advances in computer technology and the advent of film (microfilm, microfiche, etc.). I think you and your students will find "Modern Records Management" exciting and highly informative. A booklet describing the film is enclosed.

May I send you this new film instead of "Filing and Finding"? I expect a copy to be available within the next ten days, and I will reserve it for you if you wish (use the enclosed postcard). There is no charge, of course, but we do ask that you return it within a week—the demand for the film is very great.

Thank you for writing.

Cordially yours,

20–14 Returning an Unsigned Check for Signature

Situation   Mrs. Karen Thresher, a fairly new customer, places an order for calendars, enclosing her check for $116.30. The check has not been signed, and the supplier returns it for signature.

The Letter   Dear Mrs. Thresher:

Thank you very much for your order for calendars and the check for $116.30 that accompanied it.

Through an oversight, the check was not signed, and I am returning it to you for your signature. In the meantime, the order will be sent out immediately.

Sincerely yours,

20–15 Response to an Irate Customer About Sloppy Record Keeping

Situation   Refer to Letter 18–15 on page 144.

The Letter   Dear Mrs. Shaw:

You are absolutely right—you owe us nothing. I'm enclosing a new statement which provides the details, but the important thing about it is the "00" balance!

As you will see, we made an error in our extension on invoice 763. The figure should have been $443.40 instead of $466.40. For some reason, the discount to which you were entitlted on invoice 877 wasn't given you; this amounts to $60. And credit for $888.80 for the returned shipment was not given because our warehouse didn't notify the accounting department that it had arrived and my department wasn't notified that the return was imminent.

I am very sorry about these mistakes, Mrs. Shaw, and I can't imagine why they all happened to you. Nor can I explain why you got the runaround when you tried to get the matter settled.

We've made such a fuss here about the treatment you received that I think it's safe to say that your future transactions with Elko are going to receive special attention from everyone. In fact, I look forward to your next order so that I can prove that statement.

Thank you for your patience.

Cordially yours,

20-16

Bending Company Policy to Say "Yes" to a Customer

Situation

Imagine that you are supervisor in the Order Services Department of Fairfield Aluminum Company. You have received a letter from R. F. Follett, manager of the Giant Family Store, saying he is returning a shipment of lawn chairs. Follett claims that the chairs he received are not the ones he ordered, and he requests a credit memorandum for the total of the order, $477.80, plus shipping charges of $43.20.

Your investigation shows that the chairs sent to Giant Family Store are the ones that were ordered. Since you do accept shipments returned in first-class condition, there are no problems about giving Giant full credit. At the same time, you do not feel that it is fair for Follett to ask you to pay the shipping charges. It's against company poicy to do so unless an error was made by Fairfield Aluminum, and in this case the error is the customer's.

The response letter requires two answers—yes on the credit memo for the returned chairs and no on the shipping charges. But you decide to check on the latter point; company policy is often loosely interpreted, depending on the customer and the circumstances. Giant Family Store happens to be a new customer—a potentially big buyer—and getting Follett on your side could mean several hundred thousand dollars' worth of business per year. Your boss might think $43.20 is a small price to pay for keeping a customer as large as this one.

The Letter

Dear Mr. Follett:

Here is our credit memorandum for $521, which covers the returned shipment of Compac lawn chairs ($477.80) and shipping charges ($43.20).

Although the chairs we sent you seem to be the ones listed in your April 7 order, perhaps they are not what you had in mind. I'm sending you a copy of your order, together with a tear sheet of the Compac line, so that you may check. Because we think there might have been some misunderstanding, we are paying the return shipping charges, which we don't ordinarily do.

The important thing, of course, is that you have a stock of lawn chairs to meet your summer needs. Be sure to place another order soon so that you may have them for the first warm day. Separately I am sending you a section from our general summer furniture catalog; you might be more interested in the new Ezy-Fold line (pages 18–22), which is fast becoming our best seller.

Let me know, please, how I can be of further help. By the way, we can ship your next order the same day it is received.

Sincerely yours,

20–17   Saying "No" to a Customer

Situation   Agatha Covey, a retail customer, writes to the wholesaler asking to return 38 gallons of paint. She contends that one customer returned two gallons of Brand A-1 paint and, suspicious, asks permission to return the unsold paint. The request is denied.

The Letter   Dear Mrs. Covey:

I appreciate your letter in which you ask permission to return 38 gallons of A-1 paint. You indicate that one customer was not satisfied with this paint, and you are afraid others will feel the same way.

Actually, Mrs. Covey, Brand A-1 has been a very successful product for us, and our other retail customers have reported highly satisfactory experience with this excellent paint. I honestly believe that a single customer's unhappiness with A-1 is not conclusive, and I must deny your request to return the unsold paint to us.

My mind is not closed, however. If we find other customers unhappy with their purchase of Brand A-1, that places the matter in an entirely different light. Let's keep in touch and see what happens. OK?

Cordially yours,

Part 7

CREDIT AND COLLECTION LETTERS

It is an undeniable fact that buying on credit has become a way of life. Well over 90 percent of all business is transacted on credit. This includes customers who have charge accounts at various retail stores or use their bank credit cards, business firms that use credit to buy supplies and equipment for use in the business or to manufacture other products, and those that purchase merchandise that is to be immediately resold.

Businesses offer credit simply because it increases sales. Buyers expect this privilege, and if it is denied them by one organization, they turn to another that provides it. It stands to reason that with so many people charging their purchases, there will be some who will not honor their obligations. Unfortunately, no one has yet found a foolproof method of determining in advance who will and will not pay. Even some of those who score very high on the so-called three Cs of credit—character, capital, and capacity—wind up on the list of uncollectible accounts. Workers with the most honorable intentions get laid off unexpectedly, and businesses that looked so promising at birth go bankrupt because of economic conditions not of their own making. And there is that relatively small minority who use credit as a means of obtaining something for nothing.

Section 21

Credit Letters

Offering credit can be hazardous, and the bankruptcy cemetery is well populated with businesses—some small and some not so small—that were put there by their nonpaying credit customers. To reduce chances of loss from bad debts, credit personnel get as much information as possible about applicants before they grant credit privileges.

The first step is to ask the applicant to fill out an application for credit. Applicants for consumer credit are generally required to supply such information as the name of their present employer, their position, salary received, and how long employed there; the names of previous employers and dates of employment; credit references, including places where they've had charge accounts, banks where they have accounts or from whom they've borrowed; and the approximate amount of their debts. Those seeking commercial credit are usually asked about their type of business ownership, principal owners or stockholders, the insurance carried, the name of their bank, and names of businesses from whom they've bought on credit or borrowed money. If the initial order is fairly large—say, over $1000—the applicant may also be required to submit a current balance sheet and income statement.

Beyond the information supplied by the applicant and the references given, the seller may refer to other sources, such as Dun & Bradstreet (for commercial credit) and a local retail credit association (for consumer credit).

Accepting a Credit Applicant

When a consumer applicant is approved for credit, he or she may be notified by means of a printed "welcome" message, which may also include such information as the rate of interest charged (required by law) and the monthly payment required for varying amounts of indebtedness. A similar message is sent to those accepted for commercial credit, although instead of disclosing the interest rate (interest is not ordinarily charged on commercial accounts), the supplier describes its credit policy, discounts allowed, and how payment is to be made on the account.

Some sellers write personal letters to their new credit customers. Of course, the tone of such letters is warm and friendly, making the recipient feel highly valued.

Turning Down a Credit Applicant

Some of the people who apply for credit have to be turned down. This is one of the hardest of all letters to write, for in denying credit privileges the writer is saying, in effect, "We don't have sufficient trust in you to allow you to buy on credit." And no matter how tactfully this message is put, it is always a bitter pill to swallow. Here are three guidelines for turn-down letters:

1. *Express appreciation for the opportunity to consider the applicant's request.*

2. *Say as tactfully as possible why the request must be denied. (Retail stores often try to convince the applicants that they're being done a favor since additional debts would simply add to their burdens.)*

3. *Leave the door open for future credit privileges, and, in the meantime, encourage the applicant to pay cash.*

21–1 Requesting Commercial Credit

Situation   The Computer Place in Wichita not only provides computer services to local businesses, but also sells computer equipment. At a recent business show in Omaha, the owner of The Computer Place, Gretchen Rivers, saw a computer printer that sells for $1100. She thinks it will be a popular item for the businesses she serves, and she writes to the manufacturer requesting credit terms.

The Letter   Ladies and Gentlemen:

When I visited the Omaha Business Show last week, I saw your new Harrison-Fisher Laser Jet 4 printer. I think this printer would meet the needs of a number of my customers.

I would like to order three LJ 4s on 60-day credit terms and at the same time establish similar terms for future purchases up to $2500 monthly. As I understand it, the printer is priced at $1100, plus $50 for transportation, terminal checkout, and one ream of paper. This means that my first order would amount to $3350.

The Computer Place was established two years ago, and since that time we have grown very rapidly. My associates and I are convinced that the services and equipment we offer will be in increasing demand as businesses discover that only by applying sophisticated technology to their operations can they remain competitive.

For information concerning our financial responsibility and promptness in paying our obligations, I refer you to the following:

Rontech, Inc., 6200 Newman Avenue, Huntington Beach, CA 92647
Allied Data Associates, 4406 Cromo Drive, El Paso TX 79912
Winthrop Systems, 16536 Stone Avenue North, Seattle, WA 98133

If you would like additional financial information, I will be glad to supply it. Our bank is The First National Bank, 106 West Douglas Street, Wichita 57202.

Very truly yours,

21–2

Requesting Information from a Commercial Credit Applicant

Situation   Upon receipt of the order and credit application from the The Computer Place (see previous letter), the manufacturer responds promptly and with appreciation. However, many computer stores have been opened lately, some of which went out of business very quickly. The manufacturer decides to tactfully ask the credit applicant for additional financial information.

The Letter   Dear Ms. Rivers:

Thank you very much for your interest in our HF Lasers Jet 4 printer terminal. This instrument was designed with the small business in mind, and I think your assessment of it is right on target; this is where most of our orders are coming from.

I also appreciate your request to purchase three HF Laser Jet 4 on 60-day credit terms and to establish similar terms for future purchases. The references you supplied will be very helpful—thank you.

Would you please send me a copy of your most recent statements of ownership and results of operations? Or, if you prefer, you can use the forms enclosed to supply the required data.

You may be sure, Ms. Rivers, that just as soon as we have the information we need we'll attend to your request. We're eager to have the HF Laser Jet 4 in the hands of your customers, and we'll do our best to expedite shipment.

Very cordially yours,

21-3 Requesting Information from References Supplied

Situation

Refer to letter 21–1 on page 194 and Letter 21–2 on the preceding page. The manufacturer of the HF Laser Jet 4 printer terminal writes to the references supplied by The Computer Place.

The Letter

Dear Sir or Madam:

I have received a request for credit privileges from The Computer Store, Wichita (Ms. Gretchen Rivers, owner). Your company was listed as a credit reference.

I would be very grateful if you would supply the following information about this customer:

1. Credit terms extended to the customer, including limits _____
   _____

2. A brief statement concerning the customer's promptness in meeting obligations _____
   _____

3. Your reservations, if any, about the customer's financial condition and general reliability _____
   _____

I assure you that the information supplied will be treated as confidential. Thank you. (A copy of this letter and an envelope are enclosed for your reply.)

Cordially yours,

21–4 Accepting an Applicant for Commercial Credit

Situation   Johnson and Hall, a wholesale auto parts distributor, receives an order and request for short-term credit from Live Oak Auto Parts, a new retail store owned by J. C. Laughlin. The information supplied by Laughlin himself and from various credit references is very favorable. The wholesaler welcomes Laughlin as a credit customer and encourages him to use the privilege frequently.

The Letter   Dear Mr. Laughlin:

It's a genuine pleasure to welcome you as a credit customer of Johnson and Hall. Your order for four 4-way convertible tops with sun roof (totaling $799.80) is being shipped immediately by truck on credit terms described on the enclosed sheet.

We look forward to serving you and hope you will call upon us often for your parts needs. In the meantime, we wish you outstanding success in your new store.

Sincerely yours,

PS: I'm placing your name on our list to receive our monthly newsletter, *Auto Spotlight*, which will give you up-to-date information on everything new in automotive parts.

21–5 Turning Down an Applicant for Commercial Credit

Situation

Rhodes Furniture and Equipment receives an order from Premier Career Institute, a vocational school, for classroom furniture in the amount of $2800, asking for 120-day credit terms. The financial statement supplied by the school, as well as information furnished by credit references, indicates that the school's financial situation is very shaky. The most damaging information shows a current ratio of 1 to 4.7 and less than 1 percent net profit on operations during the past year. The credit manager of Rhodes writes a turn-down letter.

The Letter

Dear Mrs. Ashforth:

I appreciate your order for furniture in the amount of $2800 in which you request credit terms of 120 days.

Unfortunately, Mrs. Ashforth, the information supplied me was not at all favorable concerning the financial condition of Premier Career Institute. Not only are current liabilities far in excess of current assets, but it would appear that the school is experiencing serious difficulties in producing a reasonable profit. Under the circumstances, we feel it necessary to defer credit privileges at this time.

Of course, the situation may change. Indeed I hope so because we would be pleased to be in a position to provide the privileges you request. In the meantime, we will be happy to ship your order immediately on receipt of your certified check for $2716 ($2800 less cash discount of 3 percent).

Cordially yours,

Credit and Collection Letters

21-6   Another Letter Denying Credit

Situation   Gary Moran, owner of Oakwood Hardware Store, placed an order with Andrew Manufacturing Company for hardware items. The amount of the order is $1600 and Fields asks for credit. Fields has purchased hardware in the past but always on a cash basis. Stephanie Brown, Credit Manager for Andrews Manufacturing Company, asks Fields for current financial statements as well as a list of firms with whom he has done business on credit in the past year. When Brown receives the material, it is not at all favorable. Current liabilities are three times higher than current assets—a sad situation. The references Moran supplied indicated that Oakwood Hardware Store is not considered a good credit risk; one person said that Fields has owed money for over six months, with no attempt to pay. Brown writes Fields the following letter.

The Letter   Dear Mr. Moran:

Thank you for supplying the credit information I asked for. I wish I could say, "Yes, we'll be pleased to have you as a credit customer." However, on the basis of the information I have received about the condition of your business and the comments of those whom you owe, I must give you a reluctant no at the moment. We truly believe that it would not be wise for you to take on other obligations at this time.

I say "at this time" because I am hopeful that things will improve for you. If so, please write me again when your financial picture has changed.

In the meantime, I hope you will find it possible to order from us on a cash basis. We are proud of both our products and our services, and will do everything possible to see that you get what you want when you want it.

Cordially yours,

21–7 Accepting an Applicant for Consumer Credit

Situation   Mrs. Ming Chin was transferred by her company to Atlanta, and she immediately applied for credit at Fitch's, one of Atlanta's most popular and respected department stores. She easily met all requirements for receiving credit and is welcomed by the credit manager as a "select" customer.

The Letter   Dear Mrs. Chin:

Enclosed is your Fitch's credit card, which I am delighted to send you. This card gives you the opportunity of virtually unlimited shopping, not only in person but by mail or telephone.

We welcome you sincerely to our large family of select customers and hope you will use your credit card often!

Sincerely yours,

PS: Welcome also to Atlanta! I think you will thoroughly enjoy this area that literally has *everything*.

21–8 Turning Down an Applicant for Consumer Credit

Situation

Kermit Greene, 29, is single and lives in an aprtment on which his monthly payment is $375. Greene's take-home pay is just over $1250 a month, and his monthly payments, exclusive of rent (on a car, a loan, furniture, and credit-card purchases) amount to over $600 a month. He applies to Richert's, a department store, for a revolving credit account. The Credit Manager at Richert's decides that Green is a poor risk (he has frequently been behind on his bank credit card payments).

The Letter

Dear Mr. Greene:

I appreciate your interest in establishing a charge account at Richert's.

I have tried very hard to find a way to give your application favorable consideration, Mr. Greene. However, the fact that your present monthly payments are so perilously close to your net monthly earnings leads me to believe that it would not be wise for you to undertake further obligations at this time. If these debts were to be paid off soon, the picture would be more favorable. Yet some of your payments, such as on the car, the loan, and furniture, have from one to three years to go before they are paid off. I think that once you have thought the matter through carefully, you may feel as I do that you have possibly overextended yourself already.

When the situation changes, we will be pleased to have you reapply. In the meantime, it will be a pleasure for us to serve you on a cash basis.

Yours very sincerely,

Section 22

Collection Letters

Most credit people assume at the start of the collection process that those who owe money fully intend to pay. And they usually have every reason to feel this way. After all, the applicants were carefully investigated as to character, capital, and capacity, and the seller was satisfied that they were good risks. It makes no sense, then, to bombard them with ugly, threatening letters the minute they fall behind in their payments.

Yet the patience of the seller varies. Some credit managers will threaten legal proceedings after sending only two or three messages (especially to people they've had previous difficulty with); others will make six or more attempts to collect the money before writing an "or-else" letter.

Most large companies and retail firms have developed a collection system that, once tested adequately and found effective, is used consistently. This is often called a collection letter series, although some (often most) of the communications sent are not actually letters. A national retail chain may have four or five series of letters, each designed for a particular type of customer.

Following is the collection system used by one large company. Although the situation pertains to commercial credit, it also applies to many consumer credit situations as well.

---

1. *A monthly statement is sent to those who have account balances.*

2. *Those who do not make payment within ten to twenty days (depending on the collection policy) are sent a second statement, this time with a tactful personal message or a brightly colored sticker (available at stationery stores) on which is printed a message such as PLEASE! or HAVE YOU FORGOTTEN? (with a drawing of a finger with a string tied around it) or SECOND REMINDER or PAYMENT OVERDUE!*

3. *If there is no response to the second statement, two or three additional statements may be sent, each with an increasingly persuasive, yet low-key appeal.*

4. *If there is still no response (perhaps three months have now passed), the customer is placed on a special follow-up list and given personal attention: telephone calls, Mailgrams, and personal letters.*

5. *The final step is usually a threat to take legal action of some sort or a notification that it has already been done. (In consumer credit situations, if the amount is small, say $25 or so, the store may decide to write it off; the cost of collection may exceed the amount owed. In this case, the "or-else" letter is never sent. Retailers must be very wary of harrassing customers lest they violate the provisions of the Fair Debt Collection Practices Law.)*

22–1   First Reminder After Monthly Statement

Situation

On February 3, Greenacres Nursing Home purchases supplies and equipment from Walton Hospital Supply Company on thirty-day credit terms. Although the nursing home has been in operation only a short time, the information concerning the enterprise has been favorable and credit was granted. A regular statement is mailed on March 10. When no response is received by March 20, a second statement is sent.

First Reminder

WALTON HOSPITAL SUPPLY COMPANY
741 PERRY AVENUE
DAVENPORT, IOWA 52803

HAVE YOU FORGOTTEN?

CUSTOMER STATEMENT
Greenacres Nursing Home
P.O. Box 888
Rolla, MO   65401
Please return this stub with your check

Date	Invoice No	Articles	Amount
February 6	Y-211	Wheel chairs	$ 633.80
		Walkers	244.25
		Hospital garments	182.40
		Blood pressure units	234.90
		Total	$1,295.35

22-2 Second Reminder

Situation

Greenacres Nursing Home makes no response to the first reminder. Ten days later a second reminder is sent.

Second Reminder

This is a copy of the regular statement on which the following message appears at the bottom:

Mr. Montgomery: To date, no payments have been received from you, and we're curious to know why. Perhaps it is merely an oversight. If there are other reasons we should be aware of, please let us know. Otherwise, may we have your check for $1295.35?

22-3 Third Reminder

Situation

Greenacres Nursing Home still has not responded to the previous reminders. A third reminder is sent ten days after the second one went out.

Third Reminder

This is a copy of the regular statement on which the following message appears at the bottom:

Mr. Montgomery: Is there some reason we have not heard from you? The amount you owe us is now long past due and is beginning to concern us. Don't you think we are entitled to an explanation? Please let us hear from you at once.

22-4 Fourth Reminder—Telephone Call

Situation

The Credit Manager at Walton Hospital Supply Company has heard nothing from Greenacres Nursing Home and, on April 3, decides to telephone the owner, Mr. Montgomery.

The Telephone Call

When the Credit Manager, reaches Mr. Montgomery, she may start off something like this: "Hello, Mr. Montgomery. I'm Beth Kroll at Walton Hospital Supply Company, and I'm calling to ask about your plans for paying your account, which, as you know, is now over 30 days past due." Montgomery is given an opportunity to tell his side of the story (he has just been so busy putting the nursing home in operation that he has had to let some of his paperwork slide.) At the end of the conversation, Montgomery promises to send his check right away.

22-5 Fifth Reminder—Telegram

Situation

A week has passed since the credit manager spoke on the telephone with Montgomery, and no payment has been received. She decides that the next step is to send a telegram.

The Telegram

DURING OUR TELEPHONE CONVERSATION ON APRIL 3, YOU PROMISED IMMEDIATE PAYMENT OF YOUR ACCOUNT. YOUR CHECK HAS NOT ARRIVED, AND IF IT IS NOT ALREADY IN THE MAIL, I URGE YOU TO SEND IT TODAY.

22-6   Sixth Reminder—Personal Letter

Situation

The telegram has elicited no response from Montgomery, and the credit manager decides to write a personal letter.

The Letter

Dear Mr. Montgomery:

On February 3, we sent you hospital equipment and supplies in the amount of $1295.35. You agreed to make payment within 30 days—or by March 4. Now, 60 days later, and after four reminders, a telephone call, and a telegram, you still have made no effort to settle your account or even give us a valid reason why you have not done so.

I had every faith—especially after our telephone conversation—that you would abide by the credit terms offered you. We did, after all, supply you with materials and equipment you needed and which, so far as I know, were entirely satisfactory. Don't you think you have an obligation to reciprocate?

The idea of using other means of collecting the money owed to us has not even occurred to me until now because I know what this can mean to one's credit reputation. I know you value yours just as we do ours.

Please help me avoid other action by sending your check the minute you receive this letter.

Very truly yours,

22-7   Seventh Reminder—The Final Letter

Situation

When, after a reasonable period of time, say, 10 to 15 days, Montgomery has not sent a check, he is sent a final letter.

The Letter

Dear Mr. Montgomery:

This is to notify you that unless your check for $1295.35 is received by May 1, your account will be placed in the hands of our attorneys for collection.

Very truly yours,

Part 8

INTEROFFICE LETTERS (MEMORANDUMS)

A lot of people write more interoffice letters (memorandums) than inter-company letters. These in-house communications are usually written in memorandum form:

TO: S. Moldred Baldwin   FROM: A. R. Eylar
SUBJECT: Employee Compensation   DATE: June 14, 19XX

Many companies have memorandum stationery (usually less expensive than regular stationery), with the headings shown. Some writers include a salutation (such as "Dear Sarah") to make the message more personal.

The language of the interoffice letter is very similar to that used in regular letters, although it is more direct and lacks the "window dressing" you are likely to use when writing to a customer, a supplier, or a prospective buyer.

The suggestions for brevity in business letters also apply to memorandums. Say only what is necessary and be specific. In this part we show you a number of typical memorandums.

Section 23

"Announcing" *Memorandums*

"Announcing" memorandums include announcements of new employees, work schedules, procedures, acquisitions, promotions of executives, branch offices, and so on.

23–1   Announcing a Meeting

Situation   H. James Montgomery, Vice President, Personnel, of Columbia Products Corporation, writes the Personnel Division employees, asking them to be at a meeting on February 10. The objective of the meeting is to come up with more effective ways to welcome new employees in the company.

The Memorandum

TO: Personnel Division Employees   FROM: H. James Montgomery
SUBJECT: Employee Orientation   DATE: February 2, 19XX
       Workshops

As you know, six times a year Columbia Products Corporation conducts an orientation workshop for new employees. The purpose of these workshops is to acquaint new employees with the company: its organization, its executive personnel, its products, its objectives, and its future.

For some time I have not been satisfied with out present workshops. The meetings seem to be lifeless—even dull. Too many of those who are asked to speak give a singsong presentation, actually humdrum. We must remember that just-hired employees know almost nothing about the company, and these orientation workshops must be organized and conducted so that these new employees feel proud to work for Columbia. The workshops represent a golden opportunity for us to build esprit de corps among our new employees.

The meeting is scheduled for February 10. I hope each of you will come prepared to suggest ways in which our orientation workshops can be more interesting and productive. Please be prepared to suggest a new format for the workshops, including the use of visual aids, employee participation, and possibly "field trips" throughout the building.

                               HJM

23–2   Announcing a Moratorium on Staff Additions

Situation   The President of Winstead Fabrics Corporation, E. Lillian Hutchinson, is concerned about the poor profit picture during the past six months. Exprenses must be cut, and Hutchinson believes that a moratorium (freeze) on staff additions is one place to start.

**The
Memorandum**

TO: All Division Managers	FROM: E. Lillian Hutchinson
SUBJECT: Moratorium on Staff Additions	DATE: July 9, 19XX

Effective immediately, there will be no staff increases during the third quarter without my personal permission. This decision stems from our dismal profits in the first two quarters of the year: We simply have to reduce expenses wherever possible no matter how much it hurts. (Stand by for announcements of other cuts!)

Employees who leave the company during the third quarter will not be replaced without my approval. I realize this may be a genuine hardship in some divisions, but let's see if we can double up somehow without hiring replacements. All pending requisitions for additional staff are hereby cancelled.

I'll be willing to listen if you believe these restrictions promise catastrophe, but I warn you now that deviations from these rulings will be hard to sell.

ELH

23-3   Announcing a New Library

Situation   Avery Chemical Corporation has decided to establish a company library, to be housed on the fifth floor of the company's building. The library is open to all employees regardless of position or rank. The Vice President for research for Avery Chemical is Eileen R. Burke, and she announces the library and its services in a memorandum.

The Memorandum

TO: All Employees   FROM: Eileen R. Burke
SUBJECT: New Library   DATE: October 20, 19XX

The company library is now completed and available. It is, as you know, located on the fifth floor. All employees are cordially invited to make use of the library, which contains the following:

Books. Books of all types are stocked—professional books in many areas, including, of course, chemistry. Books in other areas include biography, economics, philosophy, sociology, philology, natural science, useful arts, fine arts, literature, history, and various dictionaries (including chemical, of course).

Pamphlets. There is a complete file of unbound pamphlets, photocopies, clippings, and other resources.

Technical and Professional Publications. These are technical and professional society publications (magazines).

Periodicals. Several periodicals are subscribed to, including *Business Week, Forbes, Fortune, Newsweek, Time,* and *U.S. News and World Report.*

Manufacturer's Catalogs. We have a very large file onmanufacturers' catalogs, including the catalogs of our largest competitors.

Company Historical Records. The library is the logical place for a complete file of the company's historical records, including annual reports.

Additional Library Services

1. Arranging for interlibrary loans and use of facilities of local and regional libraries

2. Assisting with the preparation of technical publications

3. Keeping records of publications, as well as all talks and lectures, by members of the organization

4. Assisting in preparing monthly reports

5. Answering innumerable questions on technical matters

The head librarian is Martha Lennon, who has the following assistants: Melba Crutchfield, Mike Bryan, and Marie McSpadden. The library will be open only during office hours—9:00 to 5:00.

Open House!

All employees are cordially invited to an Open House during the day of November 5. Refreshments will be served.

ERB

23-4 Announcing Final Plans for New Warehousing

Situation
Hanover Plastics is short of warehousing space and has reached the decision to build three new warehouses. Ben Fisher, Executive Vice President of Hanover, confirms the company plans in a memorandum addressed to the Operations Committee.

The Memorandum

TO: Operations Committee   FROM: Ben Fisher
SUBJECT: Confirming New Warehouse Plans   DATE: March 22, 19XX

President Falk and I have had three meetings with representatives of Reese, Inc. about our plans to build new warehouses in Schenectady, Pittsburgh, and Fort Wayne. We like their proposal and think we may have found the right people to do the job for us.

Some of the Reese people will be here the week of April 11 to learn more about our specific requirements. They are particularly interested in the procedures for receiving, storing, and shipping our products. To get ready for their visit, we'll need an updated estimate of our space needs in those three locations. Will you please reexamine your earlier reports and, where appropriate, revise your figures? I'll need your new estimates by April 2.

It is very important that you and your principal warehousing specialists be available April 11 to 13 for individual conferences with Reese people. If for any reason you plan to be away from your desk during those two days, please let me know at once.

Distribution

J. Polk
R. Cranston
M. Longyear
G. Crittenden
O. Kalb

23–5   Announcing a New High-Level Position

Situation   C. Harold Shipman, President of Butler International, occasionally issues an executive bulletin concerning a very important development within the company. This bulletin announces a new corporate-level position and the appointment of the person who is to fill it.

The Bulletin

EXECUTIVE BULLETIN 33
Office of the President

With the rapid growth of Butler International and the prospect of expanding our size substantially in the future, we have had to establish a separate executive function, long-range planning. Long-range planning embraces the following activities:

Product development

Market development

Capital budgeting

Resources development

Manager and employee development

These activities will determine largely where we are going in the next several months and years and what we must do to achieve our objective.

I am pleased to announce the appointment of Dr. Hannah R. Mancini to the position of Director of Long-Range Planning. Dr. Mancini comes to us from Martin and Ferrell Management Consultants, where she was consultant to several of the country's corporations on long-range planning. Hanna's responsibilities at Butler will relate directly to the functions of every division in the company. For this reason she will report directly to me.

I know you join me in welcoming Hannah Mancini to Butler International, and will give her your full cooperation as she pursues our important objective.

C. Harold Shipman

23-6　Announcing the Promotion of an Executive

Situation

Jeffrey C. Elliott, formerly Editor in Chief of the Business Books Division, is appointed Vice President and Editorial Director of Payne-Wyatt Book Company, effective March 1, 19XX. The announcement of this promotion is sent to all executives, managers, editors, and authors.

The Announcement

TO: All Corporate and Division Executives, Managers, Editors,
　　and Authors

Jeffrey C. Eliott is appointed Vice President and Editorial Director of the corporation, effective March 1, 19XX. This announcement is made with great pleasure and satisfaction.

In assuming this new assignment, Jeff replaces Nelson Hiatt, whose retirement was announced in my memo of December 9, 19XX.

As the Book Company pursues its role as a major factor in the publishing of U.S. and foreign educational materials, it can only maintain its leadership by recruiting and training superior editorial, design, and production personnel. This is critical and underlies our ability to reach our goals. Of equal importance is the absolute need to maintain the high standards of editorial quality that largely accounts for our success. While Jeff's assignment will embrace many functions, his greatest contribution should come in these two areas:

1. Finding and training good people

2. Helping to produce quality books and instructional materials

Reporting to Jeff and assisting him in these objectives will be Mrs. Marie Miller, Manager of Editing Services, Miss Lucille Lawson, Manager of Copyrights and Permissions, and William F. Woodson, Assistant Vice President, Production Research.

Jeffrey C. Elliot grew up in Oklahoma, graduated cum laude from Oklahoma State University and in that state began his professional life as a school teacher. He worked briefly as a sales representative for Payne-Wyatt and was Associate Dean of Beacon College, in Richmond, California. As Editor in Chief of the Business Books Division, Jeff has had a major hand in bringing that division to editorial eminence in business education.

Edward E. Meagher

Section 24

Procedural Memorandums

Procedural memorandums pertain to almost anything that has to do with the transmitting of reports and other documents, suggesting changes in company policy, solving company-wide problems, announcing important changes in personal or company organization procedures, and familiarizing recipients with important day-by-day events.

These memos are the most common because they may overlap the other types of interoffice communications discussed earlier.

24-1 Writing a Confirmation Memorandum

Situation   Among the departments in Fodge, Walker, and Taylor is the Sales Training Department, which is supervised by Brent Curtis, the Director of Marketing. Price Voiles, Sales Manager, recently met with Curtis to discuss several changes in the Sales Training Department, which were approved by Curtis. Voiles prepares a memorandum confirming the new organization.

The Memorandum

TO: Brent F. Curtis
SUBJECT: Changes in the Sales
            Training Department

FROM: Price Voiles
DATE: July 7, 19XX

This will confirm our discussion in my office on Thursday in which we agreed on the following:

1. I am authorized to hire two additional people: an instructor and an audiovisual specialist, effective August 1, at a total annual salary not to exceed $58,000. I may allocate this amount as I see fit, depending on the qualifications of the people hired. I am to talk with Allene Masters to discuss my needs and get information about her department's applications on file.

2. Two additional modular office units are to be installed on the fourth floor, and I am authorized to order these units and the equipment that will be required by the two new employees. We agreed on a total expenditure of $12,600 for these units and equipment, and I am to prepare the purchase orders for your signature.

3. Hugh Hansfield is to be promoted to the position of Coordinator of Training Materials also effective August 1, at a 15-percent increase over his present salary. I will prepare a memorandum for your signature, announcing Hansfield's promotion, which will be sent to Distribution Lists B and C.

If you have any questions or reservations about these points, please let me know. Otherwise, I will assume that we are in agreement on everything mentioned.

24–2   Reviewing the Importance of Merit Ratings

Situation

The Executive Vice President of Car Insurance Company, Donna Kingsley, is not satisfied with the manner in which supervisors and managers handle merit ratings. She issued the following memorandum.

The Memorandum

TO: All Managers and Supervisors   FROM: Donna Kingsley
SUBJECT: Merit Ratings   DATE: May 14, 19XX

Each of you will receive this week merit rating forms for the employees under your supervision.

I think it is appropriate to point out that these ratings should not be taken lightly. As you know, they play a major role in employee promotion, salary increases, and opportunities for advancement.

I am sure you know that you are expected to rate each employee with complete honesty; yet some people insist on giving an "outstanding" rating in all categories. It's hard for me to believe that there are no average or below-average employees in this company. Certainly there are numerous employees who will be given the highest ratings possible, yet when someone puts all his or her ratings in this category, I suspect the rater is taking the easy way out.

Remember, it is your obligation to discuss with each employee the rating you give her or him, pointing out tactfully what you consider to be strong and weak points and suggesting how the employee can improve attitudes, job performance, dependability, and so on.

I intend to do a random sampling of the completed merit ratings each of you turns in, and you can expect to hear from me if I think your ratings are unrealistic.

24-3   Employee Request to Attend a Convention

Situation

Beverly Byers, Supervisor of Office Training at Tabor Auto Parts Inc., wants to attend a convention of the American Society of Training Directors (ASTD) to get up-to-date information on training methods. She writes a memo asking for permission to attend this convention.

The Memorandum

TO: Adam C. Schultz   FROM: Beverly Byers
SUBJECT: ASTD Convention in New Orleans   DATE: October 14, 19XX

May I have your permission to attend the national convention of the ASTD in New Orleans on March 12–15?

This year's theme is "The Electronic Classroom" (see program attached). As you will note, there will be various presentations on the uses of the computer and other electronic equipment. Of particular interest to me is the panel "Is the Typewriter Becoming Obsolete?" Equally fascinating will be the forty exhibits featuring hardware and software supplies by most of the leading electronics distributors.

I estimate that my expenses would amount to $400, for travel, hotel, meals, etc. I honestly think it will be worth that amount if we can get a deeper insight into the applications of electronics to our training program.

Cordially,

24–4

Requesting Permission to Establish a New Position

Situation

You are Personnel Director in a large company. You have long felt that employee services are suffering from lack of commitment. Now you want to create a new department in the Personnel Division devoted entirely to employee services such as counseling, recreation, and training. You write a memo to your boss requesting permission to take this step.

The Memorandum

TO: Margaret Finch

FROM: Your Name

SUBJECT: Establishing an Employee Services Department

DATE: February 17, 19XX

Dear Margaret:

When I talked with you last week, you agreed with my suggestion to create a new Employee Services Department in the Personnel Division, and you asked me for my recommendation of an individual in the company who might fill this position.

After careful study and observation, I have come to the conclusion that Paul Moore, now supervisor of recruitment and placement, could handle this position very capably. Paul has been a member of the Personnel staff for five years and has served in various capacities. In each position he showed imagination, enthusiasm, and energy. He is well liked by his coworkers, and I am confident he would have everyone's support in this new assignment. Amelia Sturdevant, now assistant supervisor of recruitment and placement, would fill Paul's present position.

Attached is a revised job description for Paul, which incorporates the suggestion you made when we met.

24–5

The Company President Writes About a "Grabbag" of Valuable Leftovers

Situation

Like many large companies, Star Life Insurance Company has a plethora of used desks, chairs, calculating machines, typewriters, bookcases, and other office equipment. The president, Earl T. Zimmerman, writes department managers and supervisors, asking them to look over what's on hand before placing an order for new items.

The Memorandum

TO: All Managers and Supervisors   FROM: Earl T. Zimmerman
SUBJECT: Valuable "Grabbag" of Leftovers   DATE: July 11, 19XX

Have you visited Warehouse B lately?

If your answer is "no," I think you will be surprised at the quantity of "goodies" there. Filing cabinet? We have 16 of those in very good condition. Desks? We have 22 of those. Settees and divans? You'll find an even dozen of these—some in first-class condition. Want an electric typewriter? Six IBM electrics, all in usable condition, are available. Chairs. Bookcases. Lamps. Pictures. And so on.

I won't belabor the point. But remember, if you'll check Warehouse B before ordering something new, you may get a nearly free ride. I've already asked our director of purchasing, Betsy Brown, to check all requisitions to see if she might find exactly what you want in our "grabbag." And with immediate delivery!

Section 25

Memorandums as Reports

In nearly every enterprise, frequent reports are prepared on various topics. Often these reports are highly structured, including how data were gathered, procedures used in preparing the report, and conclusions and recommendations. In most businesses, the formal report is used only for subjects that are weighty and ponderous in nature. For everyday matters, the memorandum form is used.

25–1

Reporting on Heavy Turnover in a Regional Office

Situation

Tina Matthews is Assistant Sales Manager of Hopewell Incorpoated. Recently she was asked by the Sales Manager to go to Richmond to investigate the heavy turnover of sales representatives in that region.

The Memorandum

TO: Phil Simon   FROM: Tina Matthews
SUBJECT: Rep Turnover in Richmond Region   DATE: February 4, 19XX

Dear Phil:

As you suggested, I spent the past week in Richmond to see what I could learn about the heavy sales rep turnover there.

I was able to get in touch with the six representatives who resigned during the past seven weeks. Each spoke highly of our products and the company as a whole. I found that in every instance the overriding reason boils down to money. All claimed big increases in income in their new jobs—in three cases 25 percent or more. Also, the incentive plans based on increase in sales volume offered by other companies were a powerful inducement. Of the six who left, four went to McAlister, which is our toughest competitor in the Greater Richmond area.

I visited with seven of our present representatives and the subject of money came up constantly. Indeed, there were veiled threats that they may leave soon if our salary-incentive arrangement is not changed.

It seems to me, Phil, that we need to take a close look at our compensation policy, and I suggest we name a task force composed of yourself, me, the personnel director, and three regional managers (my choice would be King, in Indianapolis; Sherron, in Akron; and Rosen, in Pittsburgh). I am sure you know that time is important here, and I hope we can get this task force set up in the next week or two.

25-2   Report on Customer Correspondence

Situation

At a recent sales conference in Marathon Corporation, a number of complaints were voiced by sales representatives about letters that are being mailed to customers. Sales reps believe that most letters are poor and are losing friends for the company. Fred Ferraro, the Sales Manager, asks Katie Scott to study copies of the letters for the past month and report on her findings.

The Report

MARATHON CORPORATION
INTEROFFICE MEMORANDUM

TO: Fred Ferraro   FROM: Katie Scott
SUBJECT: Review of Customer Correspondence   DATE: July 7, 19XX

Dear Fred:

I have completed the review of customer correspondence (your memorandum of May 16) for the period May 21 through June 21. As you suggested, I read copies of all outgoing letters written by the four correspondents in the Customer Services Unit. (These were sent to me daily at your request.) During this period, 1079 letters were written and mailed to customers.

METHOD

As I read each letter, I assigned a grade to it: A (excellent), B (good), C (passable), and D (poor). The elements considered in assigning these grades were tone (friendliness), helpfulness, accuracy of information, organization, and grammatical correctness.

Findings

The findings follow:

Number of Letters	Grade Assigned
146	A
212	B
527	C
194	D
1079	

Although my evaluations were necessarily subjective, the preceding grade distributions would appear to give credence to the sales representatives' criticism. As they mentioned to you at the conference, there are many examples of indifference, carelessness with facts, repetition and circumlocution, and negativsm. It seems apparent, based on the 1079 letters examined, that the standard of customer letters in Permatrax is much lower than it should be.

As might be expected, most of the letters in the C and D categories were written by the same people, and the same is true of the A and B categories. Yet individuals predominantly in the C category, for example, frequently produced good to excellent letters and a few of those whose letters fell mostly in the A and B categories wrote some letters that were barely passable.

RECOMMENDATIONS

Based on this quick study, I recommend that we set up a special course for all sales correspondents, say, two hours a week for whatever period of time is required—perhaps 12 weeks or so. I believe the logical person in the company to teach the course is Dorothy Fasnacht in Human Resources in Training. She is a communications specialist (last year she organized and taught a course for credit correspondents and, according to the credit manager, Clark Pinson, it was a great success).

Procedure

I recommend that whoever handles the assignment might proceed as follows:

1. Prepare photocopies of perhaps 100 letters representing all categories and distribute them to the participants. All names would be concealed so that it would not be readily apparent who wrote the letters.

2. These letters would, in effect, serve as the textbook for the course. Each letter would be examined critically by the class, and everyone would be asked to contribute to a revision of those that contain flaws. In this way, we can get across all the basic elements of good letter writing in the most practical setting possible.

3. During the course the participants would continue to supply the instructor with copies of their outgoing letters to enable the instructor to measure the results being achieved in the course and perhaps schedule private sessions with those who continue to have difficulty.

I will be happy to assist in setting up the course and help the instructor in any way that I can if you think these ideas are feasible.

25–3 Suggestions for Improving the Company House Organ

Situation

The Personnel Director of Whitcraft Metals, Ray G. Archer, has issued an invitation to all employees to send him their opinions of *Tabs*, the company's house organ. Fabio Vargas, an accountant, wrote the following memorandum.

The Opinion Memo

INTEROFFICE MEMORANDUM

TO: Ray G. Archer   FROM: Fabio Vargas
SUBJECT: Suggestions for *Tabs*   DATE: September 26, 19XX

I am pleased to respond to your invitation to offer suggestions for *Tabs*.

First, let me say that there are many good things about *Tabs* that I like, such as the informal style, the editorial quality, the "Shop and Swap" column, the "What's New?" feature, and many other things. But I know you want suggestions rather than praise, and mine follow.

TITLE

Although a new title for the magazine has been suggested, I believe it would be a mistake to change it. Everyone recognizes the publication by the name *Tabs*, and it still seems to me to be entirely appropriate.

DESIGN

A new masthead would help, and I would like to see us engage a professional designer to do one. Indeed, this designer might be asked to give a new look to the entire magazine.

PHOTOGRAPHS

More photographs would help—photographs of employees celebrating anniversaries, participating in athletics and hobbies, receiving special recognition, and so on.

FEATURES

1. A "Letters to the Editor" column would be especially popular. It would have good readership and, at the same time, give employees a chance to "sound off" on their pet likes and dislikes.

2. After studying the issues for the past year, I feel that we have too many management stories and too few stories about the typical

worker. It seems to me that this should be principally a publication for and about employees—not a management PR magazine.

3. I recommend that the magazine establish an Employee of the Month Award. A committee of employees would select this person on the basis of recommendations of supervisors and department heads. You might run the employee's picture with a brief biographical sketch and story about that person's special recognition.

4. Finally, I suggest that a monthly gossip column be added. This column would be light and whimsical—nothing scandalous, of course, but fun to read and laugh about.

If you wish, I'd be glad to discuss these recommendations further with you. Certainly, *Tabs* is an excellent instrument for comunicating with employees, and I'm all for experimenting with ideas that will help to make it even better.

25-4 Report About Centralization of a Department

Situation

The Controller of Allegheny Leather Products, C. R. Amen, believes the company is wasting time and money with its purchasing system. The 12 divisions in the company do their own buying of supplies and equipment for internal use. Amen wants to see the purchasing function centralized. On her own initiative, Amen analyzes the problem and writes a report to the president.

The Report

ALLEGHENY LEATHER PRODUCTS
Interoffice Memorandum

TO: J. William Hart   FROM: C. R. Amend
SUBJECT: Centralization of the   DATE: February 16, 19XX
             Purchasing Function

I have mentioned to you several times recently that I think we should consider centralizing the purchasing function in the company. The following report represents my position.

INTRODUCTION

During the past year Allegheny Leather Products made purchases of internal-use equipment and supplies amounting to more than $380,000. The items purchased included computer equipment, automobiles and trucks, furniture and furnishings, stationery, calculators, books, and dozens of other things for company use. These purchases were made by 33 different individuals in our 12 operating departments.

After careful study I have arrived at the conclusion that under our present set-up we are spending more money than we should to obtain the materials we need. Although there are certain advantages to our present system—flexibility, primarily—it can be extremely wasteful in a large organization. For example, selecting a dozen major purchases made last year, I compared the prices of the suppliers for similar (or better) products and found that in at least seven instances we could have saved from 15 to 20 percent if we had made cost comparisons or obtained competitive bids.

PURPOSE AND SCOPE

The purpose of this report is to propose a new system for internal-use purchasing. The discussion that follows, including recommendations, is not intended to apply to purchasing for Manufacturing. The Manufacturing Division would continue to purchase raw materials, equipment, and supplies used in the production process.

ADVANTAGES OF DECENTRALIZED PURCHASING

There are some advantages to our present system of allowing department managers and supervisors to do their own buying. The buyers can tailor their purchases to their own specific requirements, for one thing. Then, too, they may get faster, more personalized since there are no in-company channels to go through.

ARGUMENTS FOR CENTRALIZED PURCHASING

I think we should consider centralizing the purchasing function at Allegheny Leather Products for five major reasons:

1. If all purchases were made in a centralized department, we would buy in larger quantities instead of piecemeal. We would therefore get better prices, higher discounts, and lower transportation rates.

2. Concentration of purchasing would allow us to hire specialists—people who know the best sources of supply and the best time to buy. This know-how should enable us to get better quality at lower prices.

3. Centralization would lead to uniformity in purchasing procedures, and at the same time permit us to pinpoint responsibility for effective buying.

4. By centralizing purchases, we would eliminate duplications in buying, overordering, unnecessary varieties, and inflated inventories.

5. Centralization would give us better control over what and how much to buy. Right now many people are authorized to contract for purchases (for which the company is liable), a situation that could be dangerous.

COST VERSUS SAVINGS

Assuming that Allegheny Leather Products will continue to make annual purchases of at least $580,000 a year (the amount will undoubtedly be larger as the company grows), and assuming that we can save a minimum of 15 percent of this amount, the saving would be around $58,000. This figure does not take into account the time of the purchasing people in the various departments, who are required to do a good deal of research to find the things they need.

We should be able to hire a Purchasing Manager for $40,000 to $50,000 a year, and a secretary for $15,000 to $18,000. Assuming the maximum in each instance, the salary costs would be about $68,000 a year; fringe benefits about $35,000. I have assumed that office space and equipment will cost no more than at present, in view of the expenses now incurred in the various individual departments.

Although the savings of $58,000 versus $76,000 in payroll costs would seem to make this a losing proposition, it should be remembered that purchases will increase substantially, perhaps dramatically, while personnel costs will remain relatively static. But, more important, the hidden savings in better products with longer lives, reduced inventories, elimination of "waste" buying, and other benefits could be very substantial. I would estimate that these hidden savings could amount to $80,000 a year or more.

RECOMMENDATIONS

Based on the foregoing analysis, I recommend that we:

1. Establish a centralized Purchasing Department and assign to it responsibility for all major internal-use purchases—that is, anything over $50.

2. Appoint a Purchasing Director—a person thoroughly trained and experienced in the purchasing function and preferably one who has special knwoledge of mechanical and automated equipment. This individual would report directly to you or, if you prefer, to me.

3. Authorize the Purchasing Director to employ an Assistant Manager and one secretary.

EFFECTIVE DATE

If this proposal is accepted, I suggest an effective date of July 1. This will give us time to find the right person for the Director's job, set up a tentative operational plan, and issue the necessary instructions to the employees affected.

CRA

Part 9

LETTERS CONCERNING GUEST SPEAKERS

Occasionally you may be asked to obtain a speaker for a meeting or conference. If the speaker you choose works in the same company that you do, you can probably get by with a telephone call or an informal memorandum. However, if the person chosen for a specific presentation is outside your company, then you may either telephone or write the person (if the first contact is telephone, you will still write a confirmation letter).

There are many types of program participants: a keynote speaker (one who addresses the general assembly and sets the stage for a series of small meetings that follow the keynote speech, a dinner or banquet speaker, a panelist, a moderator who is assisted by panelists, and so on.

If the person of your choice is a professional speaker—one who commands a sizable fee for his or her services—writing the invitation is no particular challenge. To the recipient, it is a sales opportunity. If, however, you have little or no money to spend, you may have to use salesmanship in your invitation.

Once a speaker has been invited and accepts the assignment, you will then follow up with a confirmation letter. After the speaker has made her or his presentation, you will want to write a letter of thanks and congratulation. The content of this follow-up will depend on how well the speaker performed.

Section 26

Inviting Guest Speakers

Here are guidelines for writing letters to obtain speakers:

1. *Supply complete information about the meeting or conference, including its purpose, its theme (if any), the size of the expected audience, and the time and place.*

2. *If you want the speaker to talk on a particular topic, say so and indicate how long the talk should be. However, if the speech is to be mainly entertainment (such as at a banquet where everyone is in the mood to laugh or be inspired or motivated), you may leave the topic up to the speaker.*

3. *Make it clear what you can do financially—pay expenses only, pay expenses plus an honorarium, or nothing. If the invitation is to a professional speaker, it may be a good idea to learn what the fee is before you make a commitment. You may find too late that the fee asked is well beyond your budget.*

4. *You don't need to give the speaker all the details in the first letter—travel suggestions, hotel accommodations, how expenses are to be submitted, and so on. You provide this and other information after you receive a favorable response.*

5. *The theme of your invitation, especially to "free" speakers, is "You're the ideal person to address our group, and you would do us a great honor in accepting the assignment."*

26–1   Inviting a Professional Speaker

Situation   The chairperson of the program committee of the American Association of Travel Agents must find a speaker for the banquet that closes a three-day meeting. The group has asked for a professional speaker, but the top fee that can be paid is $2000. Several people have mentioned Raymond Strobel as a good choice.

The Letter   Dear Mr. Strobel:

You have been highly recommended by several of our members as a speaker for the banquet that closes a three-day meeting of the American Association of Travel Agents. The place is the Sheraton Inn in Myrtle Beach, South Carolina; the date is the evening of October 3.

The banquet is a purely social affair, climaxing three days of hard work, and we prefer an address on the light side, but with an inspirational theme. I would leave it to you to select a topic, which I know will be appropriate for the occasion.

May I hear from you by June 14? Please indicate in your reply the financial arrangements you require. Just as soon as we have reached an agreement, I will send you more details, including a tentative convention program.

Sincerely yours,

26-2   Professional Speaker's Response to an Invitation

Situation   See Letter 26–1 on the preceding page.

The Letter   Dear Mrs. Wood:

I was very pleased to receive your invitation to speak at the closing banquet of the American Association of Travel Agents. I am appearing in Atlanta on September 29, and, as I recall, the airline flight from Atlanta to Myrtle Beach is about one hour. So no problems there!

I have spoken at least twice to regional meetings of the AATA, so I feel that they are old friends. I have a fairly good idea of the talk you want; closing banquests are my specialty! However, I will want more details from you so that I will be sure to be ready for your audience. It's on my mind to label my speech "Who Said Getting There is Half the Fun?"—a gentle spoof of the travel industry with emphasis on travel agents. All in fun, of course.

My fee is $2000 for such an appearance, Mrs. Wood. I pay all of my expenses, including travel and hotel. Let me know, please, whether this is satisfactory so that I may complete my plans.

Very sincerely yours,

26-3

Responding to the Letter from a Professional Speaker

Situation   See Letter 26–2 on the preceding page.

The Letter   Dear Mr. Strobel:

I am delighted that you can be with us on the evening of October 3 in Myrtle Beach. The title you suggested for your presentation, "Who Says Getting There is Half the Fun?" sounds just right. The $2000 fee is perfectly satisfactory.

A rough draft of the program is enclosed. Your name and the title of your talk will be on page 3, and you are scheduled for a 45-minute presentation. Our banquet will be in the Pelican Room in case you want to have a look-see in advance. I assume you will be staying at the Sheraton Inn. If you would like me to make reservations for you, give me a call at the number on the letterhead.

Our social hour begins at 6:30 in the Pirate's Cove. Why not join us and meet some of our officers and others?

I'm sure you know that US Air has a direct flight from Atlanta to Myrtle Beach. According to my schedule, flight number 427 arrives at Myrtle Beach at 4:50 p.m., and it's about a 20-minute ride to the Sheraton by taxi. If you prefer to have someone meet your plane, just let me know.

Cordially yours,

26–4

Inviting a Panel Participant— Modest Fee Offered

Situation

As a leader of a panel discussion on advertising media at a convention, you are to invite three people to serve on the panel with you. The topic is media—print, broadcast, and direct mail. The organization that sponsors the convention will pay expenses for panel members plus a modest honorarium.

The Letter

Dear Cara:

The National Advertising Directors Association will have its annual meeting September 4–6 at the Washington Hilton in Washington, D.C. I have been asked to lead a panel discussion on "Media Trends and Developments."

The panel will concentrate on three media—print, broadcast, and direct mail—and a specialist for each medium will speak for about 15 minutes. These talks will be followed by a question-and-answer period in which members of the audience participate.

Would you serve as our speaker-specialist on direct mail? I can think of no one better qualified to fill this role. NADA is prepared to pay all your expenses, and we can offer you the modest honorarium of $50 as a panel participant. The media panel is scheduled to begin at 2 p.m. on Tuesday the fifth and end no later than 4 p.m.

I do hope, Cara, that it will be possible for you to undertake this assignment. Let me know as soon as you can, please. If your reponse is favorable, I'll get more information to you.

Sincerely yours,

26–5

Panel Participant's Negative Response to an Invitation

Situation   See Letter 26–4 on the preceding page.

The Letter   Dear Ernie:

How I wish I could be on your panel at the AADA convention in Washington on September 4–6. Everything you said in your letter is just right except the date. I simply cannot get away, since I will be at Riverside Press in Hammond to oversee the printing of a massive mailing that has Number 1 priority here. The pressure is on from all the top people in the organization.

I wonder if you know Professor Glenn Lane at the University of Nebraska. A dynamic young man, Lane is a true specialist in direct mail—I often bend his ear for advice, and he always comes up with a good answer. I have not, of course, spoken to Glenn, but you may wish to invite him to be on your program, mentioning that I suggested him. He can be reached by telephone at number 4577.

Have a good conference, Ernie. I'm awfully sorry to miss it.

Sincerely,

26–6 Inviting a "Second-Choice" Panelist

Situation   See Letters 26–4 and 26–5 on pages 236–237.

The Letter   Dear Professor Lane:

The National Advertising Directors Association will hold its annual meeting September 4–6 at the Washington Hilton Hotel in Washington, D.C. I have been asked to lead a panel discussion on "Media Trends and Developments."

The panel will concentrate on three media—print, broadcast, and direct mail—and a specialist for each medium will speak for about fifteen minutes. These talks will be followed by a question-and-answer period in which members of the audience will participate.

You have been highly recommended by Cara Holt as our speaker-specialist on direct mail, and we would be very pleased if you can accept this assignment. NADA is prepared to pay all your expenses, and we can offer you the modest honorarium of $50. The media panel is scheduled to begin at 2 p.m. on Tuesday the 5th and end no later than 4 p.m.

I do hope, Professor Lane, that it will be possible for you to undertake this assignment. Let me know as soon as you can, please. If your response is favorable (and I hope it will be!), I'll get other information to you.

Sincerely yours,

26–7

Inviting a Keynote Speaker— No Funds Available

Situation

The Executive Secretary of a state organization of retired people has been asked to obtain a keynote speaker for the group's annual conference. No funds are available.

The Letter

Dear Dr. Burdette:

The Indiana chapter of the American Association of Retired People is holding its annual conference in Terre Haute on June 17–19. The theme of this year's meeting is "The Senior Citizen: A Dynamic Community Resource." As you might guess, most of our discussions will focus on the important role that AARP members can play in community affairs.

Would you be our keynote speaker for this conference? We are well acquainted with your excellent newspaper and magazine articles on the importance to older people of keeping involved. Your remarks as keynoter would set the tone perfectly for our conference. A 30- to 45-minute talk would be fine. We expect an attendance of about 275.

Although our limited treasury does not permit payment of fees or expenses for speakers, we are hoping that your interest in the problems of and opportunities for the aging will be a sufficient incentive for you to be with us.

I look forward to a favorable reply, Dr. Burdette, and just as soon as I receive it, I will send you complete details. Our meeting place is the Best Western Statesman Inn Motel on U.S. 41, just north of Indiana State University.

Very sincerely yours,

Section 27

Thanking Guest Speakers

Everyone who appears as a guest speaker deserves a thank-you letter. Some speakers do an outstanding job and thanking them is fairly easy—you simply congratulate the speaker for an excellent performance, pointing out some of the things that made the talk memorable. Other speakers turn in a so-so performance, yet they need to be thanked. Still others do a poor job (often they are last-minute substitutes for the original invitee and are not fully prepared). The not so good and pretty bad speaker letters are, of course, quite difficult to write. It's not a good idea to tell these people they weren't effective, but you can thank them for taking time to participate in the program.

27–1 Thanking an Outstanding Professional Speaker

Situation   See Letters 26–1, 26–2, and 26–3 on pages 231–233.

The Letter   Dear Ray:

Every convention-goer I've known—certainly in the American Association of Travel Agents—looks forward to the final evening banquet as "quittin' time." The "painful" cerebrations have ended, the lifeless speeches are forgotten, the arguments are mere echoes; now body and soul gasp for something refreshing. That "something refreshing" includes a period of fellowship (with the appropriate elixirs), memorable cuisine, and a good speaker to wrap it all up.

My definition of a first-rate banquet speaker is one who is easy to listen to, witty, and very wise. The eyes of the audience told me how interesting you were; you had our *full* attention. The audience also told you how much they enjoyed your stories; you must remember the number of times you had to pause to continue after an especially funny punch line.

Why do I think you were wise? You had a theme, but you did not reveal it directly: coping with stress. I'm certain no one there felt that he or she was being lectured to about stress (it's Topic A in all the media), yet no one could go away without having felt that something really important—and useful—had been said.

Thank you for a very enjoyable evening, Ray. I hope our paths will cross again; if I'm anywhere near the location of a future speech of yours, they will. Your check for $2000 is enclosed.

Sincerely,

27-2   Thanking a Successful Keynote Speaker

Situation   Dr. Theresa Worth was asked to be the keynote speaker at a two-day workshop of the National Association of Manufacturing Managers. She did a magnificent job, and the program chairman writes her a thank-you letter.

The Letter   Dear Theresa:

I'm sure you know from experience that the keynote address at a large conference is extremely important. The hope of the conference chairman is that the keynoter will establish the appropriate tone—a lead-in, if you will—for the various group meetings that follow. You did exactly that in your address, "Dynamic Manufacturing Management." I sat in on each panel group and was pleased to witness the many references made to your address; you obviously widened the perspective of all our members!

I'm convinced that this was the best national conference NAMM has had since I've served as executive director, and much of the credit goes to you. Thank you for being with us.

Very sincerely yours,

27-3

Thanking a Successful Speaker and Requesting Copies

Situation Janet Cox was asked to speak at the National Office Management Association (NOMA). Her talk was so well received that several members of NOMA asked for a copy of the talk.

The Letter Dear Janet:

The best way to tell you how well received your presentation was on Tuesday evening is to mention the many requests I've had for a copy of your remarks. I have a feeling that those who heard you want to share with their colleagues back at the office your highly imaginative evaluation of typical incentive compensation plans and your own recommendations.

If you have a copy of your presentation and would be willing to send it to me for reproduction, you'll make a lot of people happy. If this isn't feasible, I'll understand of course.

In any event, Janet, thank you for participating so effectively in our national conference. You played a major role in making it an outstanding event.

Cordially,

27–4

Thanking an After-Dinner Speaker

Situation   Doug Bryant was recently appointed Program Chairperson of the Oshkosh Lions Club. He has been very critical of the recent programs of the club, saying that there should be better speakers at the monthly dinner meetings. At the first meeting after Bryant's election, the speaker was superb. Bryant writes Phil Denton, the speaker, a thank-you letter.

The Letter   Dear Phil:

When the Lions elected me Program Chairman this year, I knew darned well it was because the members were tired of my negative comments on some of our past speakers. "OK, Doug," they said, "let's see what *you* can do," perhaps convinced I would fall flat on my face.

Thanks to you, my first selection, I remained upright! Indeed, I felt pretty smug when I got so many compliments on your presentation—several in writing. You not only kept the audience riveted—and at the right time wonderfully amused—you really gave us something to stash away in our heads for later reflection and application. You must have sensed that you had everybody with you, as evidenced by the furious notetaking during your talk and the applause and handshakes that followed.

Thank you very much for giving us such a good evening, Phil. Now if I can come even close to your performance in future selections of speakers....

Sincerely,

27–5   Thanking an Ineffective Luncheon Speaker

Situation

Avery Enright, National Vice President of Toastmasters International, recently spoke at a luncheon meeting of the Houston Toastmasters organization. The topic assigned was "Toastmaster's Goals for the Coming Year."

The talk given by Enright was badly prepared and delivered, barely touching on the assigned topic. In addition, he spoke for over an hour, when he was allotted 30 minutes. He dwelt mostly on a personal history of his role in Toastmasters and the important work he is doing in the national office.

The audience was bored, frustrated about the length of the talk, and only mildly receptive. As program chairperson, Kay Price must write Enright to thank him for his presentation.

The Letter

Dear Avery:

The Houston members of Toastmasters Intenational have asked me to write you and express our appreciation for your being with us at our May 14 luncheon. It is always a special occasion when a member of the national staff visits our chapter and shares his or her experiences with us. And, of course, it was interesting to hear about your colleagues in the national office.

I know how busy you are and the sacrifice it was for you to share some time with us, and on behalf of the Houston chapter I want to thank you for coming.

Cordially yours,

27–6

Thanking a Disappointing Substitute Speaker

Situation

Each spring, Montclair University sponsors an educational conference to which high school and college teachers are invited. One of the three speakers engaged for the conference had to bow out at the last minute, and a substitute had to be found on very short notice. His performance was disappointing, yet he is entitled to the $100 honorarium promised. The writer wants to transmit the check and express gratidue in a tactful yet truthful manner.

The Letter

Dear Dr. Barkham:

Enclosed is a check for $100, your honorarium for your presentation at the Fifth Annual Conference on Educational Innovation.

We are all very grateful to you for accepting this assignment on such short notice, Dr. Barkham. As a whole, we felt the conference was quite productive, and we thank you for participating in it.

Very sincerely yours,

Part 10

PUBLIC RELATIONS AND PERSONNEL LETTERS

Many of the letters you write will probably fall under the general category of public relations. Of course, the public is *everybody*—including your customers, suppliers, and employees—but in this part, we concentrate on those letters that have to do mainly with a company's image.

Nearly every business wants people to have a good feeling toward it. Many large organizations spend millions of dollars a year toward that end, employing a large stafff of PR specialists or engaging consultants to build and maintain a supportive attitude on the part of the public. Among the groups with whom PR departments are most anxious to establish good relations are news media, government (local, state, and federal), organized consumer groups, local civic organizations, professional associations, and others who represent centers of influence. Obviously, paying close attention to the reactions of the public makes good sense; the road to success in any endeavor is a lot smoother when you have influential friends.

But whether you're a member of the PR group or not, you're likely to write some letters to people who ask for favors or solicit donations or merely express their views—pro and con—on what your company is doing.

Section 28

General Public Relations Letters

As we mentioned earlier, some public relations letters are pleasant messages whose primary purpose is to build goodwill and enhance the company's image. In tone and style they are very much like the letters you would write to sales prospects and customers. The guidelines for writing them are simple: be warm, friendly, and persuasive.

Other letters deal with matters that are not altogether pleasant, such as saying "no" to requests that you can't grant or responding to outraged critics. In these instances, you are, of course, as tactful and cordial as possible, but you must still deliver a response that is unlikely to win applause from your readers.

In this section, we concentrate on the latter type simply because they are the hardest to write. Here are guidelines for writing such letters:

---

1. *If there's good news to report, do it first; then deliver the bad news.*
2. *When the letter you received contains a compliment, acknowledge it gratefully.*
3. *When you have to say "no," do it as gently as possible, giving reasons why.*
4. *If you're responding to an irate critic:*
   a. *Express appreciation for his or her point of view.*
   b. *Fully explain your point of view.*
   c. *End the letter with a statement that assumes the air has been cleared and no further correspondence is necessary.*

28-1　Handling a Special Request

Situation　A graduate student in communications writes the president of Widmark Corporation. She is making a study of the history of corporate annual reports and requests a copy of each of Widmark's reports for the past fifteen years. Only three can be sent, but the president has a suggestion for getting access to the others.

The Letter　Dear Miss Demeter:

Your study of the history of annual reports sounds very challenging, and I'm pleased that you want Widmark represented.

I'm enclosing copies of our annual report for the current year and the two preceding years. Although earlier reports are not available in hard-copy form, they are on microfilm. If you are in Minneapolis, you are welcome to visit us and spend as much time as you wish examining these films. Just let me know ahead of time, and I will make arrangements with the company librarian (J. C. Schultz) to set up a carrel for you with viewing equipment.

I suspect your study will prove to be quite an ambitious one, but certainly useful to a large number of people. Good luck!

　　　　　　　　　　　　　　　　Cordially yours,

28–2   Refusing a Request to Buy Advertising

Situation   Frank Traylor is Sales Promotion Director for Mott-Tillson, a company that manufactures and sells sports uniforms and equipment for schools and colleges. Every spring, Traylor receives letters from high school and college yearbook editors inviting Mott-Tillson to place ads in their yearbooks. It is not a satisfactory advertising medium (the people who see these ads are local business proprietors and other residents). The invitation must be declined.

The Letter   Dear Bill:

I appreciate your invitation to purchase an advertisement in *Reminiscence*. Thank you.

Bill, many thousands of yearbooks are published each year, and it is impossible for us to purchase advertising in all of them. I admit that there is probably equipment in your school that was purchased from Mott-Tillson, but that same is true of thousands of other institutions. National advertisers are forced to spend their money where the message gets into the hands of purchasing directors and others who buy in large quantities.

I expect, Bill, that you will have to rely primarily on local community businesses to purchase space in *Reminiscence*. Many businesses feel a strong obligation to support worthy community activities; just having their names associated with a local school project is a strong incentive. Indeed, Mott-Tillson feels that same way about Grand Rapids, which is our home base.

Thank you for thinking of us, Bill, and best wishes for the most successful *Reminiscence* that has ever been published.

Cordially yours,

28-3   Acknowledging a Request for a Donation

Situation

Most companies get many requests for donations to various causes; more often than not, they are addressed to the president, for obvious reasons. Although there is usually an amount set aside for contributions, it is almost never enough. To remove the responsibility for decisions from one person, it is standard practice to set up a committee to cull the most worthy causes for support. The first response, however, usually comes from the person addressed. The President of Halpern Associates responds to such a request, explaining the company's position in handling such matters.

The Letter

Dear Mrs. Mueller:

Thank you for writing about your need for financial support for the Duplin Youth Symphony.

Each year, our company sets aside a sizable sum of money for distribution to various charitable agencies and other groups. The requests for financial aid have multiplied many times in the past few years, and to make sure our budget is distributed in the fairest manner possible, we have established a special contributions committee, whose members have the responsibility of selecting those organizations they consider most deserving in terms of what we can give. It's a difficult job because most of the requests we receive are, like yours, for worthy causes.

I am handing your letter to the head of the contributions committee, and you may expect to hear from her within the next few weeks. In the meantime, I wish you all success in your endeavor.

Very cordially yours,

28–4   Turning Down a Request for a Donation

Situation

This is a continuation of the situation described in Letter 28–3 on the preceding page. The contributions committee of Halpern Associates decides against a donation to the Duplin Youth Symphony, and the head of the committee writes Mrs. Mueller, who made the request.

The Letter

Dear Mrs. Mueller:

Our contributions committee has, after careful study of all the requests for contributions, selected those which we think are in greatest need of our support.

Although the members unanimously agreed that the Duplin Youth Symphony contributes much to the community—as well as to the performers themselves—we can't, unfortunately, provide financial support at this time. There are so many projects that need help desperately, and we have chosen to allot our budget to child-care centers for working mothers, drug rehabilitation programs, parental counseling on child abuse, "halfway" facilities for unwed teenage mothers, and various projects for the aged.

Of course, Mrs. Mueller, we realize that any decisions our committee makes are arbitrary, but I assure you that they were arrived at thoughtfully and, we believe, fairly. I do hope that in the future we will be in a position to provide some funds for the Duplin Youth Symphony. In the meantime, we wish you success with your efforts on behalf of this excellent organization.

Sincerely,

28-5 Responding to a Friendly Critic

Situation   You're in the Public Relations Department of Transamerica Technologies, a large conglomerate that sponsors a public-service television series, "American Issues." It is your job to answer letters from viewers who comment—pro and con—on the program. One viewer writes that he likes the series a lot, but takes issue with the segment that dealt with the environment. You write to the viewer to express appreciation for his interest and point of view, present the other side, and retain his good will and support of the series.

The Letter   Dear Professor Converse:

It was very thoughtful of you to write about the television series, "American Issues," sponsored by Transamerica Technologies. Our mail from viewers has been much heavier than we expected but, as we had *hoped*, overwhelmingly favorable. Certainly, your general assessment of the series is very satisfying to us.

Your comments on "Environment versus Progress" indicate that you have given much study and thought to this subject, and I appreciate your frank appraisal of it. Several other people wrote that they, too, felt it was biased in favor of industry.

The producers were well aware in the beginning that this a highly controversial subject and were determined not to take sides. Our general mail would seem to indicate that they succeeded, for we received comments from many viewers that the program was biased in favor of the environmentalists!

Indeed, conflicting viewpoints are expected on this series, and as long as they are fairly well balanced (as they have been), we feel that the series is encouraging people to think more intelligently and deeply about the unresolved issues that face our nation.

Thank you for writing. I hope you will continue to watch "American Issues" and that you will let us have your opinions—favorable or unfavorable.

Very cordially yours,

28–6 Responding to an Outraged Critic

Situation
The president of a large corporation receives a severely critical letter from the owner of a construction business. The writer objects to the corporation's advertising in a magazine called *Bulwark*, which he feels is "militant" and "un-American." He is so incensed at the corporation's "support" of this magazine that he threatens to boycott its products. As Assistant to the President, you are asked to respond, expressing appreciation for the letter and explaining tactfully the company's position.

The Letter
Dear Mr. Coughlin:

I appreciate your writing about our advertising in *Bulwark* magazine.

Bulwark was chosen as an advertising medium simply because its circulation (about 300,000) is made up mostly of young men and women in the upper-income brackets whom we consider appropriate targets for our videocassette records. Placing advertising in a publication does not necessarily mean that we endorse its editorial views. You criticize *Bulwark* as "militant" and "un-American"—even "dangerous." I expect, Mr. Coughlin, that some people will agree with you. Yet we also receive letters equally vehement about our advertising in magazines that are broadly labeled as "conservative."

We do have a policy of not advertising in periodicals that are prurient in nature or that are essentially scandal sheets. It is our opinion the *Bulwark* does not fall into either of these categories. It is quite likely that the people in our advertising department who chose *Bulwark* do not all agree with its editorial position, but it is their responsibility to place ads where they think our products will get the widest exposure, given the constraints mentioned above. I think most national advertisers use a similar criterion in choosing media. Not one that I know of believes that spending advertising dollars means "support."

Thank you for expressing your views so frankly and for giving us the opportunity to express ours.

Very truly yours,

28-7　Turning Down a Request for Confidential Information

Situation Walter Whitcraft has seen the annual report of Treadway Industries for the past fiscal year and is greatly impressed. He asks whether he can have the figures for a recently acquired company, Southwestern Synthetics, a company in which he once held stock. These figures can be broken out; however, the Board of Directors has chosen not to release them, or any other division's figures, to the general public.

The Letter Dear Mr. Whitcraft:

I appreciate your writing about our annual report for the past fiscal year. Thank you for your remarks about our over-all showing.

We did not, in our annual report, break down the figures for the eight subsidiary operations. It was the decision of the Board of Directors that this information will not be released to the general public.

Sincerely yours,

28-8 Apologizing for Inconveniences

Situation   When Family Foods, Inc. builds a new store in the suburbs, President Carl Fisk writes a letter to residents in the area, apologizing for the inconveniences they suffer.

The Letter   Dear Hawthorne Hills Resident:

Building a new store is a messy business—as you undoubtedly noticed from the dust clouds we raise, the rerouting of traffic on Old Town Road, and the noise and general confusion we create.

Although things are still unsettled, we are doing everything we possibly can to eliminate inconvenience and discomfort for our friends. The good news is that we expect to finish the "dirty" part of the job by April 10 and then get back to normal.

Thank you for your patience. Although we regret being a nuisance, we think you will be proud of this new Family Foods outlet—a full acre of shopping pleasure—which is scheduled to open September 8 of this year.

Cordially yours,

Section 29

Personnel Letters

Every day, large organizations receive letters from people who apply for a job. More often than not, these applications must be turned down, either because there are no vacancies in the positions applied for or because the applicants are not qualified for openings that do exist.

Saying no to job applicants, for whatever reason, requires the utmost tact, since those who receive such letters are quite likely to think of the turn-down as a *personal* rejection.

In this section, we give examples of "no" letters to job applicants as well as other communications pertaining to employment.

29–1 Responding to a Qualified Applicant— No Position Available

Situation   Alice Bennett, Personnel Director of Fairchild Book Publishers receives an application from Glen Rowe for Fiction Editor. There are no openings; however, Bennett is impressed with Howe's qualifications and wants to leave the door slightly open for later consideration. Bennett writes to Howe to express appreciation, explain the job situation, and compliment the applicant on his qualifications.

The Letter   Dear Mr. Howe:

Thank you for your application for the position of Fiction Editor.

At the moment, Mr. Howe, there are no vacancies in our Trade Department. Of course, the situation may change at any moment, and I would like to keep your resume handy in case there is a staff expansion or a resignation. Certainly, it would appear that you have excellent qualifications for the position you seek.

Even though I'm reluctant to "turn you loose" on the job market, in all fairness to you I recommend that you submit applications elsewhere. I would not want you to pass up an opportunity in the hope that our situation will change soon. You may be sure, however, that, if a suitable opening does occur here, I will get in touch with you at once.

Sincerely,

29–2

Responding to an Unqualified Applicant— Position Available

Situation

Andrew Hamm, Manager of Sales Promotion at Field Enterprises, receives an application for the job of Advertising Copywriter, which was advertised in the *Oakland Tribune*. The applicant is poorly qualified in comparison with others who applied. Hamm writes the applicant to express appreciation for the application and explains the situation without giving a definite "no."

The Letter

Dear Mr. Huffman:

I appreciate your application for the position of Advertising Copywriter that we advertised in the *Oakland Tribune*.

The response to our ad has been very gratifying, and we have had applications from several people who appear to be highly qualified for the job. However, we shall want to wait until all applications are in and then study each one carefully before making a decision.

Our plan is to fill this position no later than June 10. If you have not heard from us by that time, you may assume that the job has been filled.

Sincerely yours,

29–3

Writing to an Applicant Who Failed to Qualify

Situation

Five-Star Insurance Company needed two secretaries and advertised the vacancies in the *Denver Post*. Ten applicants showed up, and each was given a proficiency test, including typewriting, shorthand, simple math, and business English. The top two scorers were hired, and the remaining eight applicants are notified by letter.

The Letter

Dear Ms. Tilton:

Thank you for coming to our office to take the proficiency test for the position of Secretary.

All the tests from the ten applicants have been graded, and, unfortunately, your score was not in the top two (the number of positions open). According to the grader, you did well in typewriting, shorthand, and math; however, your score in business English brought down the total score considerably.

If you are interested in taking another test when vacancies are announced, I suggest that you continue to keep your shorthand and typewriting skills sharp and that you undertake a thorough review of business English. A book that I think you will find helpful is *Programmed Handbook of Business English*, by Mark Stewart, published by Unity Press.

Good luck!

29–4

Responding to a Partially Qualified Applicant

Situation

Recently, Cent-West Corporation advertised in *Power* magazine for a cost and scheduling manager. An applicant met one of the two experience requirements described in the ad, but did not mention the other. You write to point out to the applicant the experience requirements of the job, leaving the matter open to further consideration in case the ad was misread.

The Letter

Dear Mr. Jacobi:

Thank you for applying for the position of cost and scheduling manager at Cent-West Corporation, which was advertised in the November issue of *Power*.

Certainly, Mr. Jacobi, your educational qualifications are superb, and your 12 years' experience in general power-plant projects is most impressive. I do not, however, find any mention in your résumeé of coal power-plant experience, which is mandatory for this position (four years minimum).

If I am incorrect in my assessment of your credentials, I would be pleased to hear from you—immediately, please, since we must make a final decision within the next two weeks.

Very sincerely yours,

29-5 Requesting Information About a Job Applicant

Situation

Angela Wheaton was employed for five years in the Personnel Department of a pharmaceutical manufacturer. At the time she left the company (her husband was transferred), she held the position of Director of Clerical Training. She has applied for a similar position in a large insurance company, listing her former boss as a reference. As Personnel Supervisor for the insurance company, you write Wheaton's former boss for information about her employment record.

The Letter

Dear Mrs. Eller:

Mrs. Angela Wheaton has applied to us for the position of Director of Office Training, and your name was given as a reference.

I would appreciate your answering the following questions about Mrs. Wheaton:

1. How long was she under your supervision? _____

2. What was her position at the time she left your company? _____
   _____

3. What reason was given for leaving? _____
   _____

4. How would you rate her overall competence? (Check one.)
   Outstanding _____ Good_____ Average _____ Fair _____ Poor_____

5. Please state briefly what you believe to be her greatest strengths and weaknesses (if any):

   a. Strengths _____
      _____

   b. Weaknesses _____
      _____

6. If you had an opening for which she is qualified, would you rehire her?
   Yes _____ No _____ . If no, please state why.

I assure you, Mrs. Eller, that any information you supply about this applicant will be held in strict confidence. If there is ever an opportunity for me to reciprocate, I will be pleased to do so. Thank you.

Very sincerely yours,

Very sincerely yours,

29-6   Offering an Executive Position to a Qualified Person

Situation

Mills-Froman Corporation, in San Francisco, is establishing a new department in the company, to be called Organization Planning and Manager Development, and is searching for a director. The Executive Vice President, C. J. Bouchard, has interviewed several people in various parts of the country and has decided to make an offer to Lawrence A. Margulies in Cleveland, who is extraordinarily well qualified. Bouchard gave no definite promises when he met with Margulies in Cleveland, but is now ready to make a written offer.

The Letter

Dear Larry:

The day I spent with you in Cleveland was very enjoyable and stimulating, and I appreciate your taking the time to meet with me. Getting acquainted with Sara was a special treat; I am indebted to her for joining us at dinner on such short notice.

I am pleased to offer you the position of Director of Organization Planning and Manager Development of Mills-Froman Corporation. As I mentioned, this is a new position that we are most anxious to fill. The growth of our company makes it essential that we centralize this function, rather than leave the responsibility with individual executives, committees, and outside consultants. President Froman and all other top executives support this idea enthusiastically. As mentioned, the person who holds this position will report directly to me.

We are prepared to offer you an annual salary of $85,000 at the outset, along with what I think is a very attractive array of fringe benefits. Our personnel policy manual is being sent to you separately, along with Executive Memorandums 14 and 26, which describe various financial incentives for which you would be eligible.

Although we discussed the responsibilities of this new position briefly, I want to outline in broad terms the function as we see it. Obviously, our principal objective is to develop managers for executive responsibilities. At the same time, we are well aware that the first step is to create the appropriate climate in which candidates for leadership can grow and flourish. At the outset, this means intelligent organization planning, which includes the following:

1. Establishing company objectives.

2. Establishing the critical success factors that affect the attainment of those objectives.

3. Developing an ideal organization structure that will favor the activities related to the critical success factors.

4. Modifying the ideal structure to achieve a satisfactory compromise between the existing structure and the ideal structure.

Only when these steps are taken will we be in a position to construct and implement a sound manager development program. As you know, the scope of such a program can be very broad, including on-the-job-training, special task force assignments, seminars and conferences, business gaming, university-sponsored courses, and so on. The director of this new department will be given wide range in selecting the most effective methods of achieving the utlimate goals.

I hope, Larry, that this opportunity sounds exciting and challenging to you. After our conversation in Cleveland, I'm convinced that you have the depth and experience in this area to perform the duties of this position highly effectively.

Please let me know your decision within the next two weeks. The starting date we have in mind is January 15, but of course that date is flexible, depending on your circumstances. Certainly, we would want you to wind up things at Corcoran amicably.

Sincerely yours,

PS: Although we touched briefly in Cleveland on such matters as moving expenses, per diem allowances for you and your family while you are being settled in the Bay Area, and certain real estate adjustments, I will provide specific details when I have your acceptance. I assure you that our company policy in these matters is very generous.

29-7 Announcing an Important Appointment— News Release

Situation

DeWitt J. Fuller has just been appointed senior consultant in small business management at Harlan Thomas Associates. As Assistant to the Personnel and Public Relations Manager, you are to prepare a news release, which will be sent to local newspapers and broadcast stations. (The same information, in slightly different form, is also sent to all employees by means of an executive memorandum.)

The News Release

HARLAN THOMAS ASSOCIATES
Management Consultants
1379 Madison Avenue
New York, NY 10028

For immediate relase

DEWITT J. FULLER JOINS HARLAN THOMAS ASSOCIATES

DeWitt J. Fuller, former manager of New Orleans Small Business Administration Field Office, has joined Harlan Thomas Associates as Senior Consultant in small business management and will assume his duties April 16, 19XX.

According to President R. B. Myers, Fuller will establish a new small business management department at Harlan Thomas Associates for the purpose of providing special counsel to those who are considering starting a business, as well as those who are already operating a business and need assistance in financial planning, marketing strategies, and general management techniques. "Small business owners have largely been neglected by management consulting organizations," Myers said, "and we are convinced that an enormous contribution can be made by our company, not only to the owners themselves, but to the business community as a whole. We feel very fortunate in having a person with Fuller's experience to head up this important new service."

Prior to joining the SBA in 1947, Fuller was owner-operator of a small electronics manufacturing firm near Phoenix and for many years taught courses in small business management at Arizona State University. He is the author of *Successful Small Business Management* (Poughman Press) and numerous articles in various trade journals.

29–8　Writing a Valuable Worker Being Discharged Because of Unfavorable Economic Conditions

Situation

Cosbro Corporation is cutting its staff because of unfavorable economic conditions. Agnes Russon is a good worker, and the manager of the department in which she works writes a letter on the occasion of her dismissal.

The Letter

Dear Agnes:

I am sorry to tell you that on May 15 you will receive your last check from Cosbro Corporation.

As you know from our previous talk, this action is taken because of unfavorable economic conditions and our increasing costs in a declining market. We simply are not producing a reasonable profit, and profit is the "name of the game" in American business. No matter how much was cut from expenses other than salaries, it simply wasn't enough; therefore, we are forced to dismiss a large number of employees. As to the future, who can say? We are not optimistic; we must somehow struggle on.

I very much hope that you will be able to find employment elsewhere, Agnes. You have been a good worker, and your immediate supervisor, Beth Southerland, speaks well of you. If in your search for another job you need a recommendation, then I invite you to use my name. You may be sure that I will say the right thing in your behalf.

Thank you for your loyalty to Cosbro, and best wishes for a fine future for you and your family.

Very sincerely yours,

29–9 Demotion of a Field Sales Manager Because of Economic Conditions

Situation Because of unfavorable economic conditions, Henderson Electronics is abolishing the position of Field Sales Manager. Those holding this position are asked to return to the field as sales representatives. The Sales Manager, Leon Hendricks, writes Milton Boone, telling him of the decision.

The Letter Dear Milton:

As discussed in my office yesterday, effective October 20 the position of Field Sales Manager will be abolished.

As you know, Milt, our profit picture is not at all healthy, and the company is forced to cut expenses to the bone. One of the positions we felt could be eliminated without undue hardship is that of Field Sales Manager.

I offer you the opportunity to travel for us as a representative in Connecticut and Massachusetts, your old territory in which you made such a fine record. As a sales representative, your salary will be $25,000 a year plus commissions on the sales in your territory. This should just about equal your present salary of $35,000, assuming your sales hold up.

I hope you will accept this assignment, Milt. You have many friends in the two states mentioned, and I know they'll be glad to see you again. (Our present representative in Connecticut and Massachusetts will be transferred to New York, and she is pleased with the decision.) If this new assignment does not sit well with you and you decide to reach out for another position, please feel free to use my name as a reference. You can be sure that I'll say the right thing in your behalf.

Cordially yours,

Part 11

WRITING RESPONSIBILITIES OF EXECUTIVE ASSISTANTS

They are called by different names—Executive Assistant, "Assistant to" the President, Executive Vice President, Vice President for Marketing, and so on, Administrative Assistants, Executive Secretaries. Whatever they are called, these people serve as the "right arm" of top-level executives, writing letters and memorandums, preparing reports, representing the executive at staff meetings. In brief, they relieve the line executives of as much staff work as possible, freeing the boss for more important activities and decisions.

In this part you will see how an executive assistant to the president of a large chain of food stores handles the president's mail when he is away on a long trip. The Executive Assistant's name is Roberta Hicks; the President's, Kenneth R. Burton; and the company's, Food Family, Inc.

Section 30

When-the-Executive-Is-Away Letters

One of the most important responsibilities of many executive assistants is taking care of correspondence when the boss is away on an extended trip. Letters that require no special attention can usually be held for the executive's return, although a short acknowledgment note is a good idea. However, often the mail for the executive requires quick responses of one type or another. The administrative assistant can often respond for the executive, knowing how he or she would respond. The most important word to remember in comunicating on behalf of the absent executive is *discretion*.

30-1

Using Discretion in Writing for the Executive

Situation

Silas J. Monk, who represents a property management firm in Lowell, Massachusetts, writes Burton that he has learned that Food Family, Inc. is in the process of selecting a site in the suburbs of Lowell for a new store. He says he has an "ideal parcel of land in a very strategic location" on which to build to build a new store. He wants Burton to fly to Lowell "immediately" to inspect this "valuable" property. Roberta Hicks knows that three possible sites are being studied, with the strong possibility that one will actually be selected (not Monk's). Hicks writes Monk an appropriate letter.

The Letter

Dear Mr. Monk:

Your letter of July 10 arrived when Mr. Burton is on an extended trip and will not return until August 10. At the moment I have no idea how to get in touch with him. He calls in from time to time, and it may be that I can talk with him about your interest in the Lowell Project. If he does call, I will discuss your letter with him and let you know his reactions to your proposal.

Thank you for writing.

Very truly yours,

30-2

Handling a Request to Participate in a Convention Program

Situation

Ernest Steele, a longtime friend of Burton's, writes from Bangor, Maine, that he is attending the Young Presidents Club convention in Miami Beach on July 27–28. He wants to know if Burton is going to the convention (Steele is this year's president). If Burton plans to go, Steele would like him to give a luncheon talk on the second day.

Burton will not be attending the Miami Beach convention since he has a stockholders' meeting on July 27 and a Board of Directors meeting on the 28th. Hicks writes an approrpriate letter.

The Letter

Dear Mr. Steele:

Mr. Burton is away on a business trip for the next few weeks, and I hasten to respond to your letter inviting him to speak at a luncheon of the Young Presidents Club in Miami Beach on July 28.

Mr. Burton has a stockholders' meeting on July 27 and a Board of Directors' meeting on the 28th. You know how much he enjoys the meetings of your organization and especially seeing many old friends. I also know how pleased he will be at your invitation to give a talk at the luncheon, which, of course, he must decline.

Just as soon as I am in touch with Mr. Burton I will mention your letter. I'm sure he will write or telephone you in Bangor as soon as he "catches up with himself."

Very sincerely yours,

30–3   Referring Problems to Others

Situation

For several weeks Harriet Evers, Vice President of Operations for Food Family, Inc. and a committee have been mulling over the problem of fixtures in the firm's new delicatessen center at the Lowell operation. None of the other stores in the chain has such a center. Evers and members of her committee have been consulting suppliers' catalogs in which such fixtures are pictured, described, and discussed.

One supplier, Springfield Equipment Corporation, writes Burton asking if a decision can be made soon so that the company can gear up to order or produce the fixtures. Hicks turns the matter over to Mrs. Evers.

The Interoffice Letter

TO: Mrs. Harriet Evers   FROM: Roberta Hicks
SUBJECT: Delicatessen Fixtures   DATE: July 14, 19XX

Attached is a letter from C. F. Bowman, of Springfield Equipment Corporation, asking about the company's decision regarding the delicatessen fixtures. Apparently he wants to know whether he should begin to place orders and/or produce the required fixtures.

I believe Mr. Burton told you that he would go along with the decision reached by you and your group studying this matter. If you are ready to commit yourselves to Springfield Equipment, perhaps you will want to write to Bowman. However, if there is still some doubt about a manufacturer, just return the letter to me and I'll write Bowman a "holding" letter.

Thanks!

30–4

"Holding" Letter About a Purchasing Decision

Situation

See Letter 30–3 on the preceding page. Roberta Hicks must write to Mr. Bowman.

The Letter

Dear Mr. Bowman:

Excuse my delay in answering your letter of July 10. I wanted to discuss the matter fully with Mrs. Evers (whom you know) and her group to learn where the "delicatessen" matter stands. Mrs. Evers feels that we should withhold a final decision until Mr. Burton returns to the office on August 10.

I am sure that Mr. Burton will write to telephone you within a day or two after his arrival.

Thank you for your patience, and be assured that you'll have our decision shortly.

Very truly yours,

30–5   Follow-Up Letter to a Company Executive

Situation

When Mr. Burton telephone the office on July 24, he asked what had been done about the automobile leasing study that was undertaken by Curtis Watson, the Purchasing Director, and Ray Robertson, the Controller. Burton is surprised that the report has not been received, and he insists that it be completed by the time he arrives on August 10 when the national sales conference takes place. In any event, he wants Watson's and Robertson's conclusions and recommendations immediately. Roberta Hicks writes the required memo.

The Memorandum

TO: Curtis Watson   FROM: Roberta Hicks
  Ray Robertson
SUBJECT: Car Leasing Study   DATE: July 24, 19XX

  When I talked on the telephone yesterday with Mr. Burton, he asked me whether the automobile leasing study has been completed. If so, please send it to me and I'll get it to him by Priority Mail. In any event, he wants your conclusions and recommendations in his hands tomorrow so that he can study them on the plane en route. Please see that I get them today.

RH

30–6   Disavowing a "True" Rumor

Situation

One of the reasons for Mr. Burton's trip east was to look into the possible acquisition of a small chain of delicatessens called The Pickle Jar. A newspaper reporter picks up the rumor that Food Family, Inc. has purchased the delis and telephones Burton's office for confirmation. Mr. Burton has not yet returned from the trip, and Roberta Hicks decides to write the reporter a letter.

The Letter

Dear Ms. Kaneer:

As I mentioned on the telephone, Mr. Burton, President of Food Family, Inc., is out of the office, and I can give you no information concerning the company's acquisition of The Pickle Jar delicatessen stores.

I'm sure you know, Ms. Kaneer, that acquisitions and mergers are very common these days. For all I know, Food Family, Inc. may be in the process of studying profitable acquisitions of a dozen different companies. Pending acquisitions are hush-hush even among employees, and nothing is announced until a particular deal is a *fait accompli*. I assure you that nothing has been said here about The Pickle Jar, and I believe I would be among the first to know of our company's plans.

Yours very truly,

Section 31

Writing for the Executive's Signature

It is the executive's display of complete trust when the "assistant to" is asked to write letters for her or his (the executive's) signature. This comes, of course, only after the two have been working together for some period of time and the "assistant to" has learned to write just as the executive would. In this section, we present four challenging examples of writing for a superior's signature.

31–1

Accepting a Speaking Invitation

Situation

Professor Marvin Klein writes Kenneth R. Burton inviting him to speak to his graduate marketing class (University of Chicago) on Tuesday, November 14. At the dinner meeting, an award will be presented to the outstanding graduate marketing student of the year. Klein suggests a relatively brief talk on "New Marketing Strategies in the Food Industry," followed by a question-and-answer period with participation by the students.

Professor Klein is getting ready to print the program and would like an immediate response. On his way to a meeting, Burton says to Hicks, "Answer that with a yes, and I'll sign it."

The Letter

Dear Professor Klein:

I am pleased—indeed honored—to accept your invitation to speak at the dinner meeting of graduate marketing students on Tuesday evening, November 14.

I am especially enthusiastic about the topic you suggested for my remarks. The need for sound market research and strategies in all phases of business, including the food industry, cannot be overemphasized.

By all means go ahead with your printing of the program. In the meantime, I assume you will send more details—place, time, length of my presentation, and the number you expect to attend. Might I ask for the name of the outstanding student selected and a brief "history" of her or his achievements?

Cordially yours,

31-2 Saying "No" to a Request for Support

Situation   A letter to Kenneth Burton arrives from Theodore Dennison, who represents an organization called Parents for Library Censorship. Dennison wants permission to show Burton's name in the organization's letterhead and other printed materials as a supporter.

Roberta Hicks knows how Burton feels about strict censorship of various institutions and organizations. Indeed, Burton recently spoke out hotly about the evils of censorship to a parent-teachers group. To save Burton's time, Hicks answers the letter for Burton's signature.

The Letter   Dear Mr. Dennison:

No, Mr. Dennison, I emphatically refuse to give you permission to use my name as a supporter for Parents for Library Censorship. Obviously you and your members feel justified in your attempts to ban from the public library books with which you quarrel. At the same time, I feel just as strongly that no one person or organization has the right to determine what is "suitable" literature for other people.

I spoke out very strongly against library censorship at a recent parent-teachers meeting, and I will do likewise when I have the opportunity.

Very truly yours,

31–3   Writing a Major Stockholder

Situation

Mrs. Estelle Weems, a major stockholder in Family Foods, Inc., writes Mr. Burton (addressing him as "Ken"), requesting that the company match her contribution of $200,000 toward a center for the performing arts in Russellville, Arkansas. She describes the need for such a center and the contribution it would make to the community.

Of all business letters, none is more difficult than one in response to a major stockholder, especially when the stockholder asks for money for various causes. Knowing this, Roberta Hicks prepares a rough draft of a response, double spaced, and not set up in pure letter form, to make it easy for Burton to edit the letter.

The Rough Draft Letter

Dear Estelle:

I'm grateful for your letter, which arrived today.

Regarding your suggestion that Family Foods, Inc. match your $200,000 in behalf of a center for the performing arts in Russellville, Arkansas, I will have to delay a definite response. As you may know, we have a Donations Committee that has the responsibility for distributing monies to worthy causes, and usually top management defers to the judgment of this group. In this particular instance, I suspect the Committee will suggest that the matter be taken up by the Board of Directors, since the amount is so large.

I will take the first step immediately with the Donations Committee. If their reaction is what I predict, I will pursue your proposal with the Board of Directors, which meets September 5. I am sorry there will be some delay in getting back to you, but I have no recourse.

My best wishes to you, Estelle. I do hope you plan to attend the stockholders' meeting on September 25. If so, I look forward to seeing you there.

Very sincerely yours,

31–4 Suggesting an Alternate Speaker

Situation

The Distributive Education Clubs of America (DECA), an organization of students who are preparing to enter the field of distribution, is holding its national convention in Boston on September 3–5. The young president, Jeanette Mills, writes Mr. Burton, inviting him to be the banquet speaker at the convention on the topic, "Distribution in the Electronic Age." Burton is well acquainted with DECA and has a high regard for the organization. He is honored at the invitation, but he will be in Canada the week of September 3 and cannot accept the invitation. He suggests, however, that the Director of Long-Range Planning for Family Foods, Clarence Wharton, might be a good choice. Wharton is a dynamic speaker and is deeply involved in market research. Burton has talked with Wharton, and he is available on September 3. Roberta Hicks writes Jeanette Mills, for Burton's signature, sending Wharton a blind copy of the letter.

The Letter

Dear Miss Mills:

I am greatly honored to be invited to be the banquet speaker at DECA's annual convention on September 3–5. I am very familiar with the work of DECA and have great admiration for the organization (I have spoken before numerous DECA groups). Unfortunately for me, I will be out of the country the entire week of September 3 and will not be able to be with you.

May I suggest an alternate? Our Director of Long-Range Planning, Clarence Wharton, with whom I have spoken about your invitation, would be delighted to address your group. I can assure you that Mr. Wharton is a fine speaker and knows as much as, if not more than, I about distribution in the electronic age. If you are interested in pursuing this suggestion, I recommend that you write directly to Mr. Wharton at this address. If you have someone else in mind, he will understand, as will I.

I hope your convention is the best you could possibly hope for!

Sincerely yours,

bcc: Clarence Wharton

31-5

Situation

Marilyn Garvey is Administrative Assistant to the President of Keystone University, Pamela Moore. Moore gave a commencement speech at the University of Fort Lauderdale in May. Shortly thereafter, Dr. Moore received a highly complimentary letter about the speech from the Dean of Students, along with a check for $500. Garvey writes a response for Pamela Moore.

The Letter

Dear Betha:

You were very generous in your comments about my address at the University of Fort Lauderdale Commencement. To tell you the truth, I enjoyed expounding on my "learning is forever" theme much more than anyone in the audience could have enjoyed hearing about it from me. A great group of graduates (how proud you must be of them!), a distinguished faculty, and overwhelming hospitality—what more could a commencement speaker ask for?

I am returning your check for $500, not because I don't appreciate the generous gesture, but because I think the money can be put to much better use—in one of your scholarship funds, perhaps. But I'll leave the decision to you.

Thank you for the many courtesies while I was in Fort Lauderdale. It was an experience that I will long remember.

Sincerely yours,

31–6   Thanking a Reader for Favorable Comments

Situation

Edward Benjamin, Director of Public Relations for Capital Cities Forest Industries, recently ran a series of advertisements in several national publications. The responses to these ads have been highly favorable. Benjamin decides to write a form letter to answer the accolades that have been received. He asks his assistant, Edwin Coulter, to draft a reply for his examination.

The Letter

Dear Ms. Parkinson:

You were very thoughtful to write praising our series of ads in several national magazines. I am delighted, of course, that you enjoy these pieces and find them provocative and stimulating. This is exactly what we and our advertising agency had in mind when the series was planned.

Your suggestion that we give more emphasis to creatures of the wild is very appropriate. We are now planning six ads that will emphasize the importance of protecting our wildlife, especially endangered species. Watch for them, and, if you have time, give us your impression of these ads.

Thanks for writing. Your letter boosted our spirits!

Cordially yours,

Part 12

EMPLOYEE RELATIONS LETTERS

In our anxiety to please customers and other people of influence, we often overlook the fact that the employees in the company are the most important "public" of all. Although executives are quick to praise, congratulate, and express appreciation to outsiders, the idea of doing the same for employees rarely occurs to some.

One of the most important rewards an employee can receive costs nothing: recognition of achievement. This can be done face to face (preferably when others are present). But on certain occasions, nothing is so meaningful to an employee as a letter from the boss or fellow employees that says he or she deserves applause. Conversations and public announcements are appreciated, to be sure, but they are fleeting. Words on paper are tangible and permanent; they can be shared with family and friends and read and reread by the recipients when they need a lift.

Section 32

Letters of Congratulation and Appreciation

Obviously, you don't write letters of congratulation and appreciation to employees for simply doing what they are paid and expected to do. Such letters should be reserved for very special achievements and outstanding performance. The problem arises in determining what is special or outstanding. There are a few people who constantly dazzle their superiors with their ideas, innovations, and productivity, and if you wrote them every time they did something creditable, your letters would soon lose meaning. Although you would certainly tell them in person when they've pleased you, write them only when their achievement falls in the "spectacular" category.

It is the more typical employee—the one who does her or his job well and is only faintly visible to those on the upper rungs of management—to whom a congratulatory letter is truly meaningful when it is really deserved. And you have to define the word *deserved* in terms of the employee. What might be a run-of-the-mill accomplishment for a truly gifted and productive employee could be a grand-slam homer for the average worker. A congratulatory message to a good, solid, unspectacular employee can have a double benefit: It should lift your spirits to have written it, and you may get increased productivity from the worker because of an uplift in morale.

There are occasions, however, when nearly every employee deserves a written congratulation from the boss: upon an anniversary with the company, for recognition achieved outside the company, and on an important promotion.

The guidelines for such letters are quite simple:

1. *They should be warm and friendly.*
2. *They should be very specific about the achievement or occasion being acknowledged.*
3. *They should be believable—that is, not grossly exaggerated.*

32–1 Congratulating an Employee on a Job Well Done

Situation

Louise Kemper, Personnel Vice President, writes a letter of appreciation to Christopher Langan, an employee in the Data Processing Division who has served effectively as chairperson of the New Employee Orientation Committee during the past year.

The Letter

Dear Chris:

Thank you for serving as head of the New Employee Orientation Committee during the past year.

Under your leadership, our employee orientation program has become the most effective instrument we have for educating new people about the company—its past, present, and future; its people, policies, and procedures; its high standing in the industry. I'm confident that new people now adapt more quickly to their new environment and bring to their jobs a good feeling about Boughton's—so important to morale and productivity.

I have been especially pleased at the variety of your programs, the professional yet interesting manner in which the speakers brought off their presentations, the effective use of visual devices, and your allowance for participation by the new employees themselves.

You ran a good show, Chris, and I am deeply grateful.

My best to you,

cc. J. R. Dykman

[Christopher's boss]

32–2   Congratulating an Employee on a New Management Concept

Situation

In visiting the suburban warehousing and distribution center located about 30 miles from the home office, the company president is impressed by the way in which the operations Vice President (also housed in the home office) has established communication between headquarters and suburban-based employees. The president writes to compliment the Operations Vice President on the idea and tell him how well it is working.

The Letter

Dear Morrie:

I enjoyed sitting in on your new Joint Management Group get-together at Industrial Park on Tuesday.

I learned a lot from the experience. I realized perhaps for the first time how important it is for home-office brass to make themselves available to employees who labor in warehousing and shipping—miles from the home office—and have up to now been sort of invisible.

Surely this new committee, with its monthly get-together, smooths the lines of communication and gives those in the hinterlands a feeling of importance and belonging. It was easy to see that a lot of problems can be quickly solved when there is complete candor in an informal setting. Everyone seemed to feel free to unload his or her pet peeves without fear of recrimination. Now *that's* communication!

The plant tour was a treat, too. After it was over, I came away feeling that the employees at Industrial Park know we know what they are doing and how well it is being done.

Congratulations, Morrie, on this idea. I hope you'll invite me another time. Can we have pizza and beer again for lunch?

Yours sincerely,

32–3 Congratulating an Employee for an Outstanding Report

Situation

The executive vice president of Engineering Resources, Inc. receives a very impressive report from a fairly new employee (an engineer) in which she proposes a new potential market for the company. He writes to offer congratulations for the excellent report and emphasize its importance to the company.

The Letter

Dear Clarissa:

Congratulations on the report, "Energy Management—A New Market for Engineering Resources, Inc."

Although I have been seeing a good deal in the trade press recently about the growth of building energy consulting, I was not really aware that the demand was so explosive. Yet your report makes perfectly clear that this is a logical development in a period of economic slowdown and escalating fuel costs. I especially enjoyed the reprints you supplied of articles from leading business papers and professional journals.

The conclusions and recommendations in your report deserve very careful study, and I am sending copies to all the members of the development and planning group for their reactions. Later this month I will schedule an all-day meeting with these people at the Olympic Club. I want you to be there, and I will let you know the date and time. For the moment, I suggest that you jot down October 26 on your calendar as a tentative date.

Sincerely,

32–4

Congratulating an Employee on an Anniversary

Situation

Martha Olson joined Atlantic Mills 15 years ago as a Secretary to the Director of Purchasing. After five years she was promoted to Assistant Director, and when her boss retired four years later, she was named Director. On the occasion of her fifteenth anniversary, a special luncheon is being held in her honor and hosted by the president. Immediately following the luncheon, the president wants to congratulate Olson again, this time by means of a personal letter (not a memorandum).

The Letter

Dear Marty:

I meant what I said at the luncheon yesterday: I really can't remember when Marty Olson was *not* our director of purchasing. Six years isn't that long, but you have filled your role so competently and all of us have relied on you with such confidence that it is hard to separate the name from the function.

But you have won our esteem for personal as well as professional attributes. You have that wonderful gift of gaining friends and loyal supporters while maintaining the highest standards of purchasing management, and few are blessed with it.

As we continue to grow, the purchasing function will have an increasingly important role at Atlantic Mills. I hope you anticipate the challenge; certainly, there's no doubt that you will rise to it.

Warm personal regards,

32–5   Congratulating a New Member of the Twenty-Five-Year Club

Situation Robbins Metals Corporation honors employees who have worked for the company for 25 years by inducting them into its Twenty-Five-Year Club. It's a gala occasion, held in a hotel ballroom, at which inductees are presented with an engraved silver bowl. Just as soon as an employee's eligibility is announced—prior to the dinner and induction ceremonies—the president writes a letter of congratulation to honor the employee and express appreciation for loyal service.

The Letter Dear Sidney:

I consider it a distinct privilege to congratulate you on the completion of 25 years at Robbins Metals Corporation and to invite you to become a member of the Twenty-Five-Year Club.

As far as I am concerned, there is no group as important, for it is they who have contributed the most to our growth and our good name. I hope you look back on those years with great satisfaction and pride. It's a grand achievement, and I want you to know how much I personally appreciate your loyalty and confidence.

Shortly you will receive an invitation to the annual Twenty-Five-Year Club Dinner at which you will be formally inducted. I look forward to seeing you there and congratulating you in person on becoming a member of this very exclusive group.

Sincerely,

32–6

Congratulating an Employee for Community Recognition

Situation   The owner of a small manufacturing company in a resort area learns that an employee has been elected president of the local Chamber of Commerce. The owner writes the employee to extend congratulations and offer support.

The Letter   Dear Julie:

I've just heard the good news that you have been elected president of the Ocean Isles Chamber of Commerce. Congratulations!

During the few years the Chamber has been in existence, it has done a remarkable job of attracting new industry, professional people, tourists, and retirees to this community. And now that you're president, I expect the Chamber to achieve even bigger things during the next three years.

The Chamber has always had our support, but our resolve is now stronger than ever to contribute to its growth and success. Best wishes and good luck.

Sincerely,

32-7 Writing a Letter of Congratulation to the Boss

Situation   Stanley Fontana, formerly Assistant Personnel Manager of Consolidated Supply Corporation, was recently promoted to the position of Vice President and Personnel Director. He received several letters of congratulation, and the following is typical. It came from the Supervisor of Recruitment and Placement in the Personnel Division.

The Letter   Dear Stan:

Your elevation to Vice President and Personnel Director was great news! Although the announcement was no surprise, count me among those who yelled "Hallelujah!" when the news became official.

I'm not only pleased about this advancement for you. I'm also happy that the Personnel Division has come to mean so much to the company that its new titular head has been awarded the title of Vice President.

You must know how I feel about this, Stan. I really enjoy working with you; you're one in a million when it comes to imagination, ideas, and human relationships. You're responsible for my being in the company, and I've never regretted the decision to join you.

                                        Sincerely,

32-8

Responding to Congratulations on a Promotion

Situation   See Letter 32–7 on the preceding page.

The Letter   Dear Pauline:

I can't think of anyone I'd rather have a letter from on my promotion than you.

You mentioned my influence that led you to join Overstreet-Wilson in 1990. Well, I'm very proud that I can claim credit for that valuable acquisition. I don't honestly know how I could do without you.

Thank you, Pauline, for your very thoughtful letter.

Yours,

Section 33

Letters on Retirement

To most people, retirement after many years of employment is a joyous occasion. Not that they haven't enjoyed their work, but they look forward to a different lifestyle and the freedom to do pretty much as they please without pressures, fixed routines, or deadlines.

A few would rather stay on the job for as long as they live. They like what they do, think they are as productive as they were forty years ago, and can't imagine occupying themselves without working. Some are forced into early retirement for health reasons.

In any event, all retirees like to receive letters from fellow employees acknowledging their accomplishments and telling them how much they will be missed.

33–1

Congratulating an Employee on Retirement—A Happy Occasion

Situation

The financial Vice President of Watson-Ferguson Corporation, an employee for 45 years, retires. He is honored at a special retirement party. The president of the company wants to follow up with a personal letter to offer congratulations and express warm appreciation.

The Letter

Dear Herb:

I was a mite surprised at the gift presented to you on the occasion of your retirement party—a really beautiful set of golf clubs. I happen to know that you are not a golfer, and when I asked someone about the gift, the answer was: "That's what Sheila said Herb wanted most of all. He doesn't play now, but he's determined to learn."

Of course, I shouldn't be surprised. You've been constantly pursuing new challenges throughout your 45 years at Watson-Ferguson, and I can't think of one that you didn't master. It's that fierce determination—tempered with a delightful Hoosier wit and practical-mindedness—that has made you such an outstanding financial executive. Why not golf, indeed!

We will miss you, naturally, but our gloom is brightened somewhat by our vision of your chasing the little white ball all over Hilton Head Island. That, by the way, sounds like a lot more fun than juggling debentures and arguing with security analysts.

Muriel joins me in wishing for you and Sheila many happy years in the Sun Belt. Be sure to drop in on the folks here at W-F when you get to Cleveland.

Best personal regards,

33–2 Extending Good Wishes to a Reluctant Retiree

Situation

Edwin Millspaugh, 70, is being retired by his company. It is not a happy event for him; he is one of those who believe that no one should be forced to retire as long as he or she is productive. However, company policy requires this action. His immediate boss, the Controller, writes a letter to express appreciation for past service and extend warm wishes for the future.

The Letter

Dear Edwin:

I know that you're not especially thrilled to be retiring at the tender age of 70, so I won't congratulate you. But I do want to express my appreciation to you.

You can always look back with pride and satisfaction on your 47 years at Gemstrand. No one knows more about manufacturing cost control than you, Edwin, and I can recall hundreds of occasions when your sharp pencil and keen mind guided us in making intelligent decisions. You have been a valuable ally and friend.

I hope you will find new and exciting ways to use your know-how, Edwin. We will certainly miss you, and I extend to you every good wish for health, happiness, and satisfaction in the years ahead.

Cordially,

33–3

Writing an Employee Retiring for Health Reasons

Situation

Patricia Brogden has been in charge of the library at McKinsey and Knoblett ever since it was set up 22 years ago. Recently she has been in poor health, and she has been advised by her doctor to seek a dry climate. She has resigned and plans to live in Arizona. Her immediate superior, the Director of Personnel Services, writes her a letter shortly before her departure to express regret on the condition of her health, review her accomplishments, and extend best wishes for the future.

The Letter

Dear Patricia:

I have already told you how distressed I am that, because of health, your doctor has persuaded you to move to a mild, dry climate. The only satisfaction I can get from this development is that where you're going, you'll be a lot more comfortable and stand a good chance of full recovery. That's the important thing; the great void your leaving creates here must not even be considered.

Some people say that those who leave a company are quickly forgotten, and I guess that's true in some instances—but *not* in your case, Patricia. You've made such an imprint here by establishing and operating one of the most respected professional libraries in the country that your presence will be felt for many years to come. My association with you has been one of the genuine rewards of working at McKinsey and Knoblett.

I hope and expect that you will find living in Arizona truly delightful. I have a suspicion that when your health permits, you may look for an opportunity to use your expertise in librarianship in that area. If you do, I would be honored to have you use my name as reference.

Warmest personal wishes,

Section 34

Letters of Sympathy

Among the most difficult messages to convey are those that try to console people who have experienced tragedy. Almost anything one can say seems trite because, no matter how sincere the writer is, grief is such a personal thing that only time can erase it. Yet to completely ignore the suffering of close friends seems heartless and uncaring.

Today, most people express their sympathy by means of a personal visit to the bereaved—either in the office or the home—where a physical gesture can be much more consoling than words. Some people send the bereaved a modest gift—a potted plant, a book, and so on—accompanied by a note such as "We loved her too," or "Jack was very special to me, and I will miss him." Printed cards that also contain a personal message are sometimes used.

There are occasions, however, when nothing but a personal letter seems suitable. Only you will know what these occasions are.

Here are four guidelines for writing letters of condolence:

1. *Express your sorrow briefly; a torrent of sympathetic words can make things worse.*

2. *Recall happy personal experiences about the deceased, but don't be maudlin.*

3. *Reveal by some modest gesture your willingness to be of help or comfort.*

4. *Always use personal stationery—never a company letterhead—and write the message by hand.*

34-1

Death of an Immediate Supervisor and Close Friend

Situation

Assume that your immediate supervisor passes away. His death was not unexpected—he had been seriously ill for months. You felt very close to him for many reasons, and you feel compelled to write a letter of condolence to his window, also a personal friend.

The Letter

Dear Sarah:

Larry's death has saddened me beyond words. Although not totally unexpected, it is still hard for me to accept.

I'm sure you know, Sarah, the enormous influence Larry had on me personally and on my career. He was the first person every to say to me: "Carl, you have a special gift. I'm going to do all I can to see that it is developed to its fullest." He then proceeded to do just that, and during our eight years together, he never lost faith in me and was, of course, largely responsible for the success I have achieved.

I suppose most successful people somewhere along the line were singled out by a wise and generous mentor who guided and shaped their careers. Mine was Larry. I shall miss his counsel. Indeed, I do already. Every time I have a hard problem to solve, I ask myself, "What would Larry have done?"

I hope, Sarah, that Emily and I can continue our friendship with you. If ever you feel the need to get away for a quiet rest, our little cottage on Sequoia Lake (which I'm sure you remember) is always open to you. I've had a key made for you, and it is enclosed.

Affectionate regards,

34-2 Sympathy on the Event of a Serious Illness

Situation

Robert Harrell, age 45, is assistant to the president of a medium-size company. Rob is a demon for work—one of those who burn the candle at both ends. Recently he has had a heart attack and is in the hospital. Early reports seem encouraging, but Rob's condition remains serious. The president writes Mrs. Harrell both to express concern and try to ease some of the worries she may be experiencing.

The Letter

Dear Kitty:

I was shocked and distressed to learn of Rob's heart attack, and I won't rest easy until I learn of his full recovery.

Knowing Rob, I suspect that when he surmounts this crisis, he will be champing at the bit to get back to his job here. But you mustn't let him. Although his presence will be sorely missed, we'll find a way to cover his desk while he is away—perhaps not nearly as well as he would like, but as best we can. Please insist that he follow the doctor's prescribed routine for convalescence, with no thought for any other responsibility he may feel. We want him back, of course, but not until the doctor says he *should* return. In the meantime, Rob will remain on full salary and benefits.

Kitty, please let me know when it is permissible for Rob to have visitors. I want to see him. Now, is there anything I can do for *you*?

Affectionately,

34–3

Serious Injury of a Close Friend and Employee and Her Family

Situation

Myra Biggers has just learned of an automobile accident involving her good friend, Frances McKinsey, and her parents, and writes a letter of sympathy.

The Letter

Dear Fran:

I was greatly shocked by the news of the automobile accident involving you and your parents. Of course, I wouldn't be writing this letter if I thought you were too incapacitated to read it, but the word I get is encouraging for your family and Emily and Claude. Triple good news!

Since you're going to be in traction for quite a spell, I'm gathering an armload of paperbacks that I think you'll enjoy and delivering them to the hospital for you. I'll be seeing you in person as soon as the hospital staff will let me.

You are missed at the salt mines, but we're doubling up to handle your work. I hope you can straighten out our goofs when you get back! All your friends are asking about you, and I plan to keep in touch with the hospital so that I can relay the latest news on your recovery.

Good luck to you (and to Emily and Claude too)!

With love,

Section 35

Letters of Recommendation

Often, you will be asked to supply information about former employees who have applied for positions after leaving your company. Some response letters will be a genuine pleasure to write because the former worker can be highly recommended in all respects. Even letters about former employees who were very satisfactory on most counts are no problem; you simply emphasize their strengths and mention only casually (if at all) any minor weaknesses.

In this section, we present two letters in response to requests for information about former employees, the first an unqualified recommendation and the second a recommendation with a slight qualification.

35–1

Unqualified Recommendation of a Former Employee

Situation   For five years Edwin Woodiak was a copywriter in the Advertising Department of Riegelwood Distributors. A little over a year ago he resigned to join an advertising agency. As Manager of the Advertising Department of Riegelwood, you receive an inquiry from Newell, Inc., about Woodiak, who has applied for the job of Assistant Advertising Manager. Woodiak has a fine record, and you want to give him a hearty recommendation.

The Letter   Dear Mrs. Needleman:

Edwin Woodiak was a copywriter at Riegelwood Distributors for five years under my direct supervision.

I considered Woodiak an excellent employee. He handled all his assignments with imagination and style and, so far as I can remember, never missed a deadline. An extremely likable young man, he had many friends here. He left Riegelwood of his own free will, believing that agency work would be more exciting and offer greater opportunities. I was genuinely sorry to see him go.

I heartily recommend Edwin Woodiak to you. I would readily rehire him if a suitable vacancy arose.

Cordially yours,

35–2

Qualified Recommendation of a Former Employee

Situation L. Richard Maxwell, Sales Manager for a national sporting goods manufacturer, has received an inquiry from the marketing director a chain of clothing stores concerning a former employee, Craig Halliburton. The position Halliburton applied for is Director of Sales Training. Although he had an excellent record as a member of Maxwell's department, his experience in training was somewhat limited.

The Letter Dear Mr. Maxwell:

I am pleased to write in behalf of Craig Halliburton, who has applied to your company for the position of National Sales Training Director.

Craig joined our organization in 1983 as our sales representative for the state of Arkansas. He quickly proved highly effective in selling, and, during the three years he was in this territory, sales increased nearly 20 percent. He had a special gift for building customer loyalty, and I received many letters of appreciation from these people for his services.

In 1985 Craig was promoted to the position of Field Manager, with the responsibility for recruiting, training, and supervising eleven sales representatives in Arkansas, Oklahoma, and southern Missouri. He was equally effective in his job, and we saw a very bright future for him. When the southwest regional manager's position became vacant because of a retirement, Craig applied for it. However, he was not chosen for it because we felt that another of our field managers, who had a good deal more experience in management and an outstanding track record in selling, was the more logical candidate. Not long afterward, Craig resigned to accept a sales position with a competing company, where he felt he would have greater opportunities for growth. We were very sorry to lose him; he is an outstanding young man—intelligent, personable, hard-working, and persuasive.

I am not familiar with the requirements of your position, so I cannot speak with any authority about Craig's ability to administer a company-wide sales training program. He did some training, of course, in his field manager's job with us, and he was extremely good at it. I suspect the chances are very good that, even though Craig may lack an in-depth knowledge of training methods at present, he would in time be able to assume the responsibilities of national sales training director very effectively.

Cordially yours,

Section 36

Unfavorable Reference Letters and Warnings to Employees

One of the most difficult letters to write is one in response to a company's request for your opinion of a former employee whom you rate very low. This can present a real dilemma. If you say exactly what you think, you will almost certainly destroy the applicant's chances for a job that he or she may desperately need. Equally serious is that existing federal laws make it mandatory that employees be given the right to see everything in their personnel files, and a defamatory letter could result in a suit against the former employer.

Before there was a federal law about such matters, many employers felt it their duty to be completely truthful about unsatisfactory employees and expected the same candor from other employers. Today, however, many personnel administrators strongly recommend that only basic data be supplied in writing to those who request information about unsatisfactory employees—dates of employment, job title(s), and salary at the time of departure. If further information is required, they contend, it can be obtained by telephone.

In this section, we give an illustration of a letter that the former employer felt had to be written in spite of the cautions outlined above. It is not a recommendation, yet it is not a particularly harsh condemnation. You can be the judge as to whether the writer did the right thing.

Occasionally, you will have an employee whose job performance is not satisfactory, and you have almost reached the conclusion that the worker must be dismissed. In some companies there is a policy that no one can be fired without first warning him or her that such action is contemplated. An example of such a letter is also included in this section.

36–1

Responding to a Request for Information About an Unsatisfactory Former Employee

Situation

Charles Edwards worked in the mailroom of a large firm for nearly two years. He was a genuine problem to the supervisor—he often arrived late and left early, was absent a good deal, and showed no interest in his work. The supervisor's talks with him were not productive, and she was eventually forced to let him go. A few weeks after Charles leaves, the supervisor receives an inquiry about Charles from a company to which he has applied for a job.

The Letter

Dear Mrs. Kimberly:

Charles Edwards worked under my supervision in the Mail Department of Atkinson-Trickett Company for nearly two years (1992–1994).

Although a cheerful and popular young man, Charles showed very little interest in his work, and I was forced to talk with him many times about his tardiness and absences, and his poor work habits and general attitude. I finally concluded that there was no way for me to motivate him and suggested that he find another job.

Perhaps, given another type of work in which he is genuinely interested, Charles would succeed. He is very bright, and perhaps that was the problem here—the work did not challenge him.

Yours very truly,

36-2 Warning Letter to an Employee

Situation

Philip Moore is Administrative Assistant to an executive in a large corporation. Although highly competent, he has one bad fault: He can't keep secrets. He has been warned repeatedly about his indiscretions, but leaks continue to occur. The most recent incident proved to be very serious, and he was called into his boss's office and read the riot act. The boss writes a letter that tactfully warns the employee that he is in danger of losing his job.

The Letter

Dear Phil:

During the three years we have worked together, I have been much impressed with your job competence. You have shown a remarkable talent in managing this office, freeing me of paperwork and people interruptions so that I could spend most of my time on long-range planning for the company. I have looked upon you as an invaluable assistant and confidant.

It would appear, however, that my use of the word "confidant" is gratuitous. During the past several months, you and I have discussed numerous leaks of confidential information, and you were always courageous enough to tell the truth. Up to this point, these indiscretions were merely embarrassing to me—the damage was slight and no one was really hurt. However, the latest episode, involving an acquisition, is much too serious to pass off. Advance knowledge of our plans by certain individuals has severely hampered negotiations and has put us in a bidding situation for which we are likely to pay a heavy price. Indeed, it is not unlikely that we will remove ourselves from contention.

You and I discussed this thoroughly in my office yesterday. I accept your statement that the leaked information seemed safe since it involved only one person—a department manager—and that you had no way of knowing that the individual was on the verge of leaving the company to join a competitor. But even so, Phil, a confidence is a confidence, and a person in your position should know by now that he can have *no* intimate friends when it comes to dispensing highly private information.

It is with great reluctance that I inform you that if such a happening recurs—no matter how harmless it may appear to you—you will be asked immediately to submit your resignation.

Sincerely,

36-3 Terminating an Employee by Letter

Situation

John Coover is a sales engineer for a manufacturer of microprocessor-based communication systems, calling on customers in three southwestern states to help them with any installation or service problems they may have. Although a knowledgeable engineer, Coover has proved to be undependable in covering the territory assigned him. He often fails to show up for important appointments or to send in the itinerary that he is required to submit each week to his superior, Jeffrey Forstner. Forstner has talked with Coover many times and received the assurances asked for, but the situation has not improved. Two months ago, Forstner wrote Coover a warning letter. Recently a situation arose in which it made clear that Coover is not going to shape up, and Forstner decides to terminate his employment. However, he has been unable to reach Coover by telephone and writes to him at his home address.

The Letter

Dear John:

I have tried several times to reach you by telephone, but have been unsuccessful. Thus I am writing to you at home.

This is notification of your termination from the company effective March 10. You and I have talked several times about your problem in covering your territory properly, John. Each time you gave me assurances that you would shape up and do the job you were hired to do. Yet last week I had clear indications that you have again violated your promise to me.

Your itinerary shows that you were to be in the Albuquerque area last week, calling on customers and staying at the Best Western Capri. Three dealers in that area who had been expecting you telephoned me to say that you did not show up. All have had serious complaints from customers about the malfunctioning of the Telemaster III communication system and desperately need professional help. When I telephoned the Best Western Capri (every day last week), I was told that you had not registered and there was no record of a reservation. Today, I asked Maurice Taylor in Phoenix to fly to Albuquerque to visit three dealers and try to solve their problem.

I am sorry, John, that this action is necessary, but I am certain that under the circumstances you will agree that I have no alternative. You will, of course, receive the standard two weeks' severance pay. Indeed, I have already requisitioned a check for you, which will be sent to your home when it is ready.

Sincerely,

Part 13

JOB-GETTING LETTERS AND OTHER EMPLOYMENT COMMUNICATIONS

Some fortunate people don't have to extend themselves much to land their first job. If they specialized in college or graduate school in a field in which the demand for people far exceeds the supply, they may have only the problem of choosing between job offers. Others are channeled into good positions by influential friends and relatives. Some simply join the family business. Most people, however, have to scramble a bit for that first job, against others who are after the same thing.

But for both groups—the shoo-ins and the scramblers—knowing how to sell oneself on paper can be enormously important. True, some people settle happily into their first job and stay with the company forever. On the other hand, people change jobs rather frequently, and the reasons vary. They don't like the company they work for, or they don't get the promotions they think they deserve, or their bosses don't allow them freedom to innovate, or they get laid off for economic reasons. Others change jobs simply because they find a better opportunity elsewhere.

Chances are good, then, that no matter how happy you are in your present setup or how rosy the future looks, you'll one day need to know how to present your employment credentials in the best possible light. That's the main purpose of this part.

Section 37

Job-Getting Communications

Aside from an employer's own application form, two basic documents are often required to obtain a job of some stature: the résumé and the letter of application.

The Résumé

Vital to your job-searching campaign is a good résumé—that is, a summary of your qualifications. (Some people call it a data sheet.) Although somewhat formal in setup—mainly for quick reading and reference purposes—the résumé is essentially a sales instrument. By this we mean that you emphasize in it those events and accomplishments that make you look good to a prospective employer. While the résumé is not a razzle-dazzle document (except for certain people in the creative arts who choose to make it so), neither is it merely a condensed biographical sketch of your life and work. It is an interesting profile of your best side.

We mentioned earlier that there is no magic formula you can use to produce an effective letter for every occasion. Most of the letters you write must be tailored to fit the particular situation you are faced with. The same is true of a résumé. Although a model will be helpful (we show four excellent résumés in this section), it's not likely that any one is just right for you. You should feel free to make whatever adjustments are needed to best tell *your* story.

Every good résumé contains four basic parts:

1. *A heading*
2. *Experience (a description of the jobs you've held)*
3. *Education (degrees, major courses taken, special training, etc.)*
4. *References (a short list of people whom an employer can contact for information about you)*

Some job applicants use additional headings, and we'll talk about those later.

To illustrate these four basic parts, let's imagine that you are very much interested in the following job that was advertised in a large-city newspaper:

DIRECTOR OF PUBLICITY for a large corporation. Minimum of three years' experience in publicity, public relations, or a related field required. Must have college degree, preferably in journalism. Position requires heavy writing and ability to deal effectively with all media. Excellent salary and benefits. Send résumé to Box 000, *Times*. An equal opportunity employer.

Although relatively brief, the above ad says a great deal. You will study the job requirements very carefully; then you can start to put together a résumé that matches what you have to offer with the job requirements.

The Heading Give your résumé a heading. It will usually contain your name, address, telephone number, and the position you are applying for. Some applicants also include the name of the company to which they are applying.

It's up to you whether you give the résumé itself a title. It isn't really necessary, since the information presented is self-identifying. Here are three examples.

EDWIN R. COULTER
225 Normandy Village
Shreveport, Louisiana 71104
(318) 865-7544

Position applied for: Director of Publicity

Qualifications of
JANET LEE FELDER
Old Lyme Road
Northbrook, VT 05663
(802) 264-5911

for the position of <u>Systems Analyst</u>
Brighton Industries Inc.

JOB RÉSUMÉ
of
P.L. Quackenbush
2160 Shelter Island Drive
San Diego, California 92106
(714) 622-9178
<u>Position desired</u>: Controller

If you're applying "blind"—that is, you don't know whether there is an opening that matches your job preference—you won't know what precise position title to use. Some people believe that naming a specific job on a blind résumé lessens their chances of being hired if that particular position doesn't exist or isn't available. They feel that if they merely indicate a general field of interest, they may find just what they want, even though it doesn't carry the title they had in mind. There is nothing wrong with this, but we think you should come as close as you can to identifying your special interest. For example:

Not: Position desired: Advertising Department
But: Position desired: Advertising Assistant (copywriting, layout, etc.)

Not: Position desired: Personnel work
But: Position desired: Personnel recruitment, placement, training

Not: Position desired: Public relations
But: Position desired: Public relations (with a special interest in publications)

Of course, if you're answering an ad that names a specific job or you're applying at the suggestion of someone who knows about a vacancy, use the title specified.

Experience

Generally, your first side head is "experience." (There are two exceptions: when you have little or no experience related to the job you are applying for and when your educational background is far more impressive than your experience. In these instances, your first heading will be "education.")

Experience is mentioned as the first (and probably chief) requirement in the want-ad on page 313, and assuming you feel you meet the requirement, start there. List the jobs you've held (with dates), starting with your present position and working backward. Describe the duties of each job—that is, what you actually did. Here is where your tailoring really begins. When you outline your duties, use every opportunity to capitalize on publicity—the job you're after. Even if most of your experience has been in, say, sales promotion, you can emphasize the publicity aspects of your work (many jobs in sales promotion involve some general publicity). We don't mean that you should fake experience you don't have. We simply encourage you to focus on any relevant experience you *do* have.

Note that the ad mentions heavy writing responsibility. Among your duties in your previous job(s), be sure to mention the volume and type of writing you were required to do.

What about the phrase, "and ability to deal effectively with all media"? If any of your job duties included contact with media representatives, you will certainly say so. For example: "Was responsible for writing all releases on new products and distributing them to the media (often by means of press conferences)."

If you can't glean any media experience from your work experience (or even if you can), you may want to list memberships you hold in organizations that have some relationship to media—an advertising club, public relations group, and so on. Be sure to include any offices you may have held in such organizations.

Education

After you've made the most of your job experience, turn to the second major area—education. First, indicate your degree, the institution that awarded it, and the year. Then, indicate your major.

B.B.A. Degree, University of Mississippi, 1989
Major: Accounting

If you're light on experience in the position you're applying for but strong in educational background, you may wish to list the courses you completed that have a direct bearing on the job and any related courses that may add clout to your qualifications.

With reference to the want-ad on page 313, let's assume that you majored in journalism. Since this is what the employer prefers, you may need to say nothing further about your education.

Suppose, however, you majored in English instead of journalism. This doesn't mean that you're automatically ruled out as a candidate for the job—the ad says *"preferably* in journalism." This leaves the door open for other majors—English, personnel administration, public relations, and so on. In these instances, however, you will probably want to augment your educational history by listing any courses you took that relate to journalism or publicity—perhaps creative writing, business communications, or copywriting, and so on.

Another thing you can do under the "education" heading is describe outside college activities that relate to journalism or publicity. Perhaps you were an editor or the advertising manager of your college yearbook, or a reporter for the college newspaper, or the publicity director for the college's Spring Festival. If you did none of these things but were an active member of professional and social organizations, you might list them. While none is likely to qualify as education or experience, your participation (especially if you held office) says something about your liking for and effectiveness in mixing with people. Simply identifying yourself as a doer could help persuade the employer that you have the "ability to deal effectively with all media."

References

Finally, list three or four references, giving their courtesy title, name, position, affiliation, address, and, if possible, telephone number. Your most important references will be those for whom you have worked—supervisors, managers, and executives. However, if you're light on experience or have other reasons for not listing former employers, you can use the names of major professors and people of some distinction in your community (a judge, a government official, and possibly a minister, priest, or rabbi). *Note:* Before you list people as references on your résumé, you ought to get their permission. You can do this in person, on the telephone, or by letter. If by letter, enclose a self-addressed, stamped envelope.

If you are presently employed, you probably will not want your company to know that you are looking for another job. In that case, simply use the heading "references" and state "supplied on request." Most employers will know what you mean and will not violate your trust by contacting your present management until they have your okay. (References are usually asked for on the application blank that you fill out.)

Job-Getting Letters and Other Employment Communications

Other Headings

In some résumés you will see such headings as "special interests and achievements," "brief personal history," "statement of philosophy," and the like. If you have something really important to say under these headings, by all means go ahead.

At one time it was standard practice to include a heading called "personal data," under which was included such information as date of birth, physical characteristics (height, weight, etc.), state of health, marital status, and so on. You may do this if you wish, but the tendency is to omit this data entirely. The information you supplied earlier in the résumé will reveal all the employer needs or should want to know.

Some applicants attach a photograph to the résumé. There is nothing wrong with this—indeed it might be a good idea. But the decision is yours; an employer cannot require it.

37–1   Job Résumé—Middle-Management Position

Situation   At the annual convention of the American Association of School Administrators, Rusell Buchanan, a field sales supervisor for a book publisher, learns that Kauffman Institutional Equipment, Inc. has an opening for a regional sales manager. He decides to apply.

The Résumé

RUSSELL R. BUCHANAN
1416 Saybrook Road
Wellesley Hills, Massachusetts 02181
(617) 944-8778

QUALIFICATIONS SUMMARY

Position: Regional Sales Manager

EXPERIENCE

1992–present   Field sales supervisor, Horton-Miller Book Company. <u>Duties:</u> Selecting, training, and supervising a field sales staff of 16. Territory includes Massachusetts, New Hampshire, Vermont, and Maine. During this period, sales in the territory have increased 22 percent.

1988–1992   Sales representative, Horton-Miller Book Company, calling on teachers and administrators in western Massachusetts.

1984–1988   Head of department of business education, DeKalb (Illinois) High School. <u>Duties:</u> Supervised eleven instructors and managed the department with an enrollment of over 800 students.

1980–1984   Instructor in accounting and data processing, DeKalb High School. Also taught evening classes in accounting at Northern Illinois University.

EDUCATION

<u>Degrees</u>   B.S. In Business Education, University of Wisconsin, 1981
M.S. in Business Education, 1983

<u>Activities</u>   Member of Pi Omega Pi (undergraduate business education fraternity—served as president in junior year), Badger diving team (placed second in Big Ten meet), and Tau Kappa Epsilon (social fraternity). As a senior, I worked part-time as a grader for accounting instructors.

BRIEF PERSONAL HISTORY

When I was associated with DeKalb High School, I had frequent opportunity to meet and talk with sales representatives of various companies that supply schools with textbooks and equipment. Although I enjoyed teaching and administration, I became interested in selling because I felt it provided broader opportunities for me.

It turned out to be a wise choice—I found that I thoroughly enjoyed selling. Meeting new people constantly and providing counsel and services to the educational community was immensely rewarding. It still is. I have not lost my basic love for education, but I feel strongly that my influence is much greater in my present capacity.

In my two years as Field Sales Supervisor at Horton-Miller, I have had an excellent opportunity to exercise what I believe is my real forte: motivating sales personnel and managing a sales organization. To me, the principles of sales management are the same, whether the product is a book, a desk, or a computer system.

REFERENCES

*Mr. A. J. Sholes, Director of Marketing
Horton-Miller Book Company
2001 Aurora Boulevard
Northbrook, Illinois 60062

Dr. James C. Hightower, Principal
DeKalb High School
DeKalb, Illinois 60015

Dr. Mary C. Hornstein
Professor of Business Education
University of Wisconsin
Madison, Wisconsin 53706

*Mr. Sholes is aware of my interest in changing positions. The opportunity to become a regional manager at Horton-Miller in the near future does not appear to be favorable because of a recent restructure in the field organization.

37-2 Job Résumé—Change of Career

Situation   Dianne Seaton started as a private secretary at Livermore Manufacturing Company five years ago, and eventually moved up to Administrative Assistant to the Executive Vice President. Although she likes the work and is competent, for years she has wanted to be a teacher. Indeed, she earned her teaching credentials in college (history), but when she could not find a teaching position, she took a secretarial course in a business school and quickly landed a secretarial job.

In spite of her success in her present work, Seaton's desire to teach remains strong. During the past two years, she has been taking university extension courses in education, thinking that one day she would enter the teaching profession. She has just seen an advertisement in *The Wall Street Journal* for Supervisor of Office Training and decides to apply.

The Résumé

DIANNE SEATON
517 Park Avenue
Omaha, Nebraska 68105
(402) 862-1175

Position applied for: Supervisor of Office Training

JOB EXPERIENCE

1993–present   Administrative Assistant to the Executive Vice President, Livermore Manufacturing Company, 7400 West Center Road, Omaha, Nebraska. <u>Duties:</u> Supervise general office activities (including one secretary and one clerk-typist) and assist the Executive Vice President with such matters as writing letters and reports, doing research, planning conferences and meetings, and representing the executive in various functions, particularly when he is away from the office (very frequent).

1988–1993   Secretary to the Manufacturing Manager, Livermore Manufacturing Company. <u>Duties:</u> General secretarial activities, such as receiving visitors, managing the appointment calendar, taking and transcribing dictation, writing routine letters and reports, assisting in the preparation of analytical and statistical reports, and handling other responsibilities assigned by the manager. <u>Reason for Leaving:</u> Promoted to higher position in the company.

OTHER EXPERIENCE

1985–1988   Taught evening courses twice a week in word processing, typewriting, and business communication, Creighton University, Omaha

1981–1985   Part-time assistant in the history department of the University of South Dakota, where I graded student exams and reports and did some tutoring of freshman students.

EDUCATION

University   A.B. Degree, University of South Dakota, 1985. Major: History, Minor: Education. Honors and Activities: Dean's list three years (B+ average): Vice President of Kappa Delta Phi (history fraternity): member of Choral Ensemble; received Award of Merit in History in senior year.

Business   Diploma in secretarial administration, Yankton (SD) Business
College   College, 1984. Courses included shorthand (two semesters), typewriting (two semesters), accounting, business mathematics, business communications, and secretarial procedures.

High School   Vermillion (SD) High School; graduated in 1985. (College preparatory course. Electives included one year of typewriting and one year of business English.)

Current   During the past two years, I have taken extension courses
Studies   at Creighton University in educational media, adult education methods, and personnel administration.

SPECIAL INTERESTS

My primary avocational interests include music (since junior high school I have always been associated with one or more school and community choral groups, often as soloist) and working with brain-damaged children at hospitals and social service agencies. I am also a sports enthusiast (especially water skiing and scuba diving), play better-than-average tennis, and am learning handball.

REFERENCES

Professor H. A. Douthit
Department of History
University of South Dakota
Vermillion, South Dakota 57069

Mrs. Janette Cellars
Yankton Business College
Yankton, South Dakota 57078

Mr. Jason Carew, Principal
Vermillion High School
Vermillion, South Dakota 57609

Note: References from the two executives with whom I have been associated at Livermore Manufacturing Company will be submitted upon request. Neither is aware that I am interested in a career change at this time.

37–3   Job Résumé—High-Level Position

Situation   Frances Rosen, an executive in a large Baltimore corporation, learns from a friend that the Director of Public Relations in a large firm in the same city is retiring. She is not sure what the company's plans are in filling the position, but she decides to make application.

The Résumé

L. FRANCES ROSEN
1703 Salisbury Road
Baltimore, MD 21201

Position desired: Director of Public Relations

PROFESSIONAL EXPERIENCE

1986–present	Manager, Corporate Communications, Regent Chemical Corporation, Baltimore. <u>Duties:</u> Responsible for employee magazine and other publications, communications with stockholders, general publicity, and media relations.
1981–1986	Assistant Director of Public Relations, Marchand Manufacturing Company, Arlington, Virginia. <u>Duties:</u> Handled PR correspondence, news releases, preparation of reports to stockholders, institutional promotion (including advertising and special brochures). Also responsible for instituting and directing a school and community relations program, which included the development of educational materials, speaking before various groups, and representing the company at most civic affairs. <u>Reasons for leaving:</u> Professional and financial advancement afforded by a larger organization.
1978–1981	Editor and Publisher of *Periscope* (employee magazine), Marchand Manufacturing Company. <u>Duties:</u> Directed a staff of five in producing the magazine and distributing

it to employees and others. Also, upon request, assisted various department heads in preparing new-product information releases.

1974–1978   Administrative Assistant to the Director of Publicity, Marchand Manufacturing Company. <u>Duties:</u> Secretarial and office management, composing drafts of news releases and other publicity, and writing routine letters and reports for the director's signature.

PROFESSIONAL ACTIVITIES

Member of the Baltimore Advertising Club (Secretary-Treasurer, 1976), National Public Relations Association, Baltimore Women Executives Club, and the Board of Directors, Baltimore Symphony Orchestra. Frequent speaker at public relations conventions and contributor of articles on public relations and management communications to various trade publications.

EDUCATION

1. A.B. degree, University of Virginia, Charlottesville, 1972, with a major in journalism.
2. I have taken graduate courses (evenings) in journalism, public relations, and management communications at the University of Baltimore and Georgetown University.
3. While at the University of Virginia, I was Editor in Chief of *Daily Cavalier* for one year and a member of Gamma Theta Pi (a journalism sorority of which I was president in my senior year). I was selected the outstanding student in the School of Journalism upon graduation.

PERSONAL PHILOSOPHY

I am deeply committed to the concept that public relations is essentially education—that is, educating people in favor of one's organization—and embraces seven basic groups: the local community, employees, customers, suppliers, stockholders, the financial community, and the general public. While I believe that those engaged in public relations have the main responsibility for developing and enhancing a positive image in the eyes of the public, I feel strongly that their end objective should be company growth in terms of sales and profits.

REFERENCES

References, including Regent Chemical Corporation executives, will be supplied on request.

37-4 Job Résumé—Little Related Job Experience

Situation

When Leonard Lambeth finished college, with a major in advertising, he took a job in the university's Athletic Department, where he organized and directed miscellaneous sports, such as fishing, boat handling, hunting, and backpacking. Although Lambeth enjoyed the work, it paid very little, and he admitted to himself that he kept the job simply because he was reluctant to leave that comfortable environment and face the real world. But after three years he became restless and decided to resign and get started on a career in his chosen field. His professor of journalism, a personal friend, told him about an opening for an assistant advertising manager of *Southern Outdoorsman*, in Charleston. He decides to apply for the position.

The Résumé

> Qualifications of
>
> LEONARD B. LAMBETH
>
> As Assistant Advertising Manager
> Southern Outdoorsman

Present address:

319 Daly Street
Loris, SC 29569
(803) 271-4660

Address after August 19:

414 Maple Drive
Columbia, SC 29205
(803) 542-1151

EDUCATION

B.S. degree, University of South Carolina, Columbia, 1990
Major field of study: Advertising

Courses in Advertising
Advertising Theory and Practice
Copywriting and Layout
Advertising Art
Advertising Media
Publishing and Printing Techniques
Advertising Department Management
Advertising Research

Related Courses
Principles of Marketing
Sales Principles and Management

Marketing Statistics
Business Communications
Business Psychology

Special Electives: Newswriting, Photography, Typewriting

Honors and Extracurricular Activities
President, Angler's Club (1990); member of university golf team (1987–1988); student member of National Advertising Council, Columbia Chapter (1989–1991); advertising manager of The Gamecock (1988); and occasional staff writer for student newspaper (1988–1990).

RECENT EXPERIENCE

1990–present   Instructor, athletic department, University of South Carolina. Duties: Organized and directed miscellaneous outdoor sports, including fishing, boat handling, hunting, and archery.

OTHER EXPERIENCE

1. Sold advertising space (part-time and summers) for a small local magazine (*The Grand Strand*), Myrtle Beach, SC.
2. Clerked at the Sportman's Place, Loris, SC, in the summers of 1988–1989.
3. Worked at the Horry County *Beacon*, a weekly newspaper, in the summer of 1990 (feature writing, copy editing, proofreading, and makeup).
4. Earned money at various times repairing fishing rods (ferrules, grip, guides, and windings).

PERSONAL DATA

Height: 5 feet, 11 inches

Weight: 165 lbs.

Health: Excellent

Marital status: Single, but engaged to be married in December of this year.

REFERENCES (by permission)

1. Dr. Sophia C. Levinthal
   Professor of Journalism
   University of South Carolina

2. Mr. Patrick L Patton
   Athletic Director
   University of South Carolina

3. Mr. C. Raymond Dykstra
   Publisher
   Horry County *Beacon*
   Atlantic Beach, SC 29577

4. Mr. Harry M. Petrie (owner)
   The Sportsman's Place
   Loris, SC 29569

The Application Letter

If you have prepared a really good résumé, the hard work is done. Now you merely transmit the résumé by means of a personal letter. The main objective of both documents is to obtain an interview; few people are hired sight unseen, no matter how impressive the written description of their qualifications is. So your objective has been achieved if you get a letter or telephone call inviting you to come for an interview; it means that you looked good enough on paper to be seriously considered for the position.

People have different ideas about letters of application. Some letters are two or more pages long and loaded with self-promoting statements. Others consist of only a line or two, saying in effect, "Here's my résumé." We think something in between is best. Do not simply repeat what is in your résumé.

A good application letter, in our opinion, contains the following elements:

---

1. *How you learned about the vacancy (unless you're applying blind).*
2. *A brief statement as to why you are interested in the job and why you believe you qualify for it.*
3. *A request for a personal interview.*
4. *Information about where you can be reached.*

Caution: Do not use your company letterhead, hotel stationery, or so on. Use plain white paper of high quality, with a matching envelope. The following application letters are to accompany the four résumés illustrated earlier.

37-5

Application Letter for Middle-Management Position

Situation   See Résumé 37–1 on page 318. Russell Buchanan decides to write to the National Sales Manager of Kauffman Institutional Equipment, Inc., whose name he obtained by telephoning the company in Milwaukee.

The Letter   Dear Mr. Hewlett:

At the recent convention of the AASA in Detroit, I learned that Kauffman Institutional Equipment, Inc. has an opening for a regional sales manager. Please consider me a candidate for the job.

A summary of my qualifications is enclosed. You will see that I have had several years' experience in education (teaching and administration) and in sales and sales administration, so I feel that I know the educational community from both the inside and the outside.

Ever since I first purchased Kauffman classroom equipment and later became acquainted with a number of your representatives, I have considered the Kauffman name synonymous with quality and style. It is with such an organization that I am eager to associate myself. Although I'm not an expert on your entire line, I'm quite familiar with much of it and, frankly, I think so highly of your products that I would consider it an honor to represent your company.

A. J. Sholes, the Director of Marketing at Horton-Miller Book Company, is aware that I am making application (you will see his name on my list of references) and has said that he would welcome a call from you if you wish to know more about me.

In the meantime, I would be glad to come to Milwaukee to see you whenever it is convenient. You may write to me either at my home or at Horton-Miller. If you wish to telephone me, you may call (312) 255-6000, which is the home office in Northbrook. The people there always know where to reach me.

                                     Cordially yours,

37-6

Application Letter for Change of Career

Situation

See Résumé 37-2 on page 320. Following is the application letter written by Dianne Seaton to accompany the résumé she prepared for the position of supervisor of office training. (The ad in *The Wall Street Journal* gave only a box number.)

The Letter

Ladies and Gentlemen:

This is my application for the position advertised in *The Wall Street Journal* (May 16)—supervisor of office training.

The résumé enclosed reveals five years of responsible secretarial and administrative office experience, a broad education that includes an academic degree, specialized training in secretarial science and related subjects, and teaching experience in classes designed expressly for working people.

You will see that my original plans were to teach history, but jobs in this area just didn't exist at the time I graduated; thus I chose a secretarial occupation where there were many opportunities. I am very glad I did. Not only do I enjoy being a part of the business world, I have learned that I have an unusual talent for administrative office work.

Yet the desire to teach remains. You will see that I have been teaching evening courses in word processing and related subjects during the past two years. I find teaching immensely exciting and rewarding—even more satisfying than my regular job.

I truly believe that responsible business experience, expertise in secretarial skills and procedures, and a sincere love of teaching make an ideal combination for the position you advertised. At age 28 I feel ready for a new challenge, and I hope you will offer that challenge to me.

Your ad indicated that the position is open in a large electronics firm in the Midwest. I would be pleased to visit the company at any time that would be convenient for you. May I hear from you?

Sincerely yours,

37-7   Application Letter for High-Level Position

Situation   See Résumé 37–3 on page 322. Frances Rosen decides to write the Executive Vice President of Farraday Plastics Manufacturing Company. This is the person to whom the Director of Public Relations reports, according to her informant who told her about the imminent retirement of the current director.

The Letter   Dear Mr. Klaff:

It has come to my attention that your current Director of Public Relations is on the verge of retirement, and that that position may be open shortly. If this is true, would you please consider this as my application for it.

The enclosed résumé indicates my broad experience in the area of public relations and management communications. It seems to me that this experience, together with my education (which continues), has given me ideal preparation to assume the role of the director of public relations in a firm such as yours. All of my professional experience has been in manufacturing organizations. My current employer, Regent Chemical Corporation, manufactures products closely allied to your own, so I am quite familiar with the kinds of issues and problems that your public relations people have to deal with.

I'd like to call your attention to page 2 of my résumé, on which I describe my concept of public relations. I am convinced that this function can make enormous contributions to growth and profits, and I am most eager to prove it to you.

Let me say that I have been very happy with my work at Regent Chemical Corporation. However, I see no opportunity in the near future to direct a full-scale public relations program (the present director is quite young and high competent), and I am eager to become established with a large company where I can assume this broader responsibility.

May I have the privilege of an interview? If you will let me know when it is convenient for you to see me, I will arrange my calendar accordingly. You may telephone me on my private line (622-4418) or write to me at the address given.

Sincerely yours,

37–8

Application Letter for a Position Requiring Different Background

Situation   See Résumé 37–4 on page 324. Leonard Lambeth accompanies his résumé with a letter of application. Professor Levinthal, who recommended that he apply for the job, supplied the name of the person to whom to write.

The Letter   Dear Mr. Reinheimer:

The position of Assistant Advertising Manager of *Southern Outdoorsman* was called to my attention by Dr. Sophia Levinthal, professor of journalism at the University of South Carolina. It is upon her recommendation that I am sending you my application.

When I graduated from the university in 1990, I accepted a job in the Athletic Department as an instructor of various outdoor sports. After three years, I decided that I would never be content until I became launched on a career in the field in which I was trained—advertising.

As you will see in the enclosed résumé, I was an advertising major at the University of South Carolina, a program that I thoroughly enjoyed and did well in. The résumé will also reveal my knowledge of and enthusiasm for all outdoor sports—all those that interest your readers. Believe me, Mr. Reinheimer, I can speak their language.

I hope you will give me the opportunity to talk with you in person. I can come to Charleston at any time and am available to begin work at a moment's notice. Incidentally, I'm a regular reader of *Southern Outdoorsman* (including the ads), and I am confident that I can quickly become an effective member of your advertising staff.

Cordially yours,

Section 38

Other Employment Communications

You may have occasion to write six other types of employment communications: requesting permission to use a person's name as reference, follow-ups on job applications, accepting a job offer, declining a job offer, letters of recommendation, and letters of resignation. These are all covered in this section.

Letters Pertaining to References

As mentioned earlier, always ask permission before you list a person's name as a reference on job applications. In some cases, you can do this by telephone, but in others you will find a letter necessary. Here are guidelines for permission letters:

1. *Describe your job-hunting plans.*
2. *Ask for permission to list the reader's name as a reference.*
3. *Express your appreciation for the favor.*
4. *Add any personal message you think is appropriate.*

When you have landed a job, you should write each of your references a letter of appreciation. Although you may not really know whether any of the references you supplied were contacted, the chances are good that they did receive an inquiry and said what you hoped they would. Here are some guidelines for such letters:

1. *Mention the position you obtained and your excitement about it.*
2. *Thank the reference for help, even though none may have been given.*
3. *Include any personal remarks that you think appropriate to the occasion.*

38-1 Requesting Permission to Use a Person as a Reference

Situation   Before Leonard Lambeth completed his job résumé (see pages 324 and 325), he wrote to various people for permission to use their names as references. One was the publisher of the Horry County *Beacon*, for whom Lambeth worked one summer while attending college.

The Letter   Dear Mr. Dykstra:

May I use your name as a reference for a job that I am interested in?

Let me bring you up to date. After I received my degree from the University of South Carolina in 1990 (my major was advertising), I accepted a job in the Athletic Department of the university as an instructor in outdoor sports. Now after three years I'm eager to get started in the advertising field.

The job I'm applying for is assistant advertising manager of *Southern Outdoorsman* in Charleston. I believe I have a good chance at it. I know I have the academic credentials, and, as you've heard so often, consider myself an "authority" on outdoor sports.

I think my experience on the *Beacon* (summer of 1990) could be very important, and I'd appreciate your support in case someone wants to make inquiry about me. A postcard is enclosed for your response.

Thanks—and leave some of the king mackerel for me!

Sincerely,

38-2   Thanking a Reference

Situation   Leonard Lambeth (see previous letter) receives word from *Southern Outdoorsman* that he has been accepted, and he writes each of his references to relay the good news. One of the persons listed on his résumé is Dr. Sophia Levinthal, professor of journalism at the University of South Carolina.

The Letter   Dear Professor Levinthal:

I think you'll be pleased to know that I have been hired as Assistant Advertising Manager of *Southern Outdoorsman*. I report to work July 21. This gives me a little time, and I hope to drop in to see you before I leave for Charleston.

At any rate, I want to thank you for your help. The job looks very challenging, but because of the thorough training I received at USC, together with your own informal coaching, I'm confident I can handle it.

Best wishes,

Follow-Up Letters

There are two instances when you may wish to write a follow-up letter on your application for employment:

1. *When you have not heard within a reasonable time from the firm to which you applied.*
2. *When you want to call attention to something about your experience, education, activities, and so on, that was omitted from your résumé. (Often this is simply a ploy to increase your chances of being hired, which says, in effect, "I still want that job and think I am the right person for it. Don't forget me.")*

Here are three guidelines for writing follow-up letters:

1. *Be brief.*
2. *Be tactful and courteous—don't pressure.*
3. *Reemphasize your interest in the position.*

38–3   Follow-Up for Reason of Elapsed Time

Situation   Russell Buchanan (see Résumé 37–4) receives an acknowledgment of his application for the job of Regional Sales Manager, with the assurance that he will hear from the national sales manager "shortly." Two weeks go by and nothing happens. Buchanan decides to write a follow-up letter.

The Letter   Dear Mr. Hewlett:

May I ask whether the position I applied for April 11 (regional sales manager) is still open?

I'm still greatly interested in the job and hope I'm still in the running for it. However, I would like to know right away so that I can make appropriate plans.

Thank you.

Very cordially yours,

38–4   Follow-Up to Present Additional Information

Situation   A few days after Frances Rosen (see Résumé 35–3) applies to Farraday Plastics Manufacturing Company, she decides to send a reprint of her recent article in the *Journal of Public Relations*. Although she could have attached it to her résumé, she decided to use it now as a follow-up device.

The Letter   Dear Mr. Klaff:

Right after I sent you my résumé, it occurred to me that you might like to see a copy of my article, "The Role of Public Relations in Corporate Planning," which appeared in the September issue of the *Journal of Public Relations*. It is enclosed.

Sincerely yours,

Accepting a Job Offer

After the interview, you may receive a letter from the employer telling you that you have been selected for the position you applied for and asking you to report to work on a certain date. If the reporting date is, say, a couple of weeks hence, it's usually wise to write a letter accepting the job and saying you will report on the date suggested. This is a good idea, even if you are not asked to accept the job in writing, for it leaves no doubt that you're going to show up and expect the job to be held for you.

Guidelines for writing job acceptance letters are as follows:

1. *Express your enthusiasm for the news.*
2. *Confirm the date you are to report to work with assurance that you will be there.*
3. *Indicate your anticipation in getting started.*

38–5   Accepting a Job Offer

Situation

A week after Leonard Lambeth (see Résumé 37–4) is interviewed, he receives a letter from Mr. Reinheimer telling him the job is his and asking him to report to work in three weeks. Lambeth accepts the job by letter.

The Letter

Dear Mr. Reinheimer:

Your letter brought wonderful news. I am delighted to accept the position of assistant advertising manager of *Southern Outdoorsman*.

As you suggested, I will report to the medical department at 9 a.m. on July 21 and then proceed directly to your office.

I thoroughly enjoyed meeting you and the others on your staff, and I really look forward to joining you.

Sincerely yours,

Rejecting a Job Offer

It sometimes happens that after people have received a letter in which they are offered a position they applied for, they have changed their minds. Maybe the present boss learned about their plans to leave and came across with a promotion, or after they left the interview, they unexpectedly received a better offer from another firm, or they were not favorably impressed with what they saw when they were interviewed, or there may be other reasons. When you decide not to accept a job offer, it is common courtesy to tactfully decline in writing.

Letters rejecting job offers are often difficult to write. Follow these guidelines:

1. *Express your appreciation for the offer.*

2. *Give the reason why you must decline. (Here you must be very careful. Obviously, you don't want to say, "I don't think I'd like working for you," even if that's your real reason. Nor will you say, "I've found something that pays a lot more." We'll supply examples of what your message might look like.)*

3. *End on a pleasant note, such as saying something favorable about the company or the people you met at the interview.*

38-6 Rejecting a Job Offer—Better Opportunity

Situation

Linda Parish applies to a large insurance company for the position of Systems Analyst. She receives notice that she has been selected for the job. In the meantime, however, a new position is offered in the publishing company where she is presently employed. It is not only a better job (including salary), but she is certain that she likes publishing better than she would like insurance. She declines the offer.

The Letter

Dear Mrs. Weiman:

I appreciate your letter offering me the position of Systems Analyst which I recently applied for.

Shortly after I arrived back at my office from my visit with you, I was told by our Administrative Vice President that I was being promoted to the position of manager of computer services. It is an excellent opportunity (which came as a complete surprise), and one that I feel I cannot pass up. Therefore, I must decline your generous offer.

Thank you for all the courtesies extended me. I enjoyed my brief visit with you.

Yours very cordially,

38-7 Rejecting a Job Offer— No Interest in the Position

Situation

Kenneth Bianca, Purchasing Manager for a small manufacturer of electronic parts in a suburb of Seattle, receives an inquiry about his availability as Purchasing Director for a large business machines manufacturer in St. Louis. Bianca is interviewed and eventually offered the job. However, he does not like the structure of the company or the job description, so he decides to decline the offer.

The Letter

Dear Louis:

I am flattered by your offer of the position of Purchasing Director of Calumet, Inc. It is very generous.

After giving the matter much thought and discussing it with my family, I have come to the conclusion that I should stay where I am. Certainly, the opportunity to work with such a prestigious firm as Calumet is most attractive. On the other hand, I do enjoy my work here at Electronics Unlimited immensely, and I guess you might say we are "addicted" to the Seattle area and the lifestyle it affords.

Thank you for your confidence in me and for the opportunity to meet with you, Jim, Alice, and Quincy in St. Louis. My best regards to all.

Cordially yours,

Letters of Resignation

When you resign from a position, there is no rule that says you must write a letter of resignation. Certainly, if you're leaving in a rage and can think of no way to conceal it, then don't write. Just tell your boss you're leaving and why (if asked). It's just not wise to leave on record an angry message with your name on it; it may very well haunt you later.

But if you want to write a letter of resignation—whether it's a genuinely friendly separation or one that has negative overtones—that's up to you. If you have regrets about leaving the company, the letter gives you the opportunity to express appreciation for the breaks you received, your high opinion of the people, and so on—a good gesture that certainly can't hurt you. On the other hand, you may have been bypassed for a promotion you expected, and you may want to register your disappointment in writing simply for the record. In this case, we recommend that you express your feelings in a straightforward manner, but avoid name calling and vituperation.

38–8   Letter of Resignation—Dislike for Travel

Situation

Craig Sherman has been a traveling sales representative for an appliance manufacturer for nearly 18 months. Although he enjoys meeting with dealers and likes the company he works for, he objects to being away from home several weeks at a time. He has discussed the problem with the Sales Manager, Gerald Bergstrom, several times, but, of course, the job requirements cannot be altered, and there are no inside positions that appeal to him. He decides to resign in writing.

The Letter

Dear Jerry:

I am sure it will come as no surprise to you that I wish to resign my position as a sales representative, effective at your convenience, but not later than June 12.

You are fully aware of my problem, Jerry. Although I like the company and the people I work with, being on the road for weeks at a time does not appeal to me. I think the situation would be entirely different if I were single or even married with no children. But with two youngsters (2 and 4 years old), traveling represents a real hardship on me and especially on my wife Gretchen. After each trip it gets increasingly harder for me to tear myself away from my family to go back on the road.

I really have no plans at the moment. I need to take some time to think about what I want to do. I may try to get back into coaching, and I'm also considering buying into a local sporting goods store. Whatever I wind up doing, it will have to be something that will permit me to stay anchored in one place.

Thank you for everything you have done for me. I really don't know how I could have received better treatment from a company or a manager.

Sincerely,

PS: In case I need a reference, may I use your name? I would very much appreciate it.

38–9 Letter of Resignation— No Opportunity for Growth

Situation

Helen Leavitt has been Administrative Assistant to Raymond Durward for three years. She quickly proved to be an excellent assistant, and frequent salary increases attest to her boss's high opinion of her. However, Durward is one of those people who will not delegate responsibility, and Leavit is eager to assume the duties of a bona fide Administrative Assistant. She has discussed the matter several times with Durward, but received only noncommittal responses, such as "I'm happy with what you're doing—why change things?" Finally, she decides to resign and writes Durward, giving the reasons for her action.

The Letter

Dear Mr. Durward:

Please consider this as my resignation from my position as your administrative assistant, effective August 10.

Although I have enjoyed working with you and have learned a great deal, I would really like to operate in a wider management sphere, and since you have not been willing to provide this opportunity, I feel that I should seek a position that allows greater freedom to make decisions and to function more independently. As you know, my job has not changed in the three years I have been with you. Although you have been very fair in terms of compensation, I feel the need to grow professionally as well as financially.

I have discussed my management aspirations with two placement counselors in Portland, and both stressed the accelerated demand for women management trainees in various areas. So I think I'll have no difficulty finding what I want.

Thank you for all your help and your many personal kindnesses.

Sincerely,

38-10 Letter of Resignation— Bypassed for Promotion

Situation

Lewis Michaels is one of three department managers (all on an equal level) reporting to the Financial Vice President, C. J. Spanswick. During the five years he has been with the company, Michaels has had several job offers at a better salary, but each time Spanswick has urged him to stay on. "You're doing a great job, Lew," Spanswick would say, hinting that he would have the first shot at Spanswick's job if it became vacant. But when Spanswick moves up to Treasurer of the corporation, the vacancy is filled by an individual outside the company. The explanation given by Spanswick is: "You're all three indispensable in the jobs you have now—it's much easier to replace me than any of you." Michaels decides to resign, giving specific reasons for doing so.

The Letter

Dear C. J.:

Please consider this as my resignation effective at once. I am writing to you rather than to the new financial vice president because I want you to know exactly how I feel.

You will recall that during the five years I have been on your staff, I have had offers from several companies, all of which promised better compensation and greater responsibilities. On each occasion, I discussed the situation with you and you gave me reason to believe that I would replace you, if and when you moved up. I confess that you did not actually say, "You're the next Financial Vice President, Lew," but that is the distinct impression I got from our conversations.

Your promotion to Treasurer of the corporation came as no surprise; certainly, no one is better qualified than you for that position. The genuine surprise was that instead of choosing one of your three department managers to replace you, you selected an individual from outside the company. I'm sorry that I cannot accept your reasoning—that we're indispensable in our present jobs; this would mean that a person can be penalized for doing *too* good a job. Clearly, this would mean that I can have no hopes for promotion here.

I leave Mariposa Industries with many pleasant memories; the experience has been rewarding in many ways. Under the circumstances, however, I'm certain you will fully understand the reason for my decision.

Cordially yours,

Note: Spanswick may have had good reasons for not naming Michaels to the vacated position. If so, they should have been revealed long before H-hour so that Michaels would have had an opportunity to overcome his deficiencies. The reason given by Spanswick is spurious, and under similar circumstances many people would, upon hearing it, simply clear their desks and walk out. Michaels wants his resentment on record, and there's nothing wrong with that.

38-11 Letter of Resignation—Better Job Offer

Situation Frances Rosen (see Letters 37–3 and 37–7) has been named Director of Public Relations at Farraday Plastics Manufacturing Company. Before accepting the position, she discusses it with her boss at Regent Chemical Corporation for whom she has a high regard. She receives his encouragement and congratulations and decides to write a personal letter shortly before her departure to express appreciation for courtesies and friendship.

The Letter Dear Whit:

Before taking my leave next Tuesday, I want to acknowledge with deep thanks your many kindnesses to me during the years I worked with you.

It's not everyone who has a boss who is consistently cooperative, generous, and understanding, and I feel that I've been blessed. Not only have I enjoyed working with you; I have learned how a really good public relations department should be run. It's really because of the training I received from you that I feel qualified to undertake my new assignment.

My best wishes to you always. Don't be surprised to get some telephone calls from me, asking for advice and perhaps a sympathetic broad shoulder. If I can return any of the many favors you gave me, all you have to do is pick up the telephone and dial 555-5649.

Sincerely,

cc: A. J. Merriam

38–12 Letter of Resignation—Personal Conflict

Situation

Walter Prevatte is an internal auditor for Bridewell Enterprises, where he has worked for three years. Although he has progressed financially at a satisfactory rate and therefore assumes that he is valued by his boss, J. Richard Allender, Prevatte gets no satisfaction from his work. Allender is demanding, demeaning, cold, and often verbally abusive—one of those executives who "knows it all" and refuses to give credit to subordinates for brains or ideas.

Prevatte decides to resign. In his letter of resignation, however, he believes it best not to reveal the real reason (Allender). Although it would feel good to get some things off his chest, he thinks he would lose rather than gain by doing so. So he decides to announce the decision to resign without revealing animosity toward anyone.

The Letter

Dear Richard:

After considerable thought and soul-searching, I have decided to resign my position as internal auditor at Bridewell Enterprises. I assure you it was not an easy decision to make.

Perhaps you have heard me mention on occasion that I would like to have my own accounting business. Ever since I graduated from Rutgers, this has been my long-range goal. I am thinking of applying to a graduate business school to earn an MBA in accounting and eventually to sit for the CPA exam.

I suggest an effective date of June 30. If, however, you would like more time to find a replacement, I am willing to extend that date by two weeks. On the other hand, if you feel that an earlier departure would be more convenient to you, I will certainly understand.

I value the experience I have received at Bridewell Enterprises. I'm confident that it will be very useful to me in my accounting career.

Sincerely yours,

Part 14

SOCIAL CORRESPONDENCE

Social correspondence includes formal and informal invitations,
formal and informal acceptances and regrets, and expressions of
appreciation for hospitality and special favors (often called
"bread-and-butter" letters). Although such communications
would seem to be appropriate only for books on etiquette, the
fact is that many are business related.

Several formal and informal messages are illustrated in this
part. Guidelines for their preparation are given in the analysis of
each communication.

Section 39

Formal Invitations and Responses

Business firms and other organizations often issue formal invitations to special events—a reception to honor a new president, a dinner to recognize outstanding achievements or anniversaries of employees, an open house to celebrate the organization's anniversary, a banquet to honor some dignitary, a reception to announce a merger of two companies and introduce key personnel to one another, and so on. Such invitations are often printed or engraved on stationery similar to that of a formal wedding announcement. Some ask for a response (R.S.V.P.) which, if no response card is included with the invitation, generally requires a formal note of acceptance or regrets.

39-1   Formal Invitation to Honor a New President

Situation

Rothmoor University has appointed a new president who will take office in late summer. A formal invitation is sent to the alumni of the university and other important people to attend a reception in the president-elect's honor.

The Invitation

THE BOARD OF TRUSTEES AND THE FACULTY

of

ROTHMOOR UNIVERSITY

invite you to attend a reception

in honor of

DR. MARTHA SILLS CLEVERDON

President-elect

to be held in American Women Patriots Hall

on the Campus

Thursday evening, June 2

at half after eight o'clock

R.S.V.P.
Dean of Faculty

Analysis of the Invitation

1. *The invitation is printed in black on high-quality white paper of postcard weight. A popular size is 4¼ by 4½ inches, although a number of different sizes may be used.*

2. *The placement of the message varies, but note that each line is centered.*

3. *The envelope is usually hand-addressed, and there is often a card of the same quality as the invitation, enclosed with the following message:*

   "I will _____ attend the reception for President-elect Cleverdon on Thursday, June 2.

   Name _____ "

4. *A stamped, self-addressed envelope is enclosed for mailing the card.*

39-2 Formal Invitation to an Annual Banquet

Situation

The Lakeport Business Council in Support of the Arts invites members and special guests to its annual banquet meeting by a formal printed invitation.

The Invitation

THE LAKEPORT BUSINESS COUNCIL IN SUPPORT OF THE ARTS

cordially invites you to its

Annual Meeting and Banquet

at the Lakeport Country Club

on Saturday, May 8, at half after six o'clock

featuring

Anton Michetti, Director of the Pine State Symphony

speaking on "What Is Good Music?"

and a special performance by the

Abelard String Quartet

R.S.V.P.   Black Tie
Pamela Webster
555-4417

Analysis of the Invitation

1. *The stationery and the setup are similar to the invitation on page 347.*
2. *Note that the response can be made by telephone, and the person's name and number appear under "R.S.V.P."*

39-3 Accepting a Formal Invitation

Situation   Cynthia Dolan, Vice President of a pharmaceutical house, receives a formal invitation from the National Medical Research Foundation to a reception in honor of Dr. Ormond Shipley, who has received the foundation's annual award for outstanding medical research. Although the invitation included an R.S.V.P., there is no card enclosed for the response. Dolan accepts the invitation.

The Acceptance

Cynthia Dolan
accepts with pleasure
the kind invitation of
The National Medical Research Foundation
to a reception in honor of
Dr Ormond Shipley
on Wednesday, the fifth of December
at five-thirty o'clock
The Century Club

Analysis of the Acceptance   The response is handwritten on a blank, high-quality card or a social note sheet either monogrammed or blank. If the sheet contains her full name, Dolan can begin the acceptance as follows:

"I accept with pleasure your kind invitation to a reception..."
Then she begins her name below the message.

39–4 Accepting a Formal Invitation with a Qualification

Situation

Janette Reichel, an executive, and her husband Kenneth receive a formal invitation from the parents of Janette's administrative assistant to a party to announce their daughter's engagement. The social hour begins at four o'clock, followed by dinner at seven o'clock. The Reichels will attend the social hour, but because of a previous engagement, cannot remain for dinner.

The Acceptance

Janette and Kenneth Reichel
are pleased to accept the kind invitation of
Mr and Mrs. Overstreet
to the party on Sunday, May fifteenth, at four o'clock.
Because of a previous engagement
we sincerely regret that we will be unable
to remain for dinner following the social hour

Analysis of the Acceptance

The message may be handwritten on a plain white card or note sheet. Note that the acceptance precedes the regrets.

39–5 Expressing Regrets to a Formal Invitation

Situation   JoAnne and Wilford Roos receive a formal invitation to a dinner dance, but must decline because they will be out of the country on the date of the affair.

The Regrets

Wilford and JoAnne Roos
sincerely regret
that because they will be in Mexico City all of September
they are unable to accept
Mr. and Mrs. Guilford's
kind invitation for the twelfth of September

Analysis of the Regrets   Again, the regrets are handwritten on formal stationery. Note there is no need to indicate the nature of the occasion or the location.

Section 40

Informal Invitations and Responses

Arrangements for informal parties, dinners, and other get-togethers are, more often than not, made by telephone or by face-to-face meetings in the office, restaurant, or elsewhere. Depending on the occasion, some people prefer to send written invitations, either on social stationery or a special executive letterhead.

Generally, responses to written invitations are handwritten.

40–1   Informal Invitation to Dinner

Situation

Edward Agajanian, Executive Vice President of a corporation, and his wife Peggy are having a farewell dinner in their home for Ted and Virginia Novak (Novak is a subordinate of Agajanian) prior to the Novaks' departure for a foreign assignment. Ten couples, friends of the Novaks, are being invited.

The Invitation

EDWARD G. AGAJANIAN
Old Mill Creek Road
Princeton, New Jersey 08540

Dear Ruth and Cliff:

Peggy and I would like it very much if you would be our guests at dinner on August 9 at seven o'clock. It's an informal farewell party for Ted and Virginia Novak who, as you know, will be leaving in a few weeks for Hong Kong, where Ted will be the managing director of our new office there. We're inviting ten couples, all of whom are special friends of the Novaks.

I know that Ted and Virginia would be delighted to have you in the group, as would we. By the way, it's not a surprise and no gifts are expected.

Will you call me or Peggy if you can't come? Otherwise, we'll be expecting you. My office number is 555-2174 and our home number is 555-6120.

Yours,

Mr. and Mrs. C. H. Renfro
120 Cedar Drive East
Briarcliff Manor, New York 10510

Analysis of the Invitation

1. *Some executives have personal stationery that can be used for messages such as this, with either the business or home address (or both). Usually it is smaller than standard letterhead size—either Monarch (7¼ by 10¼ inches) or Baronial (5½ by 8½ inches). The stock is sometimes tinted— light tan, gray, and so on.*

2. *The message may be typewritten since it is a social-business event as opposed to a purely social one. For the same reason, the letter appropriately comes from Edward Agajanian, rather than from Peggy.*

3. At a farewell dinner, anniversary event, or similar occasion, it is usually wise to indicate whether a gift is expected.

4. To reduce the business flavor of such a message, the inside address may appear below the letter.

40-2   Accepting an Informal Invitation

Situation

During the week of April 11, Dr. Russell Chancellor and his wife Maureen will attend a medical convention in Seattle. Old friends of the couple who live in Seattle have written a note inviting them to dinner at a downtown restaurant, followed by attendance at a performance of the Seattle Symphony.

The Letter

Dear Grace and Milt,

    How nice of you to invite Russ and me to dinner on April 14 when we are in Seattle and to attend a performance by the Seattle Symphony. We're delighted to accept.

    It will be wonderful seeing both of you again. We're stopping at the Sheraton, and I'll give you a ring when we are settled in. Seattle will be a new experience for me, and I'm really looking forward to it.

                Affectionately,

                  Maureen

Analysis of the Letter

1. The letter is written by hand on either plain social stationery or a personal letterhead.

2. Note that Maureen tells Grace and Milt where she and Russ will be staying in Seattle. This is always a good idea in case there is any change in plans.

Note: The letter may be written by either of the Chancellors.

Situation

Agatha and Culver Wisniewski receive an informal invitation from friends for a weekend of skiing. They are unable to accept.

The Letter

Dear Cindy and Ed —

Culver and I wish so much that we could accept your invitation to join you in Steamboat Springs the weekend of February 16. Unfortuneately, we cannot. Ed's family is having a big reunion that weekend in Salt Lake City, which is really a must for both of us.

We'll be thinking of you and the rest of the gang. Both of us have happy memories of our numerous stays at Wynward's Chalet and hope you'll ask us again one day. Have fun!

Fondly,

Agatha

Analysis of the Letter

This letter can come from either Agatha or Culver Wisniewski. It should be handwritten either on plain social stationery or a "Mr. and Mrs." letterhead. Note its informality.

Section 41

"Bread-and-Butter" Letters

All of us learn at a very early age to say "thank you" to people who do us a favor. Ninety-nine times out of a hundred, we can express our appreciation in person or by a telephone call.

There are certain special occasions, however, when a "bread-and-butter" letter is required. Two examples are given in this section.

41–1   Expressing Thanks for a Personal Favor

Situation

Lou Aldridge, an assistant purchasing manager, is discussing his summer vacation plans with Len Rogoff, the sales representative for a long-time supplier. "This year," Lou tells his friend, "Beth and I are going to take the boys on a trip through New England—you know, a little camping and fishing, sightseeing, and the like." "That sounds great," Len says, "Millie and I have a small lakefront cottage near Bridgton, Maine. You're welcome to use it if you're headed in that direction." Lou quickly accepts the invitation, and upon returning home writes Len a letter of thanks.

The Letter

Dear Len:

Here's the key to "Rogoff's Retreat," along with my deepest thanks for allowing us to stay there. We spent a couple of days and three nights there—easily one of the best memories of our trip.

The boys became fairly expert in maneuvering that 3½-horsepower motor boat around the lake and even caught a few pickerel of respectable size. Cathy and I swam, sunned, and lolled on that breezy screened-in porch, catching up on our reading, crossword puzzles, and napping. It was a great interlude for all of us. Even Fitz, the dog, was reluctant to leave—too much fun yapping at the ducks that dropped in on us every day.

It was very generous of you and Millie to lend us "Rogoff's Retreat," and we're mighty grateful.

                 Best regards,

PS: I think I fixed that drip in the outdoor shower you spoke about. I fully intended to mow the lawn, but the machine simply coughed a few times, proving (to no one's surprise) that Dad doesn't know a lot about motors.

Analysis of the Letter

The letter can be written on plain paper or on the company letterhead (we prefer the former), and it may be handwritten or typewritten, depending on how personal Aldridge wants to make it. In any event, he is appropriately warm, grateful, and whimsical.

41–2   Expressing Thanks for Generous Hospitality

Situation

Peter Hostler is a buyer of men's clothing for a department store in Dayton. On a recent buying trip to New York accompanied by his wife Lisa), the couple is given royal treatment by Bernard Jacobi, a sales representative for a men's apparel manufacturer. Upon returning home, Hostler writes a letter of appreciation.

The Letter

Dear Bernie

Lisa and I are still talking about the great afternoon and evening you gave us in New York. It is an occasion that will be long remembered.

Although you probably take New York in stride, everything we saw and did was a grad adventure: the boat trip around Manhattan Island, cocktails at the top of the World Trade Center, dinner at the Four Seasons, the Broadway revival of our favorite musical, "The Oracle," and finally the famous cheesecake at Lindy's.

The buying trip was very successful, and my boss was immensely pleased with my selections. Never again will I believe the old adage, "You can't mix business with pleasure." You provided the pleasure—and, incidentally some of the business. Thank you!

Sincerely,

Analysis of the Letter

1. *In the first paragraph, Hostler mentions the memorable afternoon and evening.*

2. *He then points out each of the treats they received, showing that none was forgotten.*

3. *The letter ends on a business-social note and with a hearty "thank you."*

Index

Accommodations, request letter/
  response, 86-87, 113
Acquisition, announcing, 105
AIDA formula, 108
Anniversary:
  announcing, 106
  congratulations to employee
    on, 290
Announcements, 103-6
  of acquisition, 105
  of anniversary, 106
  on final plans for new ware-
    houses, 213
  of meeting, 209
  memorandums, 208-15
  of moratorium on staff addi-
    tions, 210
  of new high-level position,
    214
  on new library, 211-12
  of new location, 120
  of new product, 104, 119
  of promotion of executive, 215
Application letter, 326-30
  for change of career, 328
  follow-ups, 334
  for high-level position, 329
  for middle management posi-
    tion, 327
  for position requiring differ-
    ent background, 330
Appointments, 80-84
  confirming, 101
  to see computer operation, 83
    response to request, 84
  to visit showrooms, 81
    response to request, 82

Appreciation letters, 286-94
  for past support from cus-
    tomer, 162
Attention line, 50

Big words vs. familiar words,
  21-22
Blocked letter style, 45
Bond paper, 44
Book, sales letter for, 112
"Bread and butter" letters, 356-58
  thank you for generous hospi-
    tality, 358
  thank you for personal favor,
    357
Brevity vs. common sense, 17-20
  paragraph length, 18-20
  sentence length, 18
Business letters:
  format, 44-51
  form letters, personalized, 30
  goodwill letters, 7-11

Cash order, placing, 125
Change of career:
  application letter for, 328
  resume, 320-22
Clutter words/phrases, 12-14
COD order, placing, 126
Collection:
  fifth reminder (telegram), 205
  first reminder, 203
  fourth reminder (telephone
    call), 205
  second reminder, 204
  seventh reminder (final let-
    ter), 206

sixth reminder (personal letter), 206
third reminder, 204
Color, paper, 45
Company reputation, and goodwill, 7-8
Complimentary close, 48-49
Conference accommodations:
  request letter/response, 86-87
  sales letter, 113
Confirmations, 98-102
  of appointment, 101
  in memorandum form, 217
  of oral instruction, 99
  of prices/discounts, 100
  of travel arrangements, 102
Congratulations, 286-94
  to boss, 293
  to employee:
    on anniversary, 290
    for community recognition,
      292
    on job well done, 287
    on new management con-
      cept, 288
    for outstanding report, 289
  to new member of 25-year
    club, 291
  on opening new store, 168
  on professional achievement,
    164
  on promotion, responding to,
    294
Contract, transmittal letter, 95
Copy of speech, request let-
  ter/response, 79
Credit, 192-201

Credit (*Continued*)
  commercial credit, request/response, 194-95
  commercial credit applicant:
    accepting, 197
    turning down, 198
  consumer credit applicant:
    accepting, 200
    turning down, 201
  credit applicant:
    accepting, 192-93
    turning down, 193, 199
  invitation to use, 172
  references, request/response, 196
  See also Collection
Credit card order, placing, 127
Critic, responding to, 253, 254
Customers, goodwill letters to, 9
Customers' letters to suppliers, 123-49
  cash order, placing, 125
  COD order, placing, 126
  credit card order, placing, 127
  discount, 148-49
  error in invoice, 133
  loss of conference materials, 146-47
  low-quality office product, 131-32
  "pay or else" letter received, 142-43
  poor performance on service contract, 138-39
  poor service on special order, 136-37
  sloppy record keeping, accusation of, 144-45
  supplier's sales reps:
    complaint about, 134-35
    praising, 128
  thank-you letter, 129
  unacceptable substitute, 140-41

Damaged shipment, supplier's letter to customer, 184, 185
Damaged stock returned for credit, supplier's letter to customer, 182

Delayed shipment, supplier's letter to customer, 174
Discount, customer's letter about, 148-49

Educational course, sales letter for, 111
Education section, resume, 315-16
Employee relations letters, 285-310
Employees:
  congratulations:
    on anniversary, 290
    for community recognition, 292
    on job well done, 287
    on new management concept, 288
    for outstanding report, 289
  goodwill letters to, 8-9
  terminating by letter, 310
  warning letter to, 309
Envelopes, 44
Error:
  in filling order, 176
  in invoice:
    customer's letter about, 133
    supplier's letter about, 178
  in merchandise sent, 179
  wrong size shipped, 177
Executive assistants' writing responsibilities, 269-83
  executive-is-away letters, 270-76
  writing for the executive's signature, 277-83
Executive-is-away letters, 270-76
  discretion, use of, 271
  follow-up to company executive, 275
  "holding" letter, 274
  referral of problems to others, 273
  request for convention participation, 272
  "true" rumor, disavowing, 276
Exhibit, formal invitation to, 117
Exhibit visitor, follow-up letter to, 118
Experience section, resume, 315

Federalese vs. natural writing style, 22-23
Final payment on account, transmittal letter, 93
Follow-ups:
  to application letter, 334
  to company executive, 275
  to exhibit visitor, 118
  to previous order, 159
  to rendered services, 158
  to sales representative's call, 155
Formal invitations, 346-51
  accepting, 349-50
  to annual banquet, 348
  to exhibit, 117
  expressing regrets to, 351
  to honor new president, 347
Format, 44-51
  attention line, 50
  complimentary close, 48-49
  letter style, 45-46
  margins/placement, 47
  paper, 44-45
  personal letters on plain paper, 49
  salutation, 47-48
  signatures, 50-51
  spacing, 47
  subject line, 50
Former customer, writing to, 165
Form letters, personalized, 30
Free catalog, request letter/response, 55, 56
Free products, request letter/response, 57, 58
Full-blocked letter style, 45

General memorandums, 216-21
  from company president, 221
  confirmation memorandum, 217
  employee request, 219
  merit ratings, reviewing importance of, 218
  new position, request for permission to establish, 220
Goodwill:
  building/maintaining, 8
  and company reputation, 7-8

defined, 7
promotion of, 11
Goodwill letters, 7-11
  to customers, 9
  to employees, 8-9
  to the public, 10
  to suppliers, 10
Guest speakers:
  inviting, 232-39
    keynote speaker, 239
    panel participant, 236-38
    professional speaker, 233-35
  letters concerning, 231-46
  thanking, 240-46
    after-dinner speaker, 244
    ineffective luncheon
      speaker,   245
    keynote speaker, 242
    professional speaker, 241
    and requesting copies, 243
    substitute speaker, 246

Headings, resume, 313-14, 317
High-level position:
  application letter for, 329
  resume, 322-23
Housing, request letter/re-
    sponse, 88-89

"I" approach, to writing busi-
    ness letters, 33-34
Inactive customer, writing to,
    166
Inconveniences, apologizing for,
    256
Informal invitations, 352-55
  accepting, 354
  to dinner, 353-54
  expressing regrets to, 355
Interoffice letters (memoran-
    dums), 207-30
  announcing memorandums,
    208-15
  general memorandums, 216-
    21
  as reports, 222-30
Invitations:
  formal, 346-51
  to guest speakers, 232-39
  informal, 352-55

to use credit, 172
"Ize" words, 23-24

Job-getting communications,
    312-30
  application letter, 326-30
  job offer:
    accepting, 335
    rejecting, 336-38
  references, letters pertaining
    to, 331-34
  resume, 312-25
Job resume, See Resume

Keynote speaker:
  invitation to, 239
  thank-you letter to, 242

Language, 21-27
  big words vs. familiar words,
    21-22
  federalese vs. natural writing
    style, 22-23
  new words, coining, 23-24
  stereotyped writing, 25-27
  vogue words, 25
Large order, acknowledging, 163
Letter style, 45-46
Line spacing, 47
Loss of conference materials,
    customer's letter about,
    146-47
Low-quality office product, cus-
    tomer's letter about, 131-32

Magazine reprints, request let-
    ter/response, 71, 72
Margins, 47
Materials under separate cover,
    transmittal letter, 97
Merit ratings, reviewing impor-
    tance of, 218
Middle management position:
  application letter for, 327
  resume, 318-19

Negatives, avoiding, 38-40
Newcomer to community, wel-
    coming, 121
New library, announcing, 211-12

New location, announcing, 120
New position, request for per-
    mission to establish, 220
New products:
  announcing, 104, 119
  request letter/response, 59, 60
New sales representative, intro-
    ducing, 154
New words, coining, 23-24

Open house, invitation to, 116
Oral instruction, confirming, 99
Out of stock, supplier's letter to
    customer, 175

Panel participant, invitation to,
    236-38
Paper, 44-45
  color, 45
  quality, 44
  size, 45
Paragraph length, 18-20
"Pay or else" letter:
  customer's letter about, 142-43
  suppliers response to, 187
Permission to reproduce, re-
    quest letter/response, 71,
    72, 77, 78
Personalized letters, 28-35
  form letters, 30
  "I" and "we," choosing be-
    tween, 34-35
  "I" and "you" approaches, 33-34
  and nonpersonalized letters,
    examples of, 30-33
Personal letters on plain paper,
    format, 49
Placement, 47
Positive emphasis, 36-43
  extending yourself, 40-41
  negatives, avoiding, 38-40
  stressing what you can do
    37-38
  timing for positive reaction,
    41-43
Previous order, follow-up to, 159
Prices/discounts:
  confirming, 100
  request letter/response, 62, 63
Product, sales letter, 110

Product inspection, request letter/response, 64, 65
Product/name of dealer, request letter/response, 60, 61
Professional speaker:
    invitation to, 233-35
    thank-you letter to, 241
Promotion:
    bypassed for (resignation letter), 341-42
    congratulations on, responding to, 294
    of goodwill, 11
    See also Sales promotion communications
Promptness of response, 41-43
Public, goodwill letters to, 10
Public relations letters, 247-56
    critic, responding to, 253, 254
    inconveniences, apologizing for, 256
    request for confidential information, turning down, 255
    request for donation:
        acknowledging, 251
        turning down, 252
    request to buy advertising, refusing, 250
    special request, handling, 249

Recommendation, 303-5
    for former employee:
        qualified, 305
        unqualified, 304
Redundancy, 15-17
References:
    credit, request/response, 196
    requesting permission for use others as, 332
    resume, 316
    thank-you letter to, 333
Referral, thank-you letter for, 160
Rendered services, follow-up to, 158
Repetition, 15-17
Reports, 222-30
    on centralization of department, 228-30

on customer correspondence, 224-25
on house organ, suggestions for improving, 226-27
on regional office turnover, 223
Reproduction privileges, request letters/responses, 73-76
Requests, 53-90
    for accommodations, 86-87
    for appointment, 80-84
    to buy advertising, refusing, 250
    for confidential information, turning down, 255
    for donation:
        acknowledging, 251
        turning down, 252
    for information:
        about business-related matters, 54-69
        about housing, 88-89
        about residence/vacation property, 89-90
    for permission to reproduce printed materials, 70-79
    special request, handling, 249
Residence, request letter/response, 89-90
Resignation letters, 338-43
    better job offer, 342
    bypassed for promotion, 341-42
    dislike for travel, 339
    no opportunity for growth, 340
    personal conflict, 343
Resume, 312-25
    change of career, 320-22
    education, 315-16
    experience, 315
    headings, 313-14, 317
    high-level position, 322-23
    little related job experience, 324-25
    middle management position, 318-19
    references, 316
"Retirement concept" of living, sales letter, 114

Sales letters, 107-21
    for book, 112
    for conference accommodations, 113
    for educational course, 111
    for product, 110
    for "retirement concept" of living, 114
    sales promotion communications, 115-21
    writing guidelines, 109
Sales promotion communications, 115-21
    exhibit, formal invitation to, 117
    exhibit visitor, follow-up to, 118
    new products/services, announcing, 119
    open house, invitation to, 116
Sales representative:
    follow-up call, 155
    letter about illness of, 171
    thank-you letter:
        for courtesies to, 156
        for receiving sales rep, 169
Salutation, 47-48
Second sheets, 44
Semiblocked letter style, 45-46
Sentence length, 18
Service:
    requesting information about, 68
    responding to request, 69
Signatures, 50-51
Size, paper, 45
Sloppy record keeping, accusation of, 144-45
Social correspondence, 345-58
    "bread and butter" letters, 356-58
    formal invitations, 346-51
    informal invitations, 352-55
Spacing, line, 47
Speakers, *See* Guest speakers
Stereotyped writing, 25-27
Subject line, 50
Substitute speaker, thank-you letter to, 246
Suppliers, goodwill letters to, 10
Supplier's letters to customers, 151-90

appreciation of past support, 162

company policy, bending to say yes to customer, 189-90

congratulations:
  on opening new store, 168
  on professional achievement, 164

damaged shipment, 184, 185

damaged stock returned for credit, 182

delayed shipment, 174

error:
  in filling order, 176
  in invoice, 178
  in merchandise sent, 179
  wrong size shipped, 177

first order, acknowledging, 157

former customer, writing to, 165

inactive customer, writing to, 166

invitation to use credit, 172

large order, acknowledging, 163

new sales representative, introducing, 154

out of stock, 175

"pay or else" letter, supplier's response to, 187

previous order, follow-up to, 159

rendered services, follow-up to, 158

sales representative's call, follow-up to, 155

sales representative's illness, letter about, 171

saying "no" to a customer, 190

sloppy record keeping, response to irate customer about, 188

substitute, suggesting, 186

thank-you letter:
  for courtesies to sales representative, 156
  to long-time customer, 170
  for payment/order, 161
  for receiving sales representative, 169

for referral, 160

for sending a friend, 167

unauthorized return of merchandise, 181

unauthorized use of service personnel, 183

unearned discount taken, 180

unsigned check, returning for signature, 187

Supplier's sales representative:
  complaint about, 134-35
  praising, 128

Termination letter, 310

Thank-you letters:
  to after-dinner speaker, 244
  for courtesies to sales representative, 156
  from customer to supplier, 129
  for generous hospitality, 358
  to ineffective luncheon speaker, 245
  to keynote speaker, 242
  to long-time customer, 170
  for payment/order, 161
  for personal favor, 357
  to professional speaker, 241
  for receiving sales representative, 169
  for referral, 160
  for sending a friend, 167
  to substitute speaker, 246

Training materials, request letter/response, 66, 67

Transmittal letters, 92-97
  contract, 95
  final payment on account, 93
  materials under separate cover, 97
  payment—discrepancy explained, 94
  payment on account, 93
  program draft for approval, 96

Travel arrangements, confirming, 102

Unacceptable substitute, customer's letter about, 140-41

Unauthorized return of merchandise, supplier's letter about, 181

Unauthorized use of service personnel, supplier's letter about, 183

Unfavorable reference letters, 306-10

Unsatisfactory former employee, response to request for information about, 308

Unsigned check, returning for signature, 187

Vacation property, request letter/response, 89-90

Vogue words, 25

Warning letter to employee, 309

Welcome letter, to newcomer to community, 121

"Wise-itis," 24

Words/phrases:
  brevity vs. common sense, 17-20
  clutter, 12-14
  repetition, 15-17
  See also Language

Writing for executive's signature, 277-83
  alternate speaker, suggesting, 281
  major stockholder, writing, 280
  praise about speech, responding to, 282
  request for support, turning down, 279
  speaking invitation, accepting, 278
  thank-you letter, 283

"You" approach, to writing business letters, 33-34

About the Author

Roy W. Poe is a business education consultant with extensive experience teaching communications in management development programs and in college and university extension classes. A former vice president and editorial director at McGraw-Hill, he is also author of *The McGraw-Hill Guide to Effective Business Reports,* as well as several business textbooks.